Adventures Abroad skillfully mixes personal experience with practical facts to give you the "head" and "heart" of living abroad. You'll profit from the guidance of experts in all areas of concern: housing, cost of living, medical care, recreation and culture, shopping, security...And you bask in the help of "neighbors" in settling into some of the most romantic places outside our borders...havens where the costs are lower and the climate milder...edens where you can be happier, healthier, and wealthier...

Peter A. Dickinson, author
Travel & Retirement Edens Abroad·

Exploring the Travel/Retirement Option

ADVENTURES ABROAD

Allene Symons & Jane Parker

Gateway Books

Printed in the United States of America

Gateway Books

Distributed by Publishers Group West

Library of Congress Cataloging-in-Publication Data

Symons, Allene.
    Adventures abroad : exploring the travel/retirement option /
Allene Symons & Jane Parker.
        p.   cm.
    Includes bibliographical references and index.
    ISBN 0-933469-10-1 : $12.95
    1. Americans--Foreign countries--Handbooks, manuals, etc.
2. Retirement, Places of.   I. Parker, Jane.   II. Title
E184.2.S96   1991
909′ .0413--dc20   91-13692
                                                                   CIP

10 9 8 7 6 5 4 3 2

Acknowledgments

We would like to express our sincere appreciation to the 56 people who shared their experiences of living and sojourning abroad, who welcomed us into their homes and willingly participated in lengthy interviews to provide details, opinions and advice for other Americans who are considering living or retiring abroad.

Special thanks to Martha Fink and Lynn and George Oberly, who guided Jane in her first venture into the travel industry; to Linda Watson, for her professional office managing; and to Marti Scutt, the intrepid and enthusiastic publicist and tour guide.

Thanks also to Bruce Pierce for capturing the spirit of the book in images, and to David Mead, whose Chiang Mai adventure inspired a globe-spanning study.

To Joe, who believed in Jane's idea and was tolerant of her "just one more year" to gain acceptance of a new approach to retirement living.

To Howard Thrasher, who encouraged his daughter to ride the Cyclone Racer instead of the Merry-Go-Round

Contents

Chapter 1

The Adventure of Living Abroad

Why do thousands of Americans reside year-round or part-time in another country? There could be as many answers as there are U.S. expatriates around the world. Some, of course, live abroad for a career, and some who were born abroad choose to return later in life.

But for those who make a purely personal choice to live in another country, the decision is often based on the promise of adventure and affordability. Even if the dollar doesn't match favorably against the pound, mark or yen, there are many countries with a desirable quality of life where the dollar may buy more in rental housing or investment property, in goods or produce, in dining, or recreation—and especially in services— than in the United States. You can live well in Costa Rica, Portugal or Spain, for example, on between $600 and $1,000 per month, and in Mexico or Uruguay on far less.

A primary residence or second home abroad can be more affordable to rent or buy than housing in many traditional retirement and holiday home locales such as Florida, the Berkshires or the Sunbelt. As a real estate investment, property in many countries abroad—from the British Isles and France to Thailand, the Greek Islands and Spain—is increasing in value at a greater rate than some formerly prime investment areas in the U.S.

Add to the economic benefits the unique advantage of living as an insider rather than a tourist and the chance to experience deeply a different culture with its unique history, language and cuisine. And add the opportunity to meet people of all

11

nationalities, to make new friends among native residents and with the British, French, Germans, Italians and other internationals who already know what many Americans have yet to discover: residing in a second country enhances your life while it expands your global awareness.

Adventures Abroad is for all age groups who enjoy travel: for those who are already retired but looking for retirement alternatives; for those who will soon retire and are weighing their options; for those years away from retirement who want to plan for a satisfying post-career life, or who may take early retirement—either by choice or chance—anywhere from 5 to 15 years before they reach age 65; and for those who are still actively involved with career and family but are interested in adding a purposeful dimension to travel planning.

Whether you are in your 30s or 60s, whatever your immediate or long-term goals, residing abroad adds a stimulating slice to life that is most appreciated when children are grown or moving toward independence, when the career that has absorbed your days for decades reaches a peak and begins to wind down.

Adventures Abroad is based on interviews with 56 Americans of different ages who live abroad part of the year or year-round, and with another dozen people who are in the planning stage. [At the request of many interviewees, we have changed names to assure privacy.] These expatriates (and future expatriates) offer a vivid and varied picture of what it is really like to live abroad, through the full range of experience—from choosing a country, finding a residence and going through the adjustment phase, to confidently handling all aspects of daily life ranging from banking, investments and taxes to hobbies, friends, shopping and community involvement.

The ideas and advice in *Adventures Abroad* are also based on interviews with experts and on seminars held in various countries under the auspices of Lifestyle Explorations. Over the past 10 years, Boston-based Lifestyle Explorations has organized travel seminars for more than 500 people interested in the residency, investment and retirement potential of Spain, Costa Rica, Mexico and Portugal.

Among the features of the following chapters are:

• The strategies of today's preplanners. A look at plans-in-progress of a dozen people from a wide variety of backgrounds who are already preparing to live abroad.

• Worksheets to update information as needed.

• Comparative charts offering sample housing costs, owner-ship policies for expatriates, taxation, residency status and other legal requirements in 10 different countries.

• Lifestyle Values Inventory, a self-graded questionnaire to help you discover if your lifestyle requirements match oppor-tunities in different countries.

The chapters in this book reflect the 15 categories in the Life-style Values Inventory. By identifying your priorities and needs (the results of your self-test may surprise you!), you may save time, effort and money in the planning stage.

For anyone curious about retiring or residing abroad, the firsthand accounts of Americans in more than a dozen countries provide an inside look at life beyond tourism, such as the search for a home or shopping in the marketplace—not a quest for souvenirs but for fresh produce for tonight's dinner. You'll get a taste of the expatriate experience—such as what happens when you dent a bumper in Portugal or when you visit a clinic in Spain, when you remodel a farmhouse in France or Ireland or turn a hobby garden in Costa Rica into a thriving export business.

It's all part of the adventure you're about to begin—even if, in the end, you decide not to leave your armchair after all.

Bon voyage.

ITALY

Chapter 2

Choosing a Country

"We had lunch in a wonderful old kitchen. I remember looking out the top half of a double door—at a perfectly framed scene of the rooftops of this little town. I fell in love with it."

Arthur Loeb
Loire Valley (France)

When asked their primary reasons for choosing Portugal, Mexico, France, Greece, Costa Rica, Uruguay, Thailand, Spain, an island in the Caribbean or any of the scores of countries where Americans choose to live abroad, the answer is heard time and again: "Because I fell in love with it."

On the first visit, we respond to a sense of place: the tempo of a city or the serenity of countryside; the personality of a people and the interplay of traditional and modern architecture. The best candidates for living abroad have traveled to other countries and are prepared to distinguish between vacationer's infatuation and the special recognition that in this particular country they could live and create a home.

When a person chooses to live abroad, the decisive moment may occur when and where it is least expected, as it did for Jim and Debra Erland during a Christmas holiday in Portugal. "We walked along the beach and said to each other, 'We would like to live here.' On New Year's Eve we signed our papers and we haven't regretted it," explains Debra.

But when a seasoned traveler becomes enamored of a country, a town or a particular old farmhouse that begs to be restored, nine points should be considered before setting a plan

15

in motion. Not all of these criteria are essential—but the following "points of departure" go a long way toward finding long-term satisfaction abroad:

Country Criteria Checklist

- Temperate climate
- Ease of access
- Good medical services
- Moderate- or low-cost housing
- Availability of reliable, low-cost help
- Americans in residence
- Acceptance by local residents
- Relative economic and political stability
- Availability of familiar tokens

Temperate Climate

This is less important for a younger expatriate and more important for someone approaching retirement age. Some people prefer a change of season and would miss the first snowfall of winter or notice the absence of autumn color in a subtropical clime. But when people get older, most want warmth and, especially for Easterners, relief from high heating costs.

Many Americans are international snowbirds: every winter, Veronica and George Alta escape the Philadelphia cold for their condominium in Torremolinos, Spain—but they avoid the Costa del Sol during its scorching summers. John and Sally Barber are reverse snowbirds: they escape San Francisco's damp, chilly summers by vacationing in their farmhouse near Sarlat, France. Climate is subjective; it depends upon what you are accustomed to. If you are a working or part-time expatriate rather than retiree, consider when you are likely to vacation abroad: an accountant who customarily takes off the month of May would be ill-advised to spend it in Guadalajara since May is the hottest and least desirable month.

"Moderate" doesn't only mean freedom from harsh weather. Don Hartman, who with his wife Beth has lived in Portugal's Algarve for the past five years, ranks climate high on his list of reasons for retiring abroad. He praises the year-round sunshine and the fact that their home is only a short walk from the beach.

But Don is from California—why move 3,000 miles for more sun? "We had sun, but we also had a lot of smog in California," explains Beth, who adds that Don has respiratory problems; back home, he often had to sleep sitting up because of the smog.

Climate was a priority for Diane and Hal Oster, who have retired twice so far: first to Florida (they are originally from Chicago) and then, in 1988, to Costa Rica. "Each year Fort Lauderdale got hotter and hotter—our air conditioning bills were astronomical, as high as $400 a month in Florida," says Diane. The Osters live in a suburb of San José, where they are comfortable without air conditioning in summer or heat in winter.

Another couple retired in the Algarve appreciate the climate from an East Coast perspective: "In New York our apartment was overheated—it was always 74 degrees. You'd walk around inside in shorts because you couldn't open the windows and in the summer we lived in an air conditioned world."

A mild climate doesn't have to be boring since many countries have microclimates. Mexico's largest expatriate communities are found inland at varying high elevations around Guadalajara, San Miguel de Allende and Cuernavaca where temperatures are moderate year-round. Mexico also offers three different coastal environments, all of them much warmer—Pacific, Gulf of Mexico and Gulf of California—for short trips or even a change of address. Although most Americans prefer the popular inland areas, Mat and Joan Feldman decided to retire in La Paz with its warm coastal climate and opportunities for boating, deep-sea fishing and scuba diving.

Costa Rica similarly has several microclimates, encompassing cloud forests, jungle, rolling vistas of coffee fields and two very different coastal regions facing the Caribbean and the Pacific. Carl and Nancy Thalmeyer lived in a cloud-forest climate for several years, then moved to the drier central valley.

Inland areas contrast with coastal regions in a number of ways ranging from climate to cost to culture. Portugal's Algarve is often chilled by winter winds from the Atlantic. Lisbon offers a striking alternative to the Algarve. It serves as a favored weekend getaway and also lures some expatriates to move from the south to the north. Part-time resident Barbara Moore is planning to move from the Algarve to Lisbon, where winters are cool but dry and where she can enjoy the capital city's urban lifestyle. Italy and France also offer variety in climate—from vineyards to ski slopes to the beaches of the Mediterranean—within their borders or in neighboring countries no farther away than a state line in the United States.

When considering a country with an unusual (by U.S. standards) climate, try to measure your patience against the duration of inconvenience: winters in Norway are long and dark; Thailand's monsoon season, with its inconvenient heavy rain and flooding, passes in a few weeks.

Ease of Access

Without affordable international transportation, good airports and reliable surface roads, living abroad could be a confining experience that limits visits by family and friends as well as your return visits to the U.S. Intercountry access is also important, since travel is one of the favored advantages of living abroad.

At first, living abroad is rather like a vacation: everything is fresh and different. But eventually you will find that a vacation serves the same role there as in the U.S.: a way to gain a new perspective, to avoid getting in a rut, so that you return with renewed appreciation for your home base and the comforts of daily routine.

What are your options for affordable getaways? For Americans in Uruguay, a favorite weekend sojourn is Buenos Aires, Argentina, an hour by hydrofoil from Montevideo across the Rio de la Plata. Europe offers the best opportunity for intercountry access and exploring different cultures. Bob Martinelli, a San Francisco–area lawyer and, since 1989, a part-time resident of Albisano, Italy, is quick to point out that Munich is a four hour drive over excellent highways—or it's two hours to Venice and only a half hour from a ski resort. Arthur Secunda, who rents an apartment in Paris, says, "They call Paris the navel of Europe, because you can get to many places." Of a recent trip to the North Sea Jazz Festival at The Hague, he says, "It's like driving from Los Angeles to Santa Paula (California) except it happens to be Holland."

Americans living abroad enjoy sharing (and proudly displaying) language, cultural skills and general expatriate know-how with friends and family. For a part-timer, new friendships abroad can be gratifying but primary relationships are still based in the U.S.—most full-timers do not want to cut Stateside ties. And for Americans with tourist status, rather than resident or pensioner status, it is necessary to journey across the border at regular intervals.

Visits from friends can mean reciprocal invitations, often a convenient opportunity to return to the U.S. without incurring lodging costs for those who do not keep a permanent address in the U.S. Lauren and Ben Gruning, who reside in Guadalajara, Mexico, "house sit" for friends in San Francisco every year or two, as do a couple who live on the Costa del Sol.

If you choose to live abroad full time, the fewer Americans in residence, the more important visits to and from the U.S. are likely to be. Fred Dahl tells Americans who visit the Algarve, where the expat community is largely British, "I miss you—I miss the American sense of humor."

Both inbound and outbound access are important if you expect visits to or from friends and family. If you are like many Americans, your family is scattered from coast to coast with siblings, children and grandchildren following the geography dictated by career or higher education. It's entirely possible that the lure of vacations abroad will result in your spending more time with your grandchildren than when you lived in the United States. You'll want to avoid a transportation obstacle course. The expatriate may be willing, and even regard it as a point of pride, to rough it through awkward air connections with long layovers, but such difficult access could discourage visitors. And even if your niece or grandson would adore an international adventure, their harried parents may not want to face a daunting itinerary with kids—of any age—in tow. In short, access is not just getting there: it is getting in, out and around by air and land. And if you prefer not to drive, then you'll need to choose a locale with good local transportation—reliable, secure, comfortable and affordable.

Good Medical Services

Unless you are fluent in the language of your second home abroad, you will want an English-speaking doctor and the availability of emergency facilities within reasonable distance of your home. The ability to report and accurately communicate symptoms is important for proper care. When you are ill or in pain late at night, you don't want to find out that emergency treatment is limited to nine-to-five. Medical needs differ for a retiree or a younger expatriate, but anyone could suddenly face

19

an emergency. At any age when living abroad, you should have a plan for medical care.

Most preferred retirement countries offer lower-cost medical care than is available in the U.S. For any foreign travel, it's wise to check your insurance coverage, and in some cases supplement it with short-term coverage when needed. Although your medical costs are likely to be modest abroad, in an emergency you may need to be evacuated to a larger city, another country or even to the U.S.—and that can be very expensive. The less adequate the local medical care, the more likely you will need to travel elsewhere for certain kinds of treatment.

You may choose to self-insure, as many Americans abroad do, since medical costs in many countries are surprisingly low. A typical doctor's office visit in Guadalajara, Mexico, is $12 (U.S.); for a specialist, $25, and an emergency room visit, $15. In Chiang Mai, Thailand, retired American David Mead pays $4–$8 for an office call and says of his English-speaking doctor: "He is the best doctor I've had in my life"—no small compliment from a man accustomed to Manhattan's best physicians. But it took him two years to find this doctor—two years of discouragement while searching for a physician who could treat one of David's chronic health problems. Finding good medical services abroad can take some research, and judgment about which medical problems you would be willing to have treated locally and which will require treatment elsewhere.

Moderate- or Low-Cost Housing

Almost every country abroad is affordable—if you avoid the obvious. What many Americans want is American-style accommodations at less than U.S. prices. In some places you can find them easily—expatriate communities in Mexico, Costa Rica and Uruguay, for example. If in some countries housing seems too expensive at first glance, it is usually because you don't yet know where to look. The greatest cost savings are gained by living away from expatriate neighborhoods, and sometimes this means adjusting to a somewhat different style of housing.

Style and location of housing depend on individual taste and budget. A gourmet cook may insist on a reasonably modern kitchen; for someone else, the satisfaction of residing in a cloud forest in Costa Rica, or in a two-hundred-year-old Portuguese farmhouse, could be worth the trade for kitchen conveniences. Or it may mean making structural changes.

Since her first trip at age 17, Larraine Grey had always wanted to live in Europe. In 1980, after a 15-year career as an art teacher, she moved to Portugal's Algarve and bought a small house near the beach. Larraine describes the house—and her friends' reaction: "It was a tiny old house. I decided to fix it up and everyone said I was crazy to go through the inconvenience." Several successful remodels later, Larraine found herself in a successful building business, and with a new partner: her British husband, whom she met during one of her remodeling projects.

One way to enjoy moderate- or low-cost housing is to live outside a popular tourist center. Arthur Secunda, currently an apartment dweller in Paris, is looking for a home in the South of France, where he has a choice of villas priced around $80,000—because he is willing to live 10 kilometers outside Antibes.

Similarly, when Karen and Paul Knight moved to Portugal their rental agent advised them to find a rental in Faro, an historic town in the Central Algarve and capital of the province. In Faro, they were able to negotiate a reasonable year-round rental—it would have been far more expensive closer to the popular tourist centers, where high-season prices are steep and a year-round price reflects an overheated market. Faro was comfortable for their budget, but for some people the density of this small city would not be comfortable for long-term living and would best serve as a temporary location.

Another approach to affordable housing is to find a somewhat overbuilt area—a renter's market. Mexico's Lake Chapala has experienced rapid growth in recent years (along with increased pollution) but with the result that it isn't hard to find a bargain in a rental home or apartment. The renter's advantage also applies to Guadalajara, a 45-minute drive away.

The risk of renting is the same everywhere: unless you own, the landlord has the final say about both price and occupancy. Yet among the more than 56 Americans living abroad who were interviewed for this book, not one complained about a landlord who unfairly increased rent, nor about being asked to vacate so that another tenant (family member or otherwise) could occupy the rental unit.

In European countries, housing costs in many desirable vacation areas are increasing as the 1992 European Community (EC) unification draws closer. If you plan to rent for a few months while looking for property to purchase in any of the popular vacation areas of southern Europe, then you need only be concerned with short-term rental costs. But if you plan to rent over a long period—several years—you may find that only by purchasing property in Europe, or by avoiding popular areas, will your housing costs be predictable in years to come.

Availability of Reliable Low-Cost Help

Another advantage of living or retiring abroad is affordable domestic services: cleaning, cooking, gardening, home repair. In most expatriate communities, the American employer benefits from low-cost help (by U.S. standards) and the employee benefits from fair wages (by local standards).

For the retiree, it becomes more important to have help with strenuous indoor and outdoor work; for anyone living abroad, inexpensive household help reduces routine tasks and frees time to spend in more interesting pursuits. For a family with health problems—or an elderly parent or spouse who needs extra care—it can be the difference between affordable home care abroad or, in the U.S., a costly dwindling of family savings.

In the new frontiers for living abroad or retirement, household help is surprisingly inexpensive. In Montevideo, Uruguay, Stanley Walters pays just $1 per hour for household help. In Chiang Mai, Thailand, David Mead pays under $2 per hour. Even in the heart of Spain's Costa del Sol, where prices are rising, household help is still less than $4 per hour.

Whether or not you find a bargain in household help depends on several things: availability, knowing enough Americans in residence to ask for recommendations and your attitude as employer toward the help—which can make all the difference between having good or bad luck with domestic employees. Ruth Walkington (in Heredia, Costa Rica) reports that she has had "wonderful luck" with her household help since moving to Costa Rica from San Diego in 1982. Her maid, who comes three half-days each week, costs around (1988) $7 U.S. per day and is so diligent, Ruth explains, that she washes and waxes the tile floors "until you can see your reflection." Windows, dishes, watering plants—whatever needs to be done, she does it.

Ruth has also considered the question of later-in-life care, should she become widowed: if alone, she plans to stay in Costa

Rica and says, "If I became disabled, it is so expensive to go into a care center in the U.S. In Costa Rica, I can hire a couple to do the cooking, cleaning and care for me for much less than I would have to spend in a care center in the U.S.—and I could still be in my own home and see my friends."

Americans in Residence

Some people are pioneers, undaunted by being one of only a few Americans in an area. They usually have accomplished language skills to pry their way into an unfamiliar culture. Or they belong to an international business or organization, or have a professional background that provides access to a locale where few Americans would otherwise choose to live.

Just as there are popular expatriate areas around the world, there is also a second tier of places where Americans are in residence—but where you would have to seek them out without the aid of an English-language newspaper or an American Club.

In Mexico, you will find Americans in Oaxaca, Morelia, La Paz, Guanajuato and other areas, besides the primary expatriate communities of Guadalajara, San Miguel de Allende and Cuernavaca (the last is less popular with Americans than in previous decades, since Mexico City's growth has eclipsed this formerly charming town).

Living in an area with few Americans is an opportunity to learn the language—because you'll have to. Renee Wolpert lived in an exclusively Mexican community for several years, studied Spanish intensively, adapted to Mexican customs—but missed having conversations in English. "You have no idea how lonely you get to speak the language," said Renee, who points out that Mexicans who know some English like to converse, but she adds, "you get tired of speaking 300 basic words."

Even if they have some facility with the language, most expatriates prefer to seek out a network of Americans—especially when it comes to recommendations for a lawyer, an auto mechanic or a physician. The network is a good way to find shortcuts through red tape, to locate a carpenter, the best restaurant or a good haircut, as well as to help during the transition of settling in, such as borrowing a telephone until yours is installed.

Social life abroad usually starts with other Americans and leads gradually into the international community. Our culture is

more open than cultures of other countries: the backyard intro-
duction that turns into a barbecue in New Jersey or California is
likely to elicit only a polite nod or greeting abroad.

Some expatriate communities seem to be more global; the
national barriers are dropped. Islands and some coastal areas
attract independent spirits, often singles and young couples, who
welcome into their circle of friends people of different
nationalities. Some of the Greek Islands, for example, are cosmopolitan. On Mykonos, Lily Cairns has easily made friends
with expats from Manchester, England, and Munich, Germany,
as well as Athenians who own vacation homes on the island. In
general, it is easier to make international friends as a single
person, since family "formalities" are suspended.

Even a gregarious but older single person will find friends in
the international community—with a little patience. When Charles Yarby rented an apartment in St. Croix in the U.S. Virgin
Islands, he says, "I didn't know anyone, but soon I met people
and those people introduced me to others."

Introductions through Americans can be helpful for meeting
both residents of the country and Europeans. In interviews with
Americans abroad, most report that their friendships are often
composed of different circles—other Americans, Europeans and
local residents. Close friendships are usually in the first two
groups.

Acceptance by Local Residents

No one enjoys living where they are not wanted. Acceptance
of Americans is one of the most important criteria for choosing a
country.

Retired social worker Carl Gower moved to the Dominican
Republic in 1984, after living for several months on St. Thomas in
the U.S. Virgin Islands. After experiencing high prices and a level
of crime and resentment toward visitors on St. Thomas that made
him uncomfortable, he was glad to find the Dominicans very
accepting of Americans. "They are neither hostile nor indifferent
toward us—in fact, they like us and have adopted many of our
ideas, values and goals." He also found something more, as he
explains: "What the social scientists call 'a sense of place.'"

In some cultures, a warm regard for expatriates is the norm:
Costa Ricans, Portuguese and Thais are almost uniformly
pleasant. Frustration can arise on occasion when, in an effort to

be agreeable, business and other agreements go awry. That's when most Americans would prefer to see less amiability and more directness.

On the other hand, in some cultures, attitudes are more complex and acceptance is more difficult to attain. But this doesn't always mean that residents are unwilling to accept Americans. It may mean reading between the lines, avoiding offense, working a bit harder at making friends. The effort will probably have to come from you. This can be a challenge with satisfying results, and is not the same as living in a country where Americans (or any other expatriates) are not wanted no matter how much effort is expended.

In Greece, where there is outward hostility toward Germans, sometimes Americans are mistaken for Germans. Even when that hurdle is past, there is still a kind of diffidence. Lily Cairns characterizes it this way: "You can feel what seems like an undercurrent of anti-American hostility, but it doesn't make me uncomfortable. They're warm and welcoming, which is odd because the Greeks don't seem to like each other. After six years in Mykonos, it takes me an hour to walk through town because people come out and hug me and say 'Do you want a coffee.'"

The French are not known for their friendliness toward foreign nationals. Nevertheless, among the half-dozen Americans interviewed on the subject of living abroad in France, all felt that it is possible to win acceptance. Joan Waterhouse is satisfied with her progress and says: "If you don't speak French it can isolate you. They really appreciate it if you speak their language." She is working to improve her fluency and looks forward to extending invitations to neighbors—that is, after a few more improvements are done on her old shepherd's house near Les Eyzies (purchased for $10,000 as a part-time home in 1988). "We just have to make the effort—improve our French and have people over," claims Joan.

Sometimes a spontaneously kind gesture brings you suddenly into the circle. Sally Barber paid a hospital visit, and brought a small gift, when one of the village women had a baby. In time, John Barber explains, the new mother brought her child "to pay a visit on 'Madame Barber' who had come to see her in the hospital, and within a few months Sally had been a guest in every home in the village."

Relative Economic and Political Stability

This is a variable in most countries where Americans retire today. It will continue to be a variable as global circumstances change—in Latin America, in emerging Eastern European countries, in the European Community, and in the burgeoning marketplace of Southeast Asia. Countries without some political or economic volatility are rare and may have other drawbacks; no one would choose to live in Switzerland for affordability or temperate climate.

To wait until global changes stabilize is the same as deciding against living abroad. (Perhaps the venture is not for a person unwilling to take some risks.) Investors from other countries appear to have no problem with volatility—even with Ireland's internal troubles, it is becoming one of Europe's affordable second home frontiers, especially for Germans. Nor does economic uncertainty prevent Saudi, Chinese (from Hong Kong and Taiwan), Japanese and South African individuals and groups from investing in Mexico. Few of the scores of people who were interviewed about living abroad expressed any day-to-day worry about political instability. Even in countries surrounded by troublesome neighbors, such as Costa Rica and Thailand, American residents are sanguine.

Many affordable countries abroad have a currency more solid in 1991 than the U.S. dollar. Some countries, notably in the EC, are good places to diversify investments while the dollar is uncertain. The stock markets of several countries have outperformed that of the U.S. in recent years. Many economic advisers are bullish about a number of foreign mutual funds, which have shown better performance than their U.S. counterparts. One is the Spanish Fund, which showed strong performance until a decline toward the end of 1990. For many years Texan Bob Slater has invested profitably in the Spanish Fund, and although his retirement plans point toward living in Mexico rather than in Spain, he believes in diversifying and notes that investing abroad can be one of the best ways to strengthen your dollars.

Low-cost living or a tax haven is not a sufficient reason to choose a locale abroad. For example, in the late 1980s the Philippines aggressively marketed low cost living with tax and other incentives for American retirees, yet it is unlikely that many Americans would choose to live in the Philippines.

Continuity in political leadership and solid relations with trading partners contribute to stability. For many decades, the leaders of Costa Rica have shared common views and political beliefs, so a radical change of leadership is unlikely. In Thailand, the country's strong trade position with otherwise difficult neighbors means there is little likelihood that crucial trade patterns (and needed supplies) will be broken. Trade is a good insurance policy.

One of the main concerns, especially in Latin American countries, is devaluation. Since almost everyone who lives or retires abroad maintains a primary bank account in the U.S., depositing only operating funds each month, the changing winds of currency are only of concern if the dollar declines in the world market.

The devaluation of the Mexican peso in 1982 only caused a minor setback for Peter Haddon, a retired dentist from Long Island. He and his wife have lived in a condominium club near a golf course in Guadalajara since 1981. "Most Americans were caught in the devaluation—there was no notice given," recalls Peter. In 1982 the government confiscated all dollar accounts, converted them into pesos and devalued them. Although the devaluation affected him, the impact was minor compared to other Americans he knew. The reason, he explains, is that "I only keep an operating amount of money in Mexico and advise all Americans to do the same."

The other side of devaluation, if living on U.S. currency, is a good exchange rate and even more value for the dollar. Since hard currency is sought after, street exchange rates can rise far above the official exchange rate. In a country where the currency strengthens against the dollar, the value of goods and services—and housing, if you rent—will go up, making your dollar shrink in purchasing power. In such countries, purchasing property abroad may be advisable if your budget allows.

Availability of Familiar Tokens

Living abroad isn't just a two-week jaunt, an escape from the home routine. Even when seasoned travelers find themselves in the role of resident, they are often surprised to discover that you don't miss hot dogs until you can't find them.

Primarily during the transition period, which ranges from months to a year or more, the novelty of a new life can give rise

27

to occasional bouts of homesickness. Familiar brand names can help restore balance. You'll find the American gathering spots, even if you choose not to go there except on one of those rare days. Moments of homesickness are certain to occur, especially if you choose to live inexpensively in a neighborhood apart from other Americans.

The subject of "value in the familiar" is often dismissed by seasoned travelers. The last thing most travelers want to see is Kentucky Fried Chicken or some other mass-market reminder of home. But the unfamiliar sights that make a vacation abroad so stimulating take on a different meaning when vacation becomes residency. That's when it can be restorative to gather with other Americans, to help each other with creative problem solving, to share the highs and lows of "adjustment"—and to spread out a picnic feast of beer, pickle relish and hot dogs on the Fourth of July.

Weighing the Country Criteria

These criteria should be carefully considered before you decide to move abroad. If an individual (or couple) has a highly adaptive attitude, then one or more of the nine country criteria might be dismissed as unimportant in an overall plan. But if a country misses on several counts, you could be courting failure if you make such a move. No single feature should overshadow others. A mild climate is important, but weather alone doesn't assure satisfaction. The island of Madeira, for example, enjoys abundant sunshine but offers limited cultural opportunities. Affordability is just one point for your checklist. Mexico is inexpensive, but as long-time Mexico resident Renee Wolpert points out, "You should choose Mexico because you find more than just a price tag."

Ease of access to the U.S. is important if you hope for visits from family and friends, less important if you do not. If you are in good health and do not anticipate the need to travel outside the country for special medical attention, or if you only plan infrequent air travel outside the country, then you might decide to live in an area several hours from the nearest international airport. Americans in residence are a plus—unless you are a loner who values privacy and is determined to master the language. Low-cost help may not be a priority, especially if your housing and home entertaining needs are modest—if you have an apartment, who needs a gardener? But don't discount the importance of acceptance by local residents or the need for relative political stability. Few people could adjust to a country where civil unrest threatens or where Americans are despised.

City and Suburb, Countryside and Coastline

Every country has a distinct profile as a possible living or retirement locale. The subtle differences may appear only after a second or third visit, or not until you have resided in the country for an extended time.

Your first destination may serve as a base of operation: you know that this locale meets your criteria, but with a little research you may find a place, slightly farther, that is even more appealing. On a first trip to Mexico, you might explore Guadalajara and the lakeside community of Ajijic. Venturing further, you may discover the historic city of San Miguel de Allende or decide to be one of the more adventurous expatriates in areas where Americans form small expatriate communities such as Morelia, Oaxaca or La Paz on the Baja Peninsula. On a first trip to Costa Rica you may use San José as a base to visit other cities—Heredia, Alajuela—and to explore possible homesites in the countryside.

When evaluating a country and region, consider if your preferred activities are accessible from where you plan to live. Are outdoor activities of interest, or do you prefer cultural events usually found in or near urban centers? It will take a few trial runs to determine transportation or driving time to be sure that the activities you want are not too far out of reach or too costly in transportation or lodging.

On a vacation, especially if ground transportation is part of the package, you may not be aware of how easy or difficult access is to areas you may want to visit frequently as a resident. Tours are designed to smooth the path of the vacationer but on your own it may be steeper going. By taking a realistic look at the country's leisure-time pleasures, and by estimating how often you expect to enjoy them, you will have a clearer picture of the time, effort and costs involved.

Here's a look at five different countries from the point of view of access to amenities:

Costa Rica has a compact geography. From the capital city of San José and its surrounding towns, where most Americans live, either the Pacific or the Caribbean can be reached in around a

29

half-day's drive, so that both city pleasures and outdoor activities are manageable from the central valley. But life in the valley isn't seaside living, and, realistically, neither coast is a one-day round trip. However, many Americans in Costa Rica spend occasional weekends on the Pacific coast, like John and Pat Nielson, who have time-share occupancy of a condominium every three months at Flamingo Beach on the celebrated shores of Guanacaste province.

Costa Rica also offers world-class fishing in the Caribbean, the Pacific and the Gulf of Nicoya. Quite often, fishing is the main attraction that draws Americans to live here. Costa Rica's topography and preservation programs provide opportunities for the naturalist, who can explore terrain ranging from cloud forests to volcanoes, or focus binoculars to watch over 350 species of birds. But transportation to these areas involves some planning, since not all are accessible by car throughout the year. To reach coastal areas, many Americans prefer to fly rather than drive, a cost that might not seem apparent if your first visit is on a tour-line minibus.

In Portugal, the pattern is the reverse: most Americans live in the Algarve on the southern coast and make occasional trips to the capital city of Lisbon, around a four-hour drive. Portugal's weather is not as mild as that of Costa Rica, but it offers much more variety in architecture, history and culture. Its natural amenities are less noteworthy than Costa Rica's, but there are still abundant opportunities for outdoor activities such as tennis, sailing, golf and horseback riding.

In Spain, as in Portugal, the coast—particularly the Costa del Sol—is favored by expatriates. Málaga is the largest coastal city, and many Americans live in surrounding towns such as Fuengirola and Torremolinos. Although Málaga offers some urban amenities, many Americans like to visit the elegant city of Seville, a few hour's drive from the coastal area. There, on an overnight trip, they shop and enjoy Seville's museums, lush parks, waterways and Moorish architecture. In Spain and Portugal, coastal residents may make a trip to Lisbon or Seville as often as once a month, others once a year or less. By first experiencing the distance, transportation and (if you plan to drive) highway conditions, you can forecast how well this country will satisfy your preference for either outdoor or cultural activities.

Mexico's Lake Chapala offers a resort setting less than an hour from the sizable city of Guadalajara, which provides everything from good shopping to concerts. Some choose to live in the city and vacation at the lake. One reason for the area's popularity—it has the largest community of American residents outside the U.S.—is its access to both resort and urban amenities.

In France, the affordable choice is a country farmhouse. In addition to the charm of small French villages and picturesque landscape, one of the primary amenities is great dining in restaurants undiscovered by tourists, countryside walks and bicycling, plus a drive of only a few hours for an overnight or longer trip to Paris.

Sometimes a source of conflict for a couple with varying interests is the availability or affordability of cultural events— usually a woman's preference—and outdoor activities—usually favored by men. How frequently will you want to fish, hike in a cloud forest or visit the beach? How often do you plan to travel to the city for a concert, to visit a museum or art gallery or to browse sophisticated shopping venues? Every country offers a unique combination of things to see and do. Many countries have one or more cities or areas where an expatriate can adjust satisfactorily to living abroad. Knowing what you want in outdoor activities and culture—and what a country has to offer—is important when choosing a home abroad.

The Resort Factor

Housing, culture and social life are different if you choose to live in a resort or a non-resort area. A "non-resort" area has a year-round population, rather than one that swells during the tourist season (along with prices) then shrinks back to a quiet off-season mode.

This definition applies to most of the residential areas where Americans now live in Costa Rica, as most reside in or near San José. Guadalajara, Mexico, is another year-round locale: this city is not a resort area even though the number of Americans in residence climbs in winter.

Resort and vacation areas such as Spain's Costa del Sol or Portugal's Algarve have a large influx of seasonal residents and tourists. So do other places chosen by some Americans—such as the Greek island of Mykonos, where Lily Cairns owns a home and reports that the winter population of 5,000 swells to 65,000

31

from June to August. "In the summer, the streets are a swarming mass of humanity," says Lily, who spends most of her time in Greece off season. Sometimes a compromise is possible—and a good choice when you can find it: the Martinellis' home in Albisano, Italy, is just outside a popular lakeside tourist area, in a small hillside village with a stable year-round population.

But your choice will usually be between a resort or a non-resort area. Both have advantages and disadvantages. Resort areas are a good real estate investment, but they are impacted by swelling crowds in season and lack the stability of a regular population all year. If you choose to live in a resort area, since neighbors and cultural opportunities tend to be seasonal it is important that you be socially self-reliant with interests that do not require year-round socializing—if you live on the Costa del Sol off season, where 80% of American Club members are part-time residents, you may have trouble scaring up a bridge game with other Americans during some months of the year.

Since the population in a resort area is itinerant, you may not like all of your tourist neighbors. Americans in non-resort areas often report that their neighbors look after their property when they are not in residence. In a resort area, you may have to take a different approach. Algarve resident Susan Broward takes the initiative when seasonal renters arrive, and this adds to her sense of neighborhood stability and safety: "I introduce myself and tell them that I live in this house—and I ask if there is anything I can do," she explains.

She has met many interesting seasonal visitors from different countries this way. Susan believes that a short-term neighbor relationship affords both social potential and security, since both parties are more aware if something seems amiss at either property. She advises that since Europeans are less open than Americans they are not likely to take the initiative, but she adds, "The more you know them, the more they open up to you."

Life "off season" in a resort area affords serenity for one kind of person, while another might find it disconcertingly quiet. There may be other Americans in residence, but when and for how long? If you plan to enjoy the social life of the American expatriate community, be sure your timing is right. Or, as some do, cultivate friends who plan to be there off season; make plans in advance to assure that as a social type you won't find yourself lonely and depressed when the crowds dwindle.

If you choose to live in a non-resort area, you will have year-round neighbors and more stable social relationships. Chances are you will live in a neighborhood with native residents, although you may choose to live where Americans are just a door or two away.

In a non-resort area, you may need to go further to enjoy resort-style pleasures, unless you live in a self-contained club complex or join a tennis or country club. One reason the club complex is becoming popular with Americans abroad is the fact that although you may not be denied membership in the local tennis, golf or country club, some Americans say they feel uncomfortable as a "minority" member in a club dominated by wealthy older native families. Friendships abroad are easier to cultivate with neighbors, shopkeepers and even with residents who share common interests such as art or gardening. The stratified atmosphere of a country club is a different matter: the same American would probably feel discomfort in any number of "old family" country clubs in the U.S., and when living abroad would prefer to relax in an expatriate club atmosphere.

For some Americans, the drawback of a condominium club complex is that a self-contained compound may be isolated from the flavor of local daily life. It is possible to live in a condominium club and partake of the outside community, as long as the on-site conveniences (such as a restaurant, market and other services) do not become substitutes for interacting with the outside community.

Making a Choice

Why did the Americans interviewed in this book choose their own special country abroad? One compelling attraction is the beauty of the land. Ruth Walkington, who has lived with her husband in Costa Rica for nine years, says, "I can't think of a time when I drove into the countryside of Costa Rica and wasn't amazed by the beauty."

For some, it's the people. For years, Barbara Moore wanted to live in Europe; today she lives in Portugal for what she describes as "a small fraction" of what it costs her to live in Albany, N.Y. Above all, she appreciates the people: "Things are done in a human way in Portugal, and that's one of the lovely things about living here." Barbara adds, "I'm still very much in love with this country. Maybe I'll get over it, but I don't think so."

Mexico appealed to Lauren and Bob Gruning not only because it was inexpensive but because after many trips to the country they were continually impressed by the warmth of the people. "There is a kind of courtesy, a friendliness that doesn't exist in most of North America," remarks Lauren.

Daniel Forbush and his wife Jean chose England's Lake District for its beauty—and its excellent sites for mountain walking. Joan Peters and Len Waterhouse, also walkers, selected France's Dordogne region where they enjoy the miles of footpaths developed by the French government. "In France we live differently," says Jean. "No TV, a lot of walking, good eating and a lot of reading." Arthur Secunda in Paris lives a contrasting lifestyle and says, "The quality of life, for me personally, is better than anywhere else. I like the passion for life, the formal elegance of Paris. I think it is the most livable city in the world."

For those who have given up city life, such as retired teacher Mark Rembold, there seems little reason to look back. He and his wife imported the urban pleasures they needed, and the land provides the amenities. Mark's home is 1,000 feet from the Pacific, at a remote expatriate enclave called the Beaches of Nosara in Costa Rica. "We are on the beach practically every day, looking for shells, swimming in the tide pools or just ambling in the surf," says Mark. "We taped a lot of music and brought a lot of books—and we don't miss city life."

A Home for Italian Holidays

Veteran world travelers Bob and Linda Martinelli prefer Italy to any other destination. Although Bob is a fourth-generation Italian-American, Linda (who is of Russian-Jewish descent) is even more enthusiastic about international living, and it was she who commented during a 1985 Italian vacation: "Wouldn't it be fun to own something here?"

The idea simmered until their next trip to Italy in 1989, when the idea really began to "percolate," as Bob recalls. Weeks before departure date they collected guidebooks and maps, spread them out in their San Francisco Bay Area home and began to outline the plan for a home search.

The Martinellis concluded that Tuscany (the region in which Florence is located) was so popular with Americans and Europeans that real estate prices would be too high. Bob attributes the passion for this area to the romantic notion of "a villa in Tuscany," which means that it has been overpublicized and overbought.

They turned their search to the lake district of Lago di Garda, 75 miles east of Milan. "We had stayed in Riva del Garda in 1985 and liked it a lot," Bob recalls, "but it occurred to us that if we bought around the lake, it might be too remote." With a map, guidebooks and memories of their last trip, Bob and Linda concentrated on the lake area, using the following strategy: They read about the different towns and decided that the area bordering the middle of the long lake offered the best access to highways and to the city of Verona around 25 miles away.

They also spoke with other frequent travelers to Italy and learned that some parts of this area enjoy the best sunlight. Mountains at the north end of the lake act as a curtain, bringing an abrupt conclusion to the day. Bob explains: "As a West-coaster, I'm used to the sun setting slowly in the West. I'd miss the gradually waning light."

The Martinellis' concern for variables such as natural light is important to emulate when considering purchase of a home abroad. It underlines the advisability of spending more than one season in an area or, as the second-best strategy, talking with knowledgeable people about how weather, sunlight and other factors could affect your enjoyment of a locale.

After deciding on the mid-lake section, Bob read about different towns in the area, narrowed their search to four or five and decided on the town of Torri del Benaco. "It is a charming town. We bought in a mountain village called Albisano, a suburb of Torri, with a year-round residential population of around 500," explains Bob.

The challenge of buying property abroad increases when it is far from major tourist areas or cities with sizable expatriate communities. Unless you are fluent in the language, you will need assistance. Bob tried to locate a real estate agent in advance of the trip (this would have been easy to accomplish if he were looking in Tuscany), but wasn't able to arrange any contacts and realized that finding an English-speaking broker would be difficult. Since Bob and Linda only know a smattering of Italian, they called upon friends who live in London and speak fluent Italian. Their friends were happy to sojourn in Italy for a few days.

With the help of their friends as translators, the Martinellis found and bought a two-story duplex property for $150,000. It has a stunning lake view that they can enjoy from their windows, from the patio (their yard has a sloping lawn) or while relaxing on their large upper deck, designed for summer outdoor living. The home is only a short ride away from the lake and 10 minutes from two lakeside towns—Torri (which means "towers") del Benaco and Garda.

The duplex was unfinished when they found it and began negotiations. One of the advantages of inquiring about partly-completed property is that you might have first choice of options. The Martinellis chose the southern unit: "It has the better view and more sun," says Bob, who notes that shortly after their purchase, a German family bought the second unit with the intention of using it for one or two months during the year.

"It's an expensive hobby," admits Bob, although he realizes that with the probable increase in property value, the diversification of investing abroad and the future rental potential as well as use by clients, family and friends, his home adds up to more than just an exotic vacation hideaway. However, at $150,000, it isn't pin money. Bob points out that when he and Linda decided to buy abroad, they also chose to curtail other plans. They won't remodel their kitchen in the U.S. and they won't buy an expensive new car, or as Bob explains: "Who cares if we don't have a designer kitchen or a new car—we enjoy traveling."

Their home has the advantages of access to exciting destinations and the serenity of a quiet village. Torri del Benaco attracts summer travelers and swells in population during high season, but its off-season population is actually smaller than the stable year-round population of Albisano. The Martinellis enjoy Albisano's peaceful village life: "I haven't seen a tour bus yet. That was one of the things we liked—it was close to a nice tourist town but remote enough for privacy." Bob and Linda are studying Italian in the U.S., but Bob notes: "The best teacher is being there. Every trip we learn a little more."

With so few Americans in the area, Bob and Linda are enjoying their uniqueness. "Everybody is very, very nice, and meeting the local merchants is an interesting project in itself. When we walk into a hardware store, they look at us and as soon as they realize that we're not Germans—they're delighted to see us because we're *not* German—they then assume we're British, but soon they find out we're not. Being an American in this little town is a lot of fun."

One of their criteria for a home abroad (one to enjoy for vacations during working years and as a possible retirement home later on) was to find a place centrally located for European travel. Their home is a four-hour drive from Munich, two hours from Venice, three hours from Florence. Verona, a city of 270,000, is a 45-minute drive. They are a half hour from a ski resort suitable for intermediate skiing and two hours from the excellent ski resort of Capellio.

By choosing a vacation area, the Martinellis' property is almost certain to increase in value. After buying their home, they discovered that a 27-hole golf course will soon be constructed on the road between Garda and Albisano. It is far enough away that it will not impinge on the town, but it will still increase their property value. Another of their goals, when establishing a second home abroad, was to make trips without packing a lot of luggage. In the short run, Bob points out, they are carrying along even more things than they would for a regular vacation, but soon they will have their European vacation base outfitted.

Additional European getaway opportunities arise as they meet other Americans in the expatriate network. Recently they met a couple who own a home in France's Loire Valley, and the two couples are discussing the possibility of home swaps. There are other advantages of international home ownership: when

Linda told her women's club in the Bay Area that she was purchasing a home in Italy, an interior decorator in the group offered
to decorate the home at no charge. The Martinellis received free
decorating services, the decorator benefited by adding a
European home to her portfolio and it also gave her the chance to
shop for antiques during her stay.

Experiencing daily life in a different culture is one of the
satisfactions of living abroad. The Martinellis' home is near a
wine producing area and, as Bob observes, "Like all of Italy,
every wine is local wine. You don't order Chianti if you are in
Chianti because you'll be served it automatically." With their
home-abroad base in Albisano, they won't have to travel far for
variety in scenery or cuisine, and in Italy you can count on music
to supply local color. One of Bob and Linda's favorite short trips
is a ferry ride across the lake: "Ferryboats connect the lakeside
cities," explains Bob. "Once we were taking the ferry across the
lake and a men's chorus was aboard, traveling to a concert
engagement. There were around 40 of them. They sang all the
way across the lake—everything from *Ave Maria* to bawdy
songs—and every one of them took a solo."

Chapter 3

An International Home Tour

"People say, 'I can't believe that you found this house in the heart of San José.'"

Allison Yance
San José, Costa Rica

T he decision to rent, buy or build a residence abroad is more complex than making a similar decision in the U.S. Renting for several months and in different seasons is strongly advised as a first step toward living abroad. But there are also many Americans who have plunged in by purchasing a home, condominium or lot after only a few weeks' vacation. As in a love-at-first-sight marriage, some thrive while others fail.

The best course is to take it slow, consider every possible factor and be twice as wary as you would be at home. This shouldn't seem surprising: you are about to face unfamiliar territory. But after all, the challenge of doing things differently is one of the reasons you decide to live in a new country.

Another reason to live abroad is to own property as an investment to be enjoyed for vacation or eventual retirement. Investment naturally carries some risk, although, in contrast to a few years ago, international real estate in many areas of the globe is now a prime candidate for your portfolio. European and Asian investors, both large and small, are bullish about buying homes and commercial and resort property—especially coastal property in Spain, Portugal, France, Italy, Greece and Ireland. Large investors are also developing resort property in prime areas of Mexico and Costa Rica. It is possible to take a wrong turn, but not too likely if you do your homework and follow international smart-money trends. The dollar is not as strong as a few years ago, another reason that some Americans regard international investments as a wise diversification strategy.

This also means that some locations that were bargains a few years ago are becoming more pricey. But like real estate prices anywhere, today's market value is often tomorrow's bargain in hindsight. Lily Cairns's condominium on the island of Mykonos cost $30,000 in 1983; today it is worth around $60,000 and says Lily: "I think that after 1992—when the European Community is fully in effect—it will be worth considerably more than it is now."

Arlene and Paul Dexter's French farmhouse, purchased in 1987 for $50,000, would cost twice the price in 1991. Veronica and George Alta's condominium in Torremolinos Spain cost $40,000 in 1984, and in 1991 is worth around $100,000. In Chiang Mai, Thailand, a burgeoning Pacific Rim economy has pushed David Mead's $40,000 home (built in 1987) to triple its original value by 1991. These are striking examples; on the other hand, you shouldn't assume that *any* international investment is a smart move. These home owners did careful research before purchasing their property—although none of them expected property values to increase so dramatically.

Some resort and retirement areas are overbuilt—such as Mexico's Lake Chapala—but for rental, such an area offers exceptional values. If your research and instincts tell you that the market will rise, and if you are patient, then a low market could offer opportunities for bargains now with appreciation likely in the future when demand catches up with supply.

After weighing your budget objectives, the choice of a home is a very personal decision: do you want a low-maintenance "turnkey" property, with little effort needed to move in? Or are you willing (or even eager) to modify an older residence, perhaps with a garden that needs nurturing? Would you prefer to be in or near a city with its cultural amenities, in a small village or in the countryside where inconvenience is often the price of rustic tranquility?

Once you have determined what you are looking for, the search is on. After retirement, Warren Lowry and his wife Anne traveled through Europe and the Far East, but Southern Spain held the strongest attraction. The Lowrys returned again and again, traveling the coast until they found a special area that appealed to them—about 20 miles east of Málaga and far enough from jet-set resorts to offer reasonable rent. The Lowry's apartment is a block from the beach and overlooks an 800-year-old fortress that is, quite ideally, preserved as a monument but not open to the public.

Bernice Gabler, a former New Yorker, found what she was looking for in Praia da Luz in Portugal's Algarve region. Her townhouse hugs the crest of a hill where the main road winds along the highest point in town. Bernice's condominium is one of several newer "clubs" that offer recreational facilities in the area. The townhouses are built in clusters of eight, but designed so that each roof in the complex is angled to provide privacy. In many prime expatriate and retirement areas around the world such clubs are planned for future retirement centers. For many people, one of the priorities for international living is this kind of comfort and service, and it is especially appreciated by single women. "I barely know how to change a light bulb," says Bernice, "and I certainly don't know how to fix the plumbing. It's wonderful to have a club that I can rely on—and they take care of the plumbing, too."

Libby Weston, who moved from Los Angeles to Spain in 1980, searched until she found an intimate corner of Spanish tradition. Her home, with whitewashed walls and a heavy wooden door, is half a block from the beach on a narrow street. The walls of her rented home are a foot thick, with deeply-set windows and a charming rear garden where wrought iron tables and chairs invite you to linger, and where trumpet vines lazily climb the walls. High-rise buildings abound in this popular coastal area, but Libby was able to find her home—one of the original adobe farmhouses built over a century ago—and she rents it at a modest price.

When you walk through her arched gate across slightly uneven tiles it is like entering another world: cool rooms filled with unusual pieces of furniture, walls decorated with old Spanish pictures. "I thought a house like this should have ancestors so I found these paintings in a second-hand store," says Libby, whose small home on the less-expensive edge of the Costa del Sol's prime resort area reflects Libby's journeys, her treasures and her taste.

Each person who is planning to live or retire abroad has different goals. These are best defined not from the armchair but

41

through travel and simulated living. In the appendix, you will find a planning worksheet for organizing current information and for locating a residence to fit your budget and overall goal.

First you travel. If your first trip to a country is on a standard tour, then the next visit should be more purposeful. A vacation packed with structured sightseeing is not likely to provide the kind of information you will need. Build in free time to explore, see property and look for opportunities to meet Americans in residence.

Plan your follow-up. The next step is to plan a follow-up trip or two in different seasons, because you should winter and summer in your prospective locale—to experience both climate and demographic changes.

In some countries, such as Costa Rica, seasons do not vary greatly throughout the year. If you explore living possibilities in a country with sharp weather contrasts, ask yourself frankly if you are willing to adapt to the off-season elements: a brief, blithe summer in a northern clime may be followed by a long winter. Experience winter and summer on an island in Greece or in the Caribbean to know your tolerance for heat and humidity.

In resort areas such as the Algarve and the Costa del Sol, visitors flock to the coast in high season but crowds drift away by mid-September. You may enjoy the contrast of a shifting population, or you may find that either the high-season bustle or the low-season quiet is unnerving. Experience both before choosing another country as your second home.

Simulated living. A vacation is the usual way to start a plan in motion, but the only way to determine whether you want to live abroad is to move in and make a country your home—at least provisionally. Simulated living usually takes six months to a year, and several phases of adjustment, before the average person reaches an everyday level of comfort in a new country. First you will experience the honeymoon phase—it's new and exciting. You feel more alive because your attention is constantly tickled by novelty and the steep learning curve brings a keen satisfaction. You may even feel younger, because the experience (in some ways) replicates discoveries of earlier years, before routine became established. Next, the novelty starts to wear thin and you begin to see faults. (A sign of this phase is when you hear yourself or your spouse comment "Back home, we used to..." or "Why don't they get smart and put mucilage on stamps here?") At this point, most people adjust but a few swing from the joy of novelty to despair, and move home.

Whether you are the type who acts on impulse and sometimes has to backtrack—or someone who pauses until the time seems right and then plunges with fixed resolve—it's advisable to build flexibility into your decisions. Don't leap ahead too fast, and don't make a hasty retreat; don't let the high of inflated enthusiasm cause an emotional chasm of disappointment.

Define Housing Goals

Housing is one of the most important decisions you will make; to reach a decision, you need to define your goals and timetable. Do you want a personal home for full-time or retirement residence? Or an investment to use as a vacation home and possible rental property or future retirement site?

Three general rules apply to housing: 1) rent first; 2) buy only where property shows promise of appreciating; 3) do not buy if it will tie up your savings, that is, maintain a reasonable amount of liquidity.

If a retirement home is your goal, remember that retirement planning should begin 5 to 10 years in advance. Some plans take longer to hatch. If you are five or more years away from retirement and have an opportunity to buy where land is appreciating, you could use the property as a vacation home or rental unit now and retirement home later. You will build equity in the meantime, while you decide whether this is an area where you really want to retire. We don't always have time—or the luxury of speculation—to allow our money to be tied up for four or five years, but if you have money to invest there can be advantages to buying abroad. Your research should answer the question of why real estate is appreciating (or not) in an area. Watch out for blueprint appreciation: the proposed highway or other infrastructure improvement may not materialize (in your lifetime) or a pollution cleanup plan may be delayed years before it progresses from a politician's desk to the out-of-doors.

Value and Speculation

A resort area is a good inflation hedge. Vacationers from a dozen countries travel to the Algarve and Costa del Sol, to Greece and the South of France, where Europeans are buying land for holiday and retirement homes. In anticipation of 1992, when EC provisos allow for free commercial interchange across the borders of the European member countries, a boom is already underway in the southern European coastal areas. With travelers of more than a dozen countries behind this appreciation of property, it does not rely on American tourism. In fact, the familiar American flag so commonly seen in the past at banks offering currency exchange now features flags of the most-travelled EC countries. The Ugly American seems to be disappearing through sheer attrition; in his or her place are an increasing number of knowledgeable Americans who are aware of the nuances of different cultures.

Outside of the EC countries, investment in a country such as Costa Rica is more speculative, partly due to the negative press surrounding its troubled neighbor, Nicaragua. But investment potential in Costa Rica is increasing with the growing number of Canadians who have discovered this small Central American country. Costa Rica is a living and working country with developing resort areas, but is less a magnet for waves of vacationers than are the Algarve and Costa del Sol. Yet this "working" country is beginning to attract foreign investors. Large Japanese companies are also buying land in Costa Rica, which helps replace political uneasiness about Nicaragua with a kind of "market trend" optimism.

Mexico, on the other hand, is a time-proven vacation and retirement destination for Americans. Easy and inexpensive access, along with a native language far less difficult than some (such as Greek or Portuguese), means that Mexico's popularity is likely to continue. Property investment is most speculative here in overbuilt areas, in cities with pollution problems and in underdeveloped but "promising" locales near popular resorts. If you prefer not to live in an expatriate community dominated by Germans, British or other Europeans, then in Mexico you are sure to be surrounded mainly by expatriate Americans.

Increasing property value is one reason many Americans prefer to buy rather than to rent. Whether at home or abroad, ownership is a way to control rising housing costs. As a renter, development and increased popularity of a locale causes rent increases; as an owner, the same circumstance brings property appreciation. The reverse is also true: a decline in value can mean a bargain for the renter, who can simply choose to move on if an area is no longer desirable; an owner may be stuck with a white elephant.

Securing a rental. After at least two trips to experience seasonal and demographic variations, you will already have developed some contacts or leads for real estate transactions, starting with rental property. Some inquiries can be handled by mail, once you have a grasp of desirable regions or neighborhoods and the style (among those available) of accommodations that you prefer—an apartment, townhouse (shared walls but more privacy than the average apartment) or a single family home. One of the best ways to lay groundwork is to see homes of Americans living in the area. Find out if there is a club for Americans; the American consulate may provide leads, or you can determine the favorite American gathering spot (it many be a hotel restaurant bar) where casual introductions are possible. If you are lucky, you may be invited to an American home during one of your exploratory trips and gain useful information as well as further leads.

After your exploratory trip you may want to secure a year-round rental. In a resort/seasonal area, the best approach is to negotiate off season, informing the landlord that you intend to remain through high and low season. You will be at a disadvantage if you try to negotiate during high season, but by discussing rental off season (especially in an area with high vacancies, such as outlying or newer areas) you should be able to arrange good year-round terms. Find out which districts are priced for prestige and which are priced for economy.

Limited Listings

You may not find all types of housing in an area. In the Costa del Sol, almost everyone is an apartment dweller, either in highrises or low-rise multi-unit villas. Single family homes are available, but they are much more costly than apartments. New construction is clustered, because coastal land is becoming scarce and therefore increasingly costly. Your neighbors will be mainly English, Dutch, German, French and Scandinavian. Rentals are usually handled through agencies here.

In the Algarve, you are likely to rent a single-story or two-story townhouse near a beach area. There are high-rise apartments but they are not as abundant as along the Costa del Sol. If you are interested in buying a villa in the Algarve, you will find that development (such as maximum height) is more carefully regulated than along the Spanish coast. If your Algarve villa is a half-mile from the ocean, it is not too likely that a new high-rise will block your view. Since rampant development in Spain preceded the Algarve by over a decade, Portugal has had a chance to learn a lesson in semi-controlled growth.

In Costa Rica, there is little restrictive zoning—so your neighbor could be an estate or a far more modest dwelling than yours. For the renter, this means occasional opportunities to rent small homes in the best residential neighborhoods. However, rentals are more difficult to find here than in the southern European resort areas. (Most of the construction in recent years has been government-built housing for lower-income native residents.) The best way to find a rental unit is through American contacts or recommended real estate agents.

Dwellings in Mexico and Costa Rica are similar to many structures found in the southwestern U.S. with cement—cool in summer, heat-conserving in winter—as the predominant construction material. You are likely to have a fireplace in your rental home in Costa Rica, except in the most inexpensive rentals. During the winter, you might use your fireplace or a space heater to take off the morning chill. Central heating is unnecessary. In warm areas, look for homes with cross ventilation so that with floor or ceiling fans you will not need air conditioning.

Real estate information is available in English-language publications found in areas with a sizable American or British expatriate community (see listings in the appendix), although the best rental prices are usually found in native-language newspapers. Word of mouth remains one of the best ways to find what you want; ask around for recommendations. Your landlord (or the seller, if you are in the market to buy) just might turn out to be an American.

Trading Up

Len and Tanya Kennebeck, who are in their mid 50s, own their home in Portugal, but the steps to ownership were gradual: the Kennebecks "traded up" from an undeveloped piece of property quite by accident. "We have been coming to Portugal for vacations for the past 15 years," says Len. "We discovered the Algarve in the 1970s when we diverted from a trip to Spain, and decided this was the place we wanted to retire."

While on vacation in Portugal one year, they purchased a piece of property with the intention of building a home in a few years. "Then the situation changed," explains Len. "The property became undesirable for us because it was too close to a new tennis complex, so we sold it." The advantage of the "undesirable" next-door development was that it greatly increased the value of their property. From the proceeds, they were able to buy their current home: five bedrooms, three baths, with two living rooms, a dining room, large kitchen and a downstairs multi-purpose room. The first unimproved parcel of land provided seed money for their lifestyle today.

Relying on Neighbors

For a single woman living abroad, security is a priority—although this doesn't have to limit your choice of accommodations. In 1982 Allison Yance joined her boyfriend (and future husband) who had a research grant to study in Costa Rica. They are now separated, and she is teaching in Costa Rica. Allie has created a world for herself as a single woman in San José. Her small rented house has parquet floors and hot running water (unlike some residences abroad, where water is heated per use). Her house is next to a large estate in a district of San José called Las Yoses ("the eyes"). Allie is very pleased with her $120-per-month home, which has two walls of floor-to-ceiling windows and a view of the mountains. She sees both sunrise and sunset, and at night the lights of San José. The house is well protected for a single woman: her home is adjacent to a large estate (with its own private security) and stone walls buffer the property from any sounds of traffic. Inside, the grounds are lush with trees and flowers. "People say, 'I can't believe that you found this house in the heart of San José.'" But she adds that finding a charming house with a view wasn't too difficult. Allie rents the house from a fellow member of an international running club, and she advises that one of the best ways to find rental property is through Europeans and other Americans.

Your network often includes your neighbors. Renee Wolpert has owned her home in Ajijic, Mexico, since 1975. At that time, an *inmigrante* could only own real estate in trust, but now free title is permitted except in certain restricted coastal areas. Renee's adobe house is in a five-house compound. Each structure is different in design but the compound offers the advantage of neighbors to help look after the property when other owners are away. Since a garden is shared by the five owners, there is little worry about (or expense for) maintenance of the grounds.

The Wolperts designed their home with a two-bedroom apartment downstairs and guest quarters upstairs; the latter has a small kitchen unit, bedroom and bath. Friends, family and paying guests have used the upstairs quarters. "The house has more than paid for itself—especially because we've rented it," explains Renee.

Plan to Upgrade

Living abroad seems to inspire plans to rebuild or remodel a home, perhaps because the type of person who decides to live abroad often has a creative streak and a penchant for restoration. Pamela Winger bought her 13-acre farm in the village of Kerry-on-Shannon in the middle of Ireland in 1990, at a price of $34,000.

The two story, 130-year-old farmhouse has two bedrooms, a small convertible room, a kitchen/living area and a sitting room (there are also two barns on the property). But the farmhouse does not have a bathroom, as is typical of many farms in the area. The Wingers plan to add a bath, plus a master suite with fireplace, for an estimated cost of $12,000. "So we will end up with a very nice property," comments Pamela.

In the early 1970s, John and Sally Barber purchased a home in the Dordogne region of France, 350 miles south of Paris. Their farmhouse is 300 years old, built of stone walls 28 inches thick. The single living room/dining room/kitchen has "a wonderful farm table made by a local craftsman," John explains. The floor is set with small, smooth stones. "We had it restored as it should be," says John, who notes that the French government keeps a close watch on restorations to be sure they are in keeping with the community. Craftsmanship is of old-world caliber. An example is the restored staircase in the Barber's farmhouse. It gave them pleasure and pride and enhanced the value of their property, for as John notes, "People always admire details like a beautiful staircase."

Larraine Grey, who sold her first small house in Portugal after renovating it and then bought another unusual home to remodel, offers this account: "We bought an old house positioned on a hill with a sea view. It's a strange house—with a *rua*, a little street in between two buildings, rather like a house in two parts." The

Greys took part of the house and made it into two rooms, added a bathroom and converted the *rua* by changing it into a hallway.

"So now it is like a wide center hallway with rooms off to the left and right," explains Larraine. "The purchase price of our farmhouse was $5,000 in 1984. We knew that was a really good deal, even though we had to install a new roof, aside from the other remodeling we wanted to do."

The property included a stable. "We left the big stone manger and decorated it with plants, then added a long dining room table. It looked very nice," says Larraine. The stable was so spacious that they converted one end (formerly a bread oven and rabbit hutch) into a one-bedroom apartment and a studio apartment, both of which they rented out. The stone farmhouse was a buff yellow color; although it is an Algarve regulation that homes be painted white—which creates the stunning whitewashed effect of the region—the Greys were allowed an exception since the property is over 200 years old and is true to its original color.

Or Move Right In

Many areas of Greece also impose design standards on new construction. Lily Cairns is glad that new construction is limited to two stories on Mykonos, and that the only color allowed on the whitewashed homes is trim on windows and doors.

Lily found her house only after her original plan fell through: after her first trip to Greece in 1981, she recalls, "I fell in love with the country and wanted to buy a house, originally on Patmos. I negotiated with the owner of the house for almost a year and was about to go over for final arrangements when the Aga Kahn bought a house—and the price of my Patmos house suddenly jumped from $25,000 to $60,000."

Lily began looking at homes on different islands, and finally decided on a move-in-condition property on Mykonos. The French-built organized community has a resident supervisor 11 months of the year, a pool, tennis courts, and the beach is only a short walk. Lily paid cash ("it was relatively simple") and worked with a lawyer who handles the sale of all properties in the village. She bought the house from a rendering. "I bought a concept: that with a new house, I wouldn't walk into electrical and plumbing problems—of course, electricity does go out on the island sometimes." Would she buy a home the same way again? Yes, says Lily, although she admits "it was a lucky thing."

The Joys and Woes of Building

Carl and Nancy Thalmeyer, both in their 70s, have changed residences twice since moving to Costa Rica in 1979. At first they lived on a farm in the hills, but after a decade reluctantly decided to leave their hillside retreat because of health problems. As Nancy explains: "We felt that we needed to divest ourselves of a lot of responsibility and just relax. And we needed to be closer to where we could call on people in an emergency."

Nancy and her husband (who are both retired teachers) had some contracting experience when they built their home in California. But when their contractor in Costa Rica didn't supervise his workers, the Thalmeyers had to change contractors. The result was a higher total cost than they had anticipated, and a lot of lost time.

Nancy advises obtaining a highly recommended contractor to supervise the job if you decide to build your own home, because it is not unusual for a job that would take three months in the U.S. to stretch out to six months there. Other Americans who have built homes abroad, such as Hal Mannheim (who built a home on the island of St. Lucia), have had a similar experience.

The Thalmeyers' lot and custom designed home of 2,700 square feet with a large yard cost $100,000 in 1987. The residential community in which their one-story home is located provides recreational facilities, including clubhouse, sauna, pool and tennis courts, as well as gardening and security service. For these amenities the Thalmeyers pay a maintenance fee of around $100 per month. The gardeners are more than just gardeners, as Nancy points out. "They are assigned to us one day each week, and they can do anything—wash windows, clean up debris—and that's quite comfortable for us at our age."

The Thalmeyers' house has a full basement, which may seem unusual in a temperate climate but there is a good reason. When building or planning to live in an area, it is important to inquire about the water supply. In some parts of Costa Rica (and other countries too) there can be problems in the dry season. "Most good residential construction projects have a water tank and pump in the basement, and the one we have is silent." There are three wells on the property and it is "good water," explains Nancy.

More Home for Your Money

"We decided early on that we wanted to build rather than buy," says Karen Knight, who has lived in Portugal since 1987, "because if you are willing to put in the effort, you get more house for your money." Karen would not advise building for someone who either does not have some experience with construction or a lot of time (she had renovated an apartment in New York and her husband Paul had contracting experience before they were married). They advise that it is important to be in the area—or living in a place where you can visit regularly—to keep an eye on the project.

To find their property, Karen and Paul spent a lot of time driving up and down the coast, "getting a feel for the Algarve," as she explains. "We decided we wanted to be in the central Algarve, and thought the eastern and western regions would be too remote." The activities that they found of interest were clustered in the central region; the town of Almansil, for example, is a center for businesses catering to foreigners. They wanted to be north of the highway that demarcates the coastal tourist area and inland area. The Knights' home is a 25-minute drive from the beach, but has a pool so they can enjoy outdoor living in privacy. Since they planned to be year-round residents, they did not build with the idea of using their home for a holiday rental.

Karen and Paul worked with one of the smaller but well-established estate agents in the area, a broker in business for 20 years. Initially when they were looking for a home to rent, the agent advised them to look in the town of Faro, where he explained that there are fewer tourists and more reasonable rents during high season. When they were ready to build, he located their land, which included one older residence along with ample room to build. The Knights now live in the new house and are renovating the original home, which they will sell when the renovation is complete.

Although it takes more patience to build or remodel abroad, there are rewards—usually financial, and also aesthetic, since in many countries there are attractive natural materials available and detail craftsmen whose families have practiced their trade for generations.

Going Native—or Not

Choosing to live in the country, or to buy in a remote development, can mean a bargain or a "ground floor price," but you should be aware of inconveniences that can accompany your remote hideaway. Roy Teicher, who has lived in Costa Rica since 1976, doesn't mind the downside of life in a rugged setting. He first visited Costa Rica in 1974 and only returned to the States to liquidate his property in San Diego. "I went back and had a garage sale. I put a sign on College Avenue that said 'Garage sale—going to Costa Rica.' I've met a lot of people who've moved here since then who tell me they saw that sign," he recalls.

Roy lives in a spectacular setting with a 54-foot waterfall on his property, where he built an A-frame home with a stone fireplace. The home is positioned for a close-up view (from his loft bedroom or spacious deck) of the waterfall and bright canyon foliage. Behind Roy are a few small homes, all occupied by rural Costa Rican families. Despite his edge-of-the-jungle lifestyle, he is only an hour's drive from San José.

Roy's lifestyle isn't for everyone, but he prefers his rustic surroundings and accepts inconveniences that would unnerve less hearty expatriates. One is the army ant migration that occurs every few years. According to Roy, the ants march in one door and out the other. He leaves doors and windows open to hasten their progress. "When they come I just leave for a couple of hours. Sometimes I go to a movie in San José. They just march through and leave the place as clean as it was before," says Roy stoically.

The Far Side of Development

For the adventurous, and those interested in more speculative investments, locales away from urban centers offer potential advantages. One is the chance to own coastal property, a dwindling opportunity in most accessible temperate areas of the world. An example is Nosara, on Costa Rica's Pacific Coast in the province of Guanacaste. Joan Racine, who has lived in Nosara since 1985, first heard about Nosara when she was working for an international airline over a decade ago. Property at that time was offered, as Joan recalls, "for $100 down, $100 per month." In the beginning, there were no roads and no electricity in Nosara, though in 1991 it is a community of 86 homes on plots of one-third to two acres with 12 condominiums and a hotel.

Nosara has one primary restriction: no building is allowed within 200 meters of the beach. Since Guanacaste is one of the drier areas of Costa Rica, Joan notes, "We prefer the wet or green season—no dust on the roads," although one of her fellow residents adds: "But in summer and the dry season, we're glad when the tourists leave." Although Nosara now boasts 35 miles of year-round roads, a civic association and a clinic, telephone lines are still scarce and the Gilded Iguana (bar and cafe) still serves as the message center for many of Nosara's residents—who won't have to worry about overdevelopment for many years.

Regulations Preserve Value

If you're considering a development in the country, you will no doubt have paved roads and modern amenities (and not have to worry about Roy's army ants), but you should be wary of drawbacks that might not be evident. You will be shown a prospectus, but you should visit the land under development—which may have one or more model units. Note that many countries and regions do not have zoning regulations; in outlying developments, regulations may be relaxed to encourage participation by developer and buyers. It is important to inquire about restrictions and conditions to help prevent the possibility that a neighboring property might block your view, or be built with standards far below your own.

If you want to buy near the coast in a temperate climate, you may find that ownership is restricted. In Mexico, for example, a foreign national cannot own property within three miles of the shoreline (although a bank trust may be established to circumvent this restriction). There are also restrictions on ownership by expatriates in Thailand; David Mead, for example, has a special business arrangement for his home in Chiang Mai.

Zoning and building regulations may hamper your personal plans, but usually these are agreeable as they help assure quality and contribute to property appreciation. On the Greek islands of Mykonos and Kalymnos, for example, only new homes in the Greek style are allowed—whitewashed walls with brightly colored doors. As Nancy Stangos explains, "They are trying to keep everything compatible with a certain traditional look. In the 1960s and 1970s people were putting up anything, painting houses any color. It took some experimentation but restraints were placed on builders and now they are building beautiful homes in the traditional style."

Portugal's Algarve is another area where steps are being taken to preserve the architectural heritage: whitewashed houses and countless variations on traditional ceramic chimneys add both sparkle in the sunlight and whimsy on rooftops. In Mexico, the city of San Miguel de Allende is leading the way in architectural preservation, which has inspired Ben and Laura Gruning to move from Guadalajara: "San Miguel is a national monument, and buildings must conform to the Colonial style of architecture. It's a beautiful city," says Laura.

Close-in Comforts

By far the majority of Americans living abroad choose to live in or near a town or city with access to shopping and other services. Alan Cox moved from Alameda, California, in 1986 to Alajuela, Costa Rica, which is around an hour's drive from San José. It is a self-contained town with a variety of shops, restaurants and services necessary for independent living abroad. Alan calls his rented house "better than average," and any visitor would agree: the modern, three-bedroom, 2 1/2 bath, two-story structure with a tile roof, fern-landscaped entryway and decorative wrought iron gate and sweep of bougainvillea in the courtyard would blend in with any upper-middle-class Southern California neighborhood.

"It's a peaceful life and you don't have any heating bills," says Alan, who rents the house from its American owner for $370 per month and explains that he is interested in buying a home when relations with Nicaragua become more stable. Alan remarks on the range of rental property available in Costa Rica: "For $600 you can have a palace, or you can rent a satisfactory house for as little as $200 per month." He advises that when looking for a home to rent, it's best to find someone who can provide referrals.

Group Support

Ralph Breyer, a retired banker from New York, moved to the Algarve in 1982. He and his wife Ellen bought property near Lagos, then purchased a 15-acre farm adjacent to their original property. The Breyers raise wheat on their farm and explain that although the first year they lost money, it has been profitable ever since. Before moving to Portugal, they visited twice and rented property in Vale do Lobo for six months.

Ralph is a member of the Association of Foreign Property Owners, which has 450 members in the Algarve and includes members of many nationalities, although the majority of members are British. One purpose of the Association, he explains, is to help people know and obey the law. The Association offers seminars on taxation, documentation and other topics, and also publishes a monthly newsletter.

Such support groups are a good way to stay abreast of laws concerning your property. In Spain, Veronica and George Alta are members of the American Club, which serves as a clearinghouse for Americans living in the Costa del Sol. Veronica first came to Spain in 1983 while she was director of the Department of Aging in Philadelphia, which conducted a trip to Spain. She and her husband returned together and found their apartment by driving through different areas, looking for *se vende* ("for sale") signs.

The Altas bought two apartments—one for personal use, another as a rental unit. Their hillside apartments with views of the sea each cost $40,000 in 1984 and have doubled in value since then. Among Veronica's criteria when choosing a neighborhood were transportation, safety and a post office. When they found the apartment they wanted, they contacted the owner who lived in London. The "transaction" was executed in Philadelphia, then registered in Spain. Now that Veronica and George are retired, they spend May through October in Philadelphia, where they still own property, and the rest of the year they reside in Spain.

The rental unit covers their expenses for both apartments. They arranged for rent to be paid to their bank in the U.S., which simplifies record keeping. The Altas have had no trouble keeping the apartment rented from June through September since they advertise in the American Club newsletter and in British magazine rental listings.

Their homeowners insurance, with full coverage, costs $250 per year (compared with $650 for their condominium in Philadelphia). Like many Americans, the Altas divide their year. "We don't spend the summers here," says Veronica, explaining that summer means hot streets crowded with tour groups. She notes that, although there are some vacationers throughout the year, "visitors who spend October through May are generally more seasoned travelers—less harried and far fewer in number."

Temporary Housing

When conducting housing research, you should become familiar with market conditions: Are there few apartment or home rental vacancies, or are they plentiful? If your preferred type of housing is not easy to find, you may need to adjust your timetable until you find that old farmhouse to remodel or a condominium in the right neighborhood. Until then, it shouldn't be difficult to find temporary housing until you locate a more permanent address. One of the advantages of the rental option, of course, is freedom to change locales whenever you choose.

After many years of visiting Mexico on vacations, the Grunings sold their retail business in San Francisco, sold their home (carrying back a mortgage) and decided to skip the simulated living phase: they simply bought a pair of one-way airline tickets to Guadalajara. As Lauren explains: "We carried most of our worldly possessions in two big suitcases."

Their first residence was the Suites Bernini in Guadalajara, a multi-story apartment with hotel services. Their accommodations included one room and a kitchen—the small space motivated them to look more quickly for an apartment since they lacked a living room. Their initial housing or "suite" is typical of that found in Guadalajara and other larger cities in Mexico, and it served as their base of operations. "They are wonderful places to stay for a while or for snowbirds," Lauren recommends. When searching for their apartment, the Grunings turned to all available resources, including classes and tours on retirement in Mexico. They looked in want ads in the *Colony Reporter*, checked bulletin boards of the American Society and other places where Americans gather. Then they walked all over the city, as Lauren describes it, "in every direction, miles and miles."

Over a two-week period they rejected some apartments as too small, unfurnished or suitable for someone staying only a few months, but then they found what they were looking for: the apartment was furnished, the right size, and in one of the neighborhoods they liked best as a result of their exploratory walks. For $350 per month, they rented a two-bedroom, two-bath apartment with a large living room and dining area, plus an extra room for hobbies.

Home Buying Abroad

Home buying abroad differs for each country, but there are some general guidelines for all. When considering the purchase of an existing home or condominium, or property for renovation, or land on which to build, you should note the following points:

1. Identify the different types of property available in the area. Note restrictions to spare yourself wasted time and expense. Does zoning allow you to build on rural land? What zoning restrictions affect possible remodeling plans? After identifying available property, narrow down your options, noting the advantages for each:

• A club complex offers security, recreation and maintenance provisions, but its self-contained country club environment may not be enjoyed by those who want a lifestyle more integrated with the native community. Services such as a market, restaurant and cleaning may be available on the premises, but the convenience (often at a premium price) may mean that you become dependent on club facilities rather than experiencing daily life in your new country.

• Condominiums (purchase) or apartments (rental) are usually near community shops and services. Some builders cater to expatriates and you may feel more comfortable to know that there are other Americans (as well as Europeans) in the building.

• A single-family or freestanding home requires more maintenance, security and transportation considerations (the last, if it is in a rural area) than common-wall housing. Advantages include privacy and land for cultivation or recreation. If you are concerned about liquidity, research how long the home (as well as other properties in the same area) has been on the market. You may find that homes sell quickly—or that you may need to wait a long time before finding a buyer if you choose to sell.

2. Understand taxes involved in property transfer. Usually transfer fees are modest (but they can be as high as 14% of market value). Be prepared for them, in order to avoid problems with fund transfer or liquidity.

3. Find out who pays the commission. In the U.S., the seller pays the commission and the agents for buyer and seller

cooperate by dividing a percentage based on the selling price of the home. In many countries the buyer pays the commission or a flat fee.

4. Define the terms used in a transaction, using a translator if necessary, since real estate terms abroad and in the U.S. may differ in intent. Know your liability for property and capital gains tax.

5. In the early stages of a real estate transaction, determine who holds title to the property. In rare cases, family disputes over ownership may tie up property much longer than you want.

6. Determine other fees, such as the cost of registry and the fee charged by a notary, auctioneer or other official involved in the transaction.

Whenever possible, seek advice from respected professionals in the country. In Portugal, seminar speaker David Oddy of Samson & Co. offered the following advice. He analyzes available property into six types: 1) a house or condominium in existing or older developments; 2) a house or condominium in a newer development, which includes facilities for which the buyer must pay an ongoing maintenance fee (usually much lower than comparable properties in the U.S.); 3) an existing apartment structure in which the developer handles rental for you part of the year, or which you may choose to use exclusively for family and friends; 4) a plot of land in a developed area, where you may be required to have the developer build for you—or you may have an option to contract your own builder; 5) a parcel of land in the country, which is a more adventurous approach since you will need building permits and must be sure that this is an area where residential construction is allowed (i.e., not designated for agriculture only) and that services such as electricity, road access and water supply are obtainable; 6) an older building or farmhouse that you buy for renovation.

Playing the System

David Mead in Thailand built his home at the edge of the municipality of Chiang Mai and thereby avoided paying property tax or transfer tax. In Portugal, the transfer tax or *sisa* tax is payable on both unimproved and improved property. However, if you buy improved property, it is based on the cost of the whole parcel—but if you buy land and enter into a building contract, you pay tax only on the lot purchased and not on construction costs. (For this reason, in some areas it may be cheaper to build than to buy.)

Tax incentives and subsidies are also possible: Barbara Moore plans to buy a loft property in Lisbon, where tax credits make such an investment very desirable. Her goal is to develop part of the space for her own residence; the other part would comprise a second unit to rent to Americans and other expatriates. Pamela Winger in Ireland will be able to apply for an EC subsidy to help improve her rural property.

Sometimes there are other strategies—all very legal—that can make your life abroad easier or more inexpensive. An American couple in Portugal discovered a way to minimize bureaucratic hassles when building a home. They decided to keep the road to their new house in muddy disarray. The well-dressed official who came to inspect their home—not wanting to muddy his shoes—said, "It looks like you're doing a fine job here. You obviously know what you are doing, so it should be fine for us to approve the house from your blueprint." You can learn tricks from fellow Americans—about taxes, loopholes, ways around official red tape—but remember that sometimes what seems a smart play could end up as a costly mistake.

Estate Agents and Notaries

The professionals with whom you will conduct a real estate transaction—whether renting, buying or building—will vary in different countries. In the U.S., a typical ensemble of professionals involved in a transaction would be two real estate agents (the buyer's and the seller's), in most cases a loan officer, an escrow officer, and a title insurance representative (usually arranged by the buyer's agent), and in some cases a lawyer is retained by the buyer and/or seller.

In other countries, a notary is often the most important professional involved in a real estate transaction. He or she signs the deed and officiates at the presentation of purchase price, since cash rather than a mortgage is usual in an expatriate real estate transaction. A deposit of 10%–30% is usually required, with the balance due within a designated number of months. A promissory contract to buy and sell a particular property is usually required as documentation to import the purchase price, which will be arranged through a designated bank or in some cases through the national bank of the country.

One of the more unusual customs when purchasing property abroad is a two-tiered purchase price. In many countries—such as Italy, France and Portugal—there are two "prices" involved in a real estate transaction: one price is agreed upon as the official sale price, on which transfer taxes will be based, and the other "real price" is achieved through a supplementary payment. Such transactions are not uncommon, but it is advisable to talk with Americans and other expatriates in residence to be sure you fully understand the consequences (i.e., penalties) if the two-price procedure is discovered by officials. It may not be a problem—or it might jeopardize your visitor or residence status. If the terms of the official contract do not reflect the entire price, and buyer and seller agree to make a separate undisclosed arrangement, the national bank may act as regulating agent and disapprove the price. Some countries do not monitor this—others, such as Portugal, conduct an assessment to be sure that the "official price" is not too low.

After the deed is notarized, your title is registered and proof of title is established by entry in the local land registry or its equivalent, depending on the country. In each country there are slight variations. The better prepared you are by obtaining current information (including pending changes of law that might affect your purchase), and by talking with Americans who have been through this before you, the smoother your real estate transaction will be.

Since home financing is rare in most countries abroad, the terms of purchase are usually worked out over a period of a few months. During a two-week period in 1989, Bob and Linda Martinelli negotiated a down payment of $20,000 on their $150,000 duplex in Albisano, Italy, with a few thousand dollars up front as a "good faith" payment. (Bob points out that the *total* price is equivalent to a down payment for similar property near their home in Marin County, California.) The Martinellis agreed to provide the rest of the down payment a month later, and the remainder of the purchase price in four months. When purchasing a property abroad, if you are not in the country when a purchase is to be finalized, it is common practice to appoint a representative with power of attorney. Although Americans are wary of granting this power, it has a very limited scope in most other countries, unlike a power of attorney in the U.S. The power of attorney may be granted for specific circumstances, such as to buy (i.e., finalize purchase of) a single property. This can usually be handled from the nearest consular office of the country where the transaction will occur.

Legal Precautions

In the U.S., we are accustomed to taking our grievances to court and assume that there is a legal safety net to protect us, despite the adage *caveat emptor* ("let the buyer beware"). The legal system in many countries does not allow for property problems to be resolved as readily through the courts as in the U.S., although at home cases can also drag on for years.

If you buy land, you pay the price and get what you have agreed upon—or should. Do not frame a convoluted contract or think that if there is a problem it can be solved in court. You should be sure that what you *think* you are buying is what you *actually* are buying, and you should always be satisfied before you sign any contract. In the U.S., when you tell a real estate agent that you want a house, he or she produces a contract, you sign it and the house is yours after title search and a period in escrow. In many countries abroad you may be presented with what appears to be an orderly contract—but the title may not be clear, and there is no automatic "falling out of escrow" as there is in the U.S. You (and your good faith payment) may end up in a lengthy legal limbo until a complicated title problem is resolved. It is important to ask questions—and to find your own lawyer, being sure that he or she represents you and preferably has no business relationship with the seller or developer. If an agent does represent the developer—as did Lily Cairns's—look for assurance by other owners in the development that they were satisfied with their agent-client relationship. Your lawyer should be experienced in foreign purchases and as a precaution you should be sure that the lawyer is acting only for you and has no conflicting interests.

THAILAND

Chapter 4

Vacation Home Today, Retirement Home Tomorrow

"Having a vacation home would be better than just having a vacation."

Robert Slater
Dallas, Texas

Y ou may not have a lot of time to spend abroad now, but you may want to spend more time—or even retire—in another country in a few years. Advance planning can open a financially advantageous door to the future, especially for a family with children at home or in college.

When you add up the numbers, it becomes apparent why some busy and farsighted people choose to buy abroad: if a two-week vacation abroad costs $3,000 for a couple, it may take 15 years to offset the price of a $45,000 home—but you will have an investment as well as vacation memories to show for it. If you are considering a home or condominium abroad, make sure that the location is appreciating (or at least is likely to retain its value), otherwise the justification as investment could turn out to be a disappointment. If you buy in or near a resort area, it's a safe bet that the value of your property will climb. Chances are, you will get more use from your overseas property than a two-week vacation, in addition to the personal appreciation you will gain by offering it to friends and family.

Most employees with job longevity receive at least two weeks of vacation. Some have sabbaticals—or even unexpected time out when a retreat is just what they need. Lily Cairns started with short spring and fall vacations in her Greek island home. Her latest trip—between jobs—was over two months, and she is now in the process of arranging consulting work that will allow her to live a split year with six months in New York and six months in Greece. She shares her home with friends and family members too, and this year she plans to rent her home for $700–$800 per week during high season through a local agent who is respected for carefully screening tenants.

With time on your side, you may be able to buy property at the edge of resort development and wait for appreciation to reach you. Be sure to do your homework regarding city planning, such as hotels and resorts slated for construction and highway expansion. If development exceeds your expectations and the area becomes too crowded, appreciation should allow you to choose a less developed area and "trade up" with your well-invested dollars.

Coastal areas are not the only magnets for tourism. Any area with natural or historic attractions is almost certain to increase in value. John Barber's farmhouse is not far from the famous prehistoric caves of Lascaux. Bob and Linda Martinelli's home is near a popular lakeside resort in Italy and not far from a major ski resort. They avoid the higher prices of the tourist center but benefit from the proximity. Another reliable long-term investment choice is a weekend or holiday area that serves a major city. Uruguay's Punta del Este, located between the Atlantic Ocean and the estuary of the Rio de la Plata, is a favorite getaway for business people from Buenos Aires and Montevideo. Many of them spend the South American summer vacation (December to February) in the cool and breezy "Punta," where ocean and river views are protected since the area from roadside embankment to waterline is, by law, free from development or private use. Knowing the restrictions—or lack thereof—will help you make a good investment decision.

Bargain Surprise

During exploratory trips, while you are learning about property value in the area, it may be difficult to resist the temptation to buy. What happens if you find what seems a good bargain, but your retirement or living-abroad plan is several years in the future? Such a good buy may not arise on the next trip (you may reason), or the dollar may have reduced purchasing power later on. If your financial position allows, here are a few points to consider before buying a vacation home abroad:

• The most obvious advantage of buying property abroad is appreciation, and location is key. The area's value and growth should be such that when it is time to move abroad or retire (or if you decide to sell at that time) your investment should have increased in value.

• If your home is in a popular vacation area and you hope to rent it out part of the year, you should consider whether the area is becoming overbuilt, which may result in a higher vacancy factor.

• It is not advisable to rely on rental income—period. Consider it as "frosting" and you won't find yourself in a bind and unable to cover cash flow requirements at home. But one of the advantages of buying before you are ready for full-time (or split-year) residency abroad is rental potential: the opportunity to defray some costs while your property is appreciating. If it is too far from a popular area, you are not likely to find regular renters. Renting out a vacation house isn't for everyone; you may find yourself uncomfortable with the idea that strangers have been living in your home. Rental income can be hard won. It may not be easy to assure occupancy, especially if your home suits you but may not have the right number of rooms or amenities for the international tourist crowd. Or, you may need to change rental agents a few times until you find one who books reliable tenants.

Often you will find that high rental rates apply to the desperate and disorganized, like "scalped" tickets to events. This does not assure quality renters. You may have to settle for less income than the prime monthly rate quoted to you by an estate agent or seller, so be skeptical about rental potential.

Lily Cairns was discouraged by her first renters, who stole blankets, pans and household objects. Now she has a different rental agent and is about to resume renting again. Debra and Jim Erland have also changed their minds about renting.

"We had no intention of buying abroad," says Debra, explaining that she and Jim were already seasoned travelers by the time they decided on Portugal for their retirement home. A broker showed them several plots of land and they viewed some available homes with an estate agent before choosing one with the amenities Debra wanted: fully furnished, an English-speaking maid and an installed telephone. "These things were vital to me because I had children in high school and one in college, and I knew they would be coming with their friends," she explains.

For 10 years the Erlands came twice a year on vacation and rented the house through an agent during the winter. The income covered the cost of maintaining the house. For the first few years they rented through friends; later on they used a rental agent. Within six years, Jim was ready for a permanent move. They sent over a shipment of goods and started painting the rooms of the house, a project they decided to do themselves. But Debra decided that her children were not ready for her to leave, so they delayed their emigration four years and decided to rent again.

This time they used a different rental agent. "They didn't pay top rental," Jim says of his choice of agent at that time, "but they were a decent shop and had clean tenants." From April to October they had 100% occupancy of their property, reserving two weeks for themselves. "And we had income, which more than covered the cost of running the house," says Jim, adding that in his opinion renting out a house does not make money because "there is damage, there are repairs, and I don't think you can count on having a 10% or 20% return. You cover your expenses, you get three holidays out of it each year, but it is not a source of income."

Rental Ups and Downs

The disadvantages of renting your property abroad include some loss of privacy and security, as well as some limit on your ability to spontaneously occupy the property. If you choose to have a rental agent in the area handle the home for you, housekeeping and maintenance are usually part of the arrangement. By working with a reputable rental agent, you should feel confident that in the event repairs are needed you can trust the agent to negotiate the repairs at a reasonable cost. This may mean quickly coming up with payment for the service—which can be an unpleasant surprise (just as it can be at home when you need plumbing, roofing or other kinds of repairs). In short, you should have a contingency plan in your budget for such expenses. To keep your home abroad producing rental income, repairs cannot wait. Since these repairs will be needed in the course of ownership anyway, with a rental agent monitoring the condition of your property it means that you are less likely to spend the first several days of your vacation on maintenance.

The advantage of owning property in a complex rather than a freestanding structure becomes apparent when you are an absentee owner. A home in any area is more vulnerable than property with shared walls: for this reason, rental homes (unless you arrange for a live-in caretaker) should be sparsely furnished, although your home can be enhanced with inexpensive, easily replaced decorative touches. Wait until you are the only resident—preferably full time—before you add expensive or heirloom pieces.

Renting to Friends

Another strategy is to rent only to friends and family, or to individuals recommended by friends and family. In this case, you will probably have a high vacancy factor (the local rental agent might keep your property occupied through the holiday season, at least). Another financial drawback of renting to friends and family is that you may find yourself charging little or nothing for the favor. When your favorite niece asks to use it as a honeymoon getaway, are you likely to charge her the going rate? Or your best friend, suddenly faced with a divorce, who needs some time to sort out his life?

When loaning your home to friends and family, it may not seem like a rental property to you, but some resort areas base taxes on a rental scale and you must be aware of your tax obligations. If you claim that the home is not for rental, but a steady stream of people are visiting your home, it will appear that you are renting it. Tax on global income is becoming more closely monitored by some countries, notably the 12 members of the EC. Computer information is making this kind of international data available, and in one resort area taxi logs are used to track property used for rental (e.g., if your friends pay rent to you in the U.S.), so be cautious if an expatriate recommends that you slide past a law "that isn't enforced." Often this is true, but be sure to get several opinions before you conclude that any law, income tax or otherwise, is generally ignored by officials, especially if the person offering an opinion is selling you something.

Sharing and Home Exchange

Renting out a vacation home is only one of the ways to defray costs when you are not a full-time resident. Another approach—that of Arthur Loeb and his wife, who own a vacation home in

France's Loire Valley—is to buy a vacation home with another couple.

The Loebs and their co-owners are old friends who understand each other's foibles, a prime requisite for such a joint venture; that is, since there are many potential complications with ownership of a home abroad, starting with the terms of purchase, it is best to have excellent communication with your partners. The arrangement between the two couples allows each to have the home part of the year, with occupancy half of the summer (so that one can enjoy spring, the other autumn). Repairs are split evenly, as are taxes. If the owner is not in residence, the home is available for use "off season" by the other with permission—and so far, the entire arrangement has worked smoothly since 1984.

Home exchange is a good way to experience different areas before deciding where to buy. Arlene and Paul Dexter spent four years vacationing through a home exchange before they bought their home in the French countryside. Of the home exchange experience, Arlene says, "It was often very hit-or-miss. You received the magazine in the spring, you tried to match yourself up with a house that seemed comparable to yours." Only one year out of four were they able to get their first choice. "Other years we ended up in places we would not have dreamed of going, but they all turned out marvelously," she explains.

"You have to explore to find the right spot," Arlene advises. On their last exchange vacation, the Dexters were walking through a small town when they saw a photograph of a small house in the window of an estate agent's office. The agent came out and said he would be glad to show it—if they were seriously interested. "Obviously we had looked at a fair number of properties by that time. We'd go to agents and say we were interested in a certain price. We had been looking for three or four years."

Sometimes there is a descriptive term that will help the estate agent understand what you are looking for. In France it is *maison secondaire*, a country or holiday house. "That implies simplicity," Arlene notes. The agent showed the Dexters beautiful old barns, which they thought were lovely and inexpensive but required a large amount of work. "If you put the money in, in five years it would be gorgeous, but we wanted to move in right away and not waste a year fixing it or managing long-distance renovations with an architect you'd only see once a year."

Of their vacation home purchase, Arlene says: "It was much cheaper than many areas we had looked at. We didn't buy anything grand because we didn't want high maintenance, and because—for the time being—we can only go for one week in the winter and a month in the summer." Paul will soon have a sabbatical, when he will be able to spend six months in France.

The Dexters' home has one large room upstairs and two small bedrooms, a bath and a larger room downstairs. The kitchen is adequate, but the Dexters plan eventually to remodel. There is a generous garden. Maintenance of the home is low because it is constructed of stone, which requires little work. The traditional shutters are natural wood penetrated with a stain. They take little upkeep and also serve as a safeguard. "You can't get in the shutters without waking the whole town," says Arlene. She comments about her security concerns with a free-standing house: "We were careful about that. The original plan was to be near a town or village so neighbors could keep an eye out. It turns out we are in a little *bourg* with a few houses, and a neighbor—a wonderful woman—keeps an eye on the place."

Including agent's fees, they paid $50,000 in 1987. The property is near Bergerac, where summers are mild and the climate is pleasant. Winters are cool, however. But since they are close to Spain and not far from the French Riviera, "If it seems chilly, we can take a short trip to the Mediterranean," Arlene points out. The Dexters have outfitted their home sparsely, but it has everything they need for their preferred kind of vacation.

A vacation home abroad provides the comfort of familiarity—with space, linen and cooking utensils arranged for your individual needs, perhaps vacation clothing in the closet, an easel for painting, a typewriter, bicycles and hobby supplies. It is your home base for exploring new byways, which may be across the nearest border or not far from your front door.

Changing Plans in
the Caribbean

A vacation home abroad can turn out to be just a pleasant getaway, rather than a profitable investment or even a hoped-for retirement haven. It might be compared to buying a painting by an undiscovered artist: be sure you will derive personal enjoyment, because there is no guarantee that your purchase will appreciate in value or meet your long-term expectations.

In 1965, Hal Mannheim of Wilmington, Delaware, bought plantation property on the island of St. Lucia with a beautiful vista of the Caribbean for $50,000. During the next few years, the Mannheims built a home with a pool on the property's best view site. They planned to use it as a vacation home and rental, then occupy it full time after Hal retired from his medical practice. The home, designed by an American architect, has three bedrooms, two baths and maid's quarters; it features a 40 ft. by 40 ft. living room with a unique beamed ceiling, spectacular windows over-looking the sea and a private beach. "We're isolated," explains Hal, "and it was exactly what we wanted at the time."

Building on a remote site has drawbacks. One is the difficulty of finding a reliable contractor who will not only travel to the site but also complete the project. Hal's first contractor gave him a bid, but halfway through the project said he needed more money to complete the job. With a half-built house, Hal had to choose between providing more money for the first contractor, or finding someone else to complete the home. He chose the second alternative, but only after a more careful search for a reputable builder. Hal was told that electricity would soon be available in the area—but it was several years before electricity could be installed, and this caused another problem: water had to be gathered in cisterns until electricity allowed him to pump water to the home.

Hal traveled to the island every few months while the home was under construction. On one trip he found that the contractor had taken a larger job, with the result that work on Hal's home only progressed when the construction crew was not engaged in their priority project. Delays were not the only problem, and as

Hal advises: "You need someone beside the contractor to be sure that all specifications are followed precisely." He eventually hired an engineer to oversee the completion of the job, and his home was finally ready for occupancy much later than planned.

Hal believed the opinion of the estate agent who sold him the property and assured him, "There will be no problem finding a capable manager to run the plantation profitably while you are away." The dream of a vacation home today/retirement home tomorrow plus an investment providing extra income sounded too good to be true—and in Hal's case, it was.

For an absentee owner who keeps household help or a manager all year Hal suggests: "You have to let the help know that you own the property and they do not. You also should be there now and then, and above all, be involved in the planning and decision making." He discovered that property in a tropical area requires a lot of maintenance, since materials deteriorate more rapidly in a hot, moist climate. One way for the owner to be involved is to help plan a replacement and maintenance schedule, suggests Hal.

Despite the beautiful setting, the Mannheims found St. Lucia lacking in cultural stimulation. At first he noticed what seemed to be an excessive preoccupation with alcohol among expatriates, which he assumed was a way of beating boredom. Over the past decade, however, technology has improved the quality of passive entertainment: satellite brings in television from around the world, and there are videos to while away the hours. With increasing airline service to the island, more hotels and restaurants have appeared, providing more places for entertainment and dining.

Such embellishments help, but Hal misses the kind of cultural life found in most other countries where he has traveled. Realizing that St. Lucia is not his choice for retirement, Hal has offered the home for sale by advertising it in exclusive property listings, but he has had few offers. "There isn't a great market for American-style Caribbean homes, except perhaps on St. Barts," he explains.

Undaunted, Hal continues to explore retirement options. He is still active in his medical practice, and divides his vacation time between his island home and trips to other countries with retirement potential. Currently he is considering Costa Rica, where he found the pace to be relaxed yet the culture more stimulating than that of St. Lucia. "You can see that there is a lot going on all the time in San José and in many of the smaller towns. In Costa Rica, you could become as involved as you want." Among the residential offerings in Costa Rica, Hal found two that he liked: One was just outside San José, a planned community of custom-built homes developed by a reputable builder who demonstrated great care in maintaining high architectural standards. The other was a beachfront development in Guanacaste Province, where architectural standards were more casual (that is, the neighboring home could be a modest cottage or a mansion). The appeal, however, was improved beach-front parcels priced at around $50,000 in 1988. As Hal explains, "I think this motivates a lot of people—especially Californians, who can no longer afford to live near the water."

Although Hal advises caution—and avoiding impulse—when buying abroad, he is still enthusiastic about international living. He counts himself among those who are not afraid to try: "I'd say that 99% of Americans are afraid to do something different. We've had people rent our house who were afraid of the isolated beauty of the place, so they moved into a Holiday Inn in town—others have rented it again and again. We have a lot of repeat rentals." Even though they do not plan to retire on St. Lucia, the Mannheims do not regret building their island hideaway. Says Hal: "It is a beautiful, beautiful island, and we've had a lot of pleasure from our home."

Chapter 5

Adjusting to a New Country

*"Sometimes I just go to the club restaurant or head for the beach
and forget about what it was I was supposed to adjust to."*
Bernice Gabler
Praia da Luz, Portugal

The surprises of a new country have two sides: stimulation of novelty—and absence of the familiar. You leave part of your life behind when you move abroad. But which part? It may be layers of life you prefer to shed, such as your former role as a harried commuter who sat fuming in gridlocked traffic or packed into an urban subway, the bombardment of consumer advertising in the media or the pressure of too many demands from extended family. On the other hand, you may miss the many conveniences: telephones that work (almost) without fail, speedy banking at automatic teller machines or a hobby/pastime/interest group that isn't transferable to another country. The key to making a bridge between the familiar and the novel is flexibility: "You have to be adventuresome, outgoing, flexible and able to roll with the punches," advises Ruth Walkington in Costa Rica.

For most people, absence of the familiar is a minor problem and one soon remedied. No matter where you live, new activities, landmarks and even trademarks eventually become familiar to you. One of the tradeoffs, when the excitement of the exotic or of "novelty" begins to pale a bit, is that at the same time you will have gained a comfort level with new habits and routines. For many people the shift from tourist to resident is smoothed by familiar tokens during the adjustment period. So don't think you have made a grave mistake by moving abroad when suddenly the thought of a quarter-pounder and fries makes your mouth water, or when you yearn for a first-run American film.

After a move abroad you may find yourself in circumstances that seem like the proverbial trade of the frying pan for the fire. A long wait in a slow postal or bank line can give rise to doubts, but new experiences come in all moods—from impatience to inspiration. Sharon Alberts in Portugal says, "I can always tell newly-arrived Americans because they are fussing and fuming in line. Long ago I learned to take along a paperback book. It does wonders for the blood pressure."

The process of adjustment is best accomplished by applying problem-solving and creative skills that you have always used in managing your job and home. To shorten your waiting time at the post office, you may need to figure out which times and days of the week have the shortest lines. Figuring out the moves makes you street smart. Tips are gained from Americans and other expatriates who have lived in the area longer than you have. Don't reinvent the wheel unless necessary: keep a list of questions, including problems with everyday logistics such as shopping, cleaning, car repair and bureaucratic paperwork. Residents love to trade information; soon you'll be one of the old-hand residents with information to offer newcomers.

Opportunities for creative problem solving are plentiful when you first move to a new country. At first, this can be daunting. Some inconveniences—such as a long wait for telephone installation or red tape to untangle before you can proceed with home remodeling—simply require patience and persistence rather than problem solving. You'll need to assess a situation to determine whether it requires stoicism or a solution. Willingness to find alternatives and substitutes is important for adjustment abroad. But you should be careful not to leave the best part of yourself behind. Without the satisfaction of self-esteem, the experience of living abroad can be disappointing or depressing. Consider, for example, the following:

• You love to play in a chamber music group. Will you be able to find such a group in the country and area where you plan to live? Perhaps not immediately, but it is a realistic goal to plan on forming such a group after your circle of friends and acquaintances widens.

• You are a voracious reader. Is there an English-language bookstore or library where you plan to live? If it is in another city, you could plan an occasional trip to browse the shelves and stock up or arrange for mail order. If there isn't a good English language bookstore around, you may be the person to spearhead a book club or book exchange library, especially since many people you meet will travel to the U.S. regularly and could carry back requested books. Alan Cox asks visitors to bring books when they visit; he passes them along to Americans as well as to Costa Rican residents who want to improve their English.

• You like to be part of a club or social organization. Is there a club for Americans in the area or a women's, garden, camera or other specialty group? If there is such a club, how do you become eligible to join? If not, you can plan to begin a club with people you meet who share common interests.

Adjustment often requires taking initiative. By expressing interest in living abroad, you are already reaching out for new information, a pattern that pays off in well-being. Americans living abroad who adjust most successfully seek out the people and activities they need for expression and self-esteem.

Among people who live abroad, those who have traveled for business or pleasure are the best adjusted. "To be born and raised in Hoboken for 50 years, with only an occasional short cruise, then suddenly to uproot and move abroad could be a mistake," notes Ruth Walkington in Costa Rica, who adds, "but I know people who had the same problem when retiring in Florida after living in Ohio all their lives." Allie Yance of Costa Rica, who is in her 30s, asserts: "If you want to move here, it's good to be a dynamic person. A lot of my friends are artists—the kind of people who would pick up and come to a new place. We have that in common."

A New Timetable

Adjustment is needed through all phases of a move abroad, from business and interpersonal relations to shopping. Arthur Loeb, who owns a home in France's Loire Valley, adjusted to delays when remodeling his home: "The workmanship has been superb, but there is a different attitude than in the U.S. about the timetable for a job. We're used to getting things done tomorrow, particularly if we're willing to pay a premium. Here they take their time, and if you want work done on a holiday you can't pay them enough to do it."

John Barber took a similar approach when he bought a farmhouse in southwestern France, in a village where there are no American or British residents. "It took time," says John, before he and his wife were comfortable with their French neighbors. With no other Americans around, they had to learn the ropes on their own. The Barbers learned that the time it took a craftsman to restore special features of their home "was so long it was almost unbearable," but that the work was outstanding. "Now we know to hire a local repairman to do quick and dirty work when that's what we need. We still use the craftsman, who does beautiful work, but we don't expect him to do something in six weeks."

When Yes Means No

An important part of adjustment is learning to read between the lines. Americans are more direct and forthright than most other nationalities. Answers do not always mean the same thing abroad as they do in the U.S., especially when you are negotiating a service or home improvement. David Mead points out that, in Thailand, a gracious response is "yes—even if the party means no." Just as you may need to slow down your timetable abroad, similarly it is advisable to practice a relaxed skepticism about promises. Renee Wolpert, who has owned a home in Ajijic, Mexico, for over a decade, says, "You have to develop a feel for it. If you take things too much at face value, it doesn't work." Everyone from the butcher to the maid to the auto repairman may give unrealistic estimates. Some might call this lying, but Renee explains, "They don't call this lying. They just give you a polite answer—the one they think you want to hear. It takes a while to get used to filtering answers by asking yourself, 'What did he or she really mean?'" The way you phrase a question can be the difference between getting the results you expect or not. Misplaced courtesy prevails in many countries, although with increased global business and communication you are more likely to get a straight answer tomorrow than you will today.

You will find out that there are other ways of getting results. In Costa Rica and in Latin American countries in general, results are best obtained if you do not push or pressure. One American resident advises prefacing a request, whether of domestic help or in a business transaction, with "when possible, would you please." Whichever country you are considering, find out from resident Americans just what are the dos and don'ts of conduct. Is it customary to give a gift or cash when someone does you a favor? To make the wrong choice is to run the risk of insulting the person you are trying to please. If a gift is customary, what and when is it to be presented? Poor timing could render the gesture pointless or, at worst, be an offense.

When to Tip

The bestowing of mandatory gifts (called *mordida* in Mexico) is not as foreign a concept as it might seem at first. In the U.S., we are accustomed to tipping everyone from the hairdresser and maitre d' to an apartment doorman, and we regard these "mandatory" cash outlays as part of our daily routine. We know that the omission of gratuities can result in poor service. It's not so surprising, then, that in other countries a consideration is often expected. To stubbornly refuse to do so (or not to do your homework and be uninformed of expectations) can cause problems for you. Dara Glass, who lives in Mexico City, recounts the story of an American friend who refused to offer the customary *mordida* to an auto emission control inspector. Not surprisingly, his car was found to need repairs; so probably a cash consideration would have saved him money in the long run. To avoid unnecessary payoffs, though, find out from other Americans when gratuities are expected. Make it part of your research when planning a move or extended stay abroad and keep some extra money at all times for the unexpected "favor."

Sometimes you will find that when you think a payment for work is expected, it isn't. Arthur Loeb has tried to compensate an elderly gardener who looks after his home when the Loebs are not in residence. But when Arthur asks, "What do I owe you?" he is always told "Oh...next time." Lauren Gruning found the same thing in Mexico when she called in repairmen for her VCR. She and her husband finally traded it in for one of similar value, but with suitable power compatibility since it turned out that a voltage problem caused the trouble. "The repairmen went back and forth from their shop to our apartment as we all tried to figure out why it wouldn't work. After all that, they wouldn't take any money for their time."

Revise Your Calendar

Adjusting to the local calendar requires some reorientation, so be prepared to revise plans around a different set of holidays and customs. Christmas, of course, is observed in all countries where you are likely to live abroad. But even with this major international holiday, social conventions may differ somewhat.

As a traveler you have probably experienced the frustration of planning to cash traveler's checks but being thwarted by a bank holiday. Or perhaps your plans to conduct business or visit a museum were blocked by some unexpected holiday.

"There are around 40 different holidays in Costa Rica," estimates Alex Rosarian, who has lived in Costa Rica over a decade yet now is comfortably in step with the calendar of his second home. But Alex recalls that at first he was frustrated by the slower pace imposed by having so many holidays, and that it made him angry with what seemed the "inefficiency" of Costa Rica. Alex points out that an easier pace is one of the reasons to leave a rush-rush life behind. He advises avoiding value judgments to keep your temper cool—especially during the adjustment phase: "Better to mutter to yourself that it's 'just different,' rather than to work up a useless ulcer and a false feeling of homesickness." (Remember the freeway? The mall at Christmas? And if you scratch your memory, you'll recall "blue laws" of your childhood, when stores were closed on Sundays and late-night hours.) So enjoy the pace and charm while accepting the price in patience when you choose to live where people do not place more importance on commerce than on holidays, and where this often results in a more old-fashioned way of getting things done.

The Price of Efficiency

We take efficiency for granted in the U.S.: good telephone service, fast food and one-stop shopping. In many countries, you should expect not only a long wait for telephone installation; you may find that once installed, or if you are using a public phone, bad connections are not uncommon. It is important to lower your expectations of just how many errands you can accomplish in a day. When you first arrive with your list of To Do items—such as driver's license, telephone arrangements, banking and various kinds of paperwork—it can seem as if you are the victim of a

Kafkaesque tangle of waiting lines and officials (who may decide to close their window for lunch, just when it is your turn).

"It takes more hands-on work and patience than you are used to," says an American resident abroad, recalling his initial weeks after the move. One of the benefits of anticipating delays is that you soon learn not to overschedule your life, as we tend to do in the U.S. That can be healthy for some of us who live in the grip of an overextended schedule with little time to smell the flowers. Here we are not prepared to wait in a society that has become ultra-efficient—yet has computers that still "go down" from time to time, plunging us into a worse state of delay than a bank line or telephone re-dial abroad. In the U.S., to be told "Call back in a few hours, the computer is down" is cold consolation if you need confirmation of an airline plan, just as it is disheartening when your after-hours bank machine is out of service before a weekend trip out of town.

Once you have moved abroad, don't forget that occasional glitch in American efficiency, and practice patience: with the move toward a more global economy, electronic communication is sure to improve. Until then, you just find a way to cope—as did Lily Cairns. In 1990, her condominium complex in Greece finally got a telephone. Until then, Lily had to arrange to receive business calls from the U.S. during the weeks she spent in Mykonos. "For five and a half years, I had to make appointments with the office in New York. Three times a week I would sit by a phone in the village and wait for my call. That's how you do it."

The Art of Substitution

Food can be a major adjustment. Many imported items are available worldwide, but the best strategy is to be prepared for substitutes. One American abroad says she is not bothered by an occasional gap in import shipments. "For two months there was no All-Bran—so I didn't eat All-Bran for two months." A gourmet cook, Debra Erland has turned adapting into a specialty: "I use turkey breasts for all my veal recipes. And it's hard to get celery in the Algarve, but there is a rib in the back of cauliflower and you can substitute it for salads. It's almost like celery."

"You adjust to almost anything," says Bernice Gabler, who moved to Portugal from New York City. "I still have trouble adjusting to the supermarket because I can't go buy a package of skinned chicken breasts—I have to buy the whole damned thing.

But you get used to it." What about those days when it seems there is an adjustment overload? Maybe it's time for something familiar and comfortable. Bernice, who lives in a club complex, observes, "Sometimes I just go to the club restaurant or head for the beach and the sun and forget about whatever it was I was supposed to adjust to."

Sometimes the country seems to adapt to your style of living, which is usually because of inroads of technology and more sophisticated retail practices. Tanya Kennebeck offers this example: "When we first moved to Portugal in 1983 we went to buy a chicken at the farmers' open-air market. They gave it to me live on a string, and I was supposed to walk it home, kill it, clean it and cook it." Tanya says that the vendor finally agreed to kill it, but she had to pluck it. "Now chicken is presented quite differently, just as most of us are used to finding it in supermarkets." A few years ago, she notes, you had to go to five different shops, but that's changing because of supermarkets. "You can still find a lot of little shops. But before, meat used to be horrendous. The cow would hang in the window, they'd cut a piece off and that was that. Now you have different cuts with labels and prices. Before, you never knew just what you were buying."

Along with the advantages gained when a country becomes more efficient, Americans abroad point out that there are some negative side effects. In a resort area that is developing rapidly, progress can give rise to an abundance of entrepreneurs who leap into business prematurely. "As soon as they learn a trade, some decide to open their own business, and that can cause problems because although they might be, say, a good electrician, they may not have learned how to deal with customers. Sometimes they take on too many jobs," cautions Karen Knight. One way to avoid a bad experience in such a booming market is to beware of bargain prices from unknowns, and instead use established vendors recommended by other expatriates (even if they are of the old school and work slowly but with care). Another casualty of changing times—notes a resident of Mexico—is that there may be fewer artisans than in years past, as many young people choose not to follow a family trade and instead find work in service industries, including tourism.

Adjustment Aid

Most people rely on other Americans to help them adapt. On your exploratory trips, seek out more than one American in the area in order to get a well-rounded picture. The first person you speak with may paint an overly rosy picture (perhaps because they adapted easily) whereas the next person might detail a laundry list of negatives (perhaps a person who griped ceaselessly about Chicago, too). The country does make a difference— some are easier for adjustment than others. Judith Henderson, commercial attaché with the American Embassy in Costa Rica, who has lived in six countries, offers this opinion: "If you haven't lived abroad, Costa Rica is a relatively easy place to adjust to." In an area with few resident Americans (or English-speaking expatriates), it may take somewhat longer for you to adjust since others have not paved the way for local residents: after all, the local merchants play a role in your adjustment. If they know other Americans, their preferences and foibles, it will be easier for them to meet you halfway.

Gender Adjustment

In almost any country, a woman faces a different kind of adjustment than does a man. If you are considering a move abroad with a husband, friend or as a single woman, you may discover that women's liberation is best practiced behind camouflage. In their careers, women in most countries are respected and treated on a par with men. They often own businesses, practice professions from medicine to law and hold political positions. But socially, especially in Latin countries, whether in this hemisphere or in Europe, you are likely to encounter a *macho* attitude. Divorcée Allie Yance (whose current male companion is an American resident of Costa Rica) agrees: "Costa Rican men are very macho. One night I was singing in a club and received two marriage proposals. I said, 'If I were your wife, would you let me sing?' No way. They want to possess you." Beth Hartman finds a similar attitude (i.e., a woman's place is in the home) in Portugal. "Many times my husband and I will go to a restaurant and I am the only woman. The Portuguese will go out for a family meal on Sundays, but if you go into a restaurant at any other time, you are likely to find few, if any, women."

Single women abroad often report that their male companions are Americans or Europeans. Barbara Moore in Portugal reports that she enjoys being a single woman abroad (and has an active social life), but notes that most of the men she sees socially are not Portuguese but other Europeans. Whether you are male or female, as a resident of any country you will need to learn various rules for social conduct. For example, how is public affection regarded? What is proper attire for different occasions, for different times of year or for day and evening? When and where are shorts acceptable or jackets for men required? During the adjustment period, make an effort to question your assumptions about routine by asking yourself (or someone else) if this or that is customary, even if it is common in the U.S. Soon your questions turn into confident answers, and you have passed your adjustment period, so give yourself a treat. Maybe a burger, after all.

Arthur Secunda sums up his adjustment experience, and many Americans in different countries would agree with his conclusion: "The French are very different and there are frustrations adjusting to their ways. You go for a loaf of bread and it's not just a loaf of bread, it's an adventure," says Arthur. "There is a huge bureaucracy and everyone has a role. A question about a telephone bill could take two months for a reply. The main difference is that the French are not consumer-oriented. Money is not their primary concern." Efficiency and such niceties as standard packaging are not the norm. Questions such as "How much is it?" are not as important as "Is it right?" "That is very difficult to get used to, but all these things add spice to living here. Each project has a sense of mystery."

Chapter 6

New Careers and Avocations Abroad

"I decided to go commercial to support my hobby. Once you collect orchids—each one is a little different—the pleasure is right up there with sex."

Roy Teicher
Costa Rica

Don't skip this chapter, even if you are tempted to jump ahead to recreation. The prospect of moving to a new country may seem to be challenge enough—planning and exploratory trips, finding a residence, the logistics of the move. But once settled, the type of person who chooses to live abroad may need to direct his or her energy (and curiosity) into other channels.

You may be a man who has recently retired from a challenging career and is looking for a new project. If you are a woman whose family is grown, or who has recently retired from a career, the task of researching international living may seem like a new job—especially if you are the organizing half of a couple—but you may want to plan for some kind of engaging gratification outside of the home once you have moved abroad.

Both men and women frequently find opportunity to use existing skills and experience and to enjoy new satisfactions—often with extra income. Chances are, you fit one of the following categories:

1. You are looking for a midlife career change, have some savings and equity and wish to use these resources to begin a

new chapter of your life in a fresh, different (and possibly exotic) location.

2. You may not plan to retire soon, yet retirement may arrive earlier than you think. In the past decade, thousands of workers faced early retirement when their employers were involved in a merger, acquisition or restructuring. Many were not psychologically or financially ready to retire on a reduced pension package.

3. You are a professional or self-employed. You may decide to retire from your practice or sell your business, but are concerned whether golf or other leisure activities will hold your attention after the intense demands of a profession or business.

There are many opportunities abroad for the professional, entrepreneur and hobbyist. The subject of avocations abroad is especially of interest to men approaching retirement, whose pattern for decades is usually a single-focus career with leisure pursuits limited to weekends and vacations. Women, we have found in interviews, are accustomed to juggling several needs and interests at one time, whether it is work and family, philanthropy or creative expression. When moving abroad, women often find social groups and projects. Since men are usually less diversified, when retiring at home or abroad they often feel severed from the drive of daily accomplishment and business friends. Sometimes the result is a sense of loss or a diminishing of self-esteem.

A post-retirement or new midlife career abroad can offer personal advantages over a former career. With a basic budget for living expenses, your new job or avocation is extra income. This adds pleasure while preventing the stress of necessity. And if you are not enjoying Phase 2 of your career, you can simply tie up the loose ends and retire again or try something else.

You are entitled to earn $70,000 abroad per year, free of U.S. income tax. Of course, you will be subject to local income taxes. If you choose to work primarily for satisfaction and do not want the added complication of foreign income tax, some Americans find the practice of barter adds perquisites with a minimum of paperwork. An American retired in Costa Rica does occasional photographic assignments for an airline or resort; they show their appreciation in free travel and lodging. Retired advertising executive David Mead in Thailand occasionally offers marketing advice to a Thai firm; they show appreciation through honoraria, which have included a car and driver and use of a corporate condominium in a resort area. As an informal associate of the firm, he enjoys many of their business/social functions, which introduces him to new international friends.

Your Profession Abroad

In most countries, job restrictions apply to positions that otherwise would be filled by a local resident. If you are not displacing a skilled worker, you may be allowed to pursue your plan. Be sure to check out the restrictions well in advance. In most of the European Community countries, professions such as law and medicine are open only to an expatriate professional whose country is part of the EC. If you have a parent or grandparent born in Ireland, you may qualify for an Irish (and therefore EC) passport, at no risk to your U.S. citizenship. With this document, some career opportunities will be available that otherwise would be closed to a U.S. citizen.

In Costa Rica and most other non-EC countries, there are also restrictions on expatriates practicing certain types of professions. But a professional such as a lawyer might practice on a consulting basis, or arrange to act as a "liaison" with a local firm, which may be glad to benefit from your experience and connections within the American expatriate community. Harold Parr, who lives in Torremolinos, Spain has practiced law this way for two decades.

In most countries, you may own your own business (a restaurant or real estate company, for example) as long as you do not fill a job that otherwise would be held by a native resident. Tourists are not allowed to work (without special worker's visas, such as that issued to a journalist on assignment). Other types of restrictions apply on a country-by-country basis: in Costa Rica, for example, as a resident you may own a business but must hire native resident employees to do the work. Elsewhere, you may be required to have a native business partner or conduct business as an independent contractor under a native employer. (For example, to practice real estate in Portugal, you must be employed by a Portuguese estate broker.)

There are four basic types of second-career and avocational opportunity for people who move abroad—that is, for those who do not move primarily for job relocation. They are:

1. Opportunities that arise within the expatriate community such as translation, communications-publications (newsletters

and magazines), importing and exporting, real estate and other services for English-speaking residents.

2. You may be offered a chance to use your professional background in a new application, often as a consultant.

3. A hobby or avocation may provide a business opportunity. At home perhaps you have discounted this possibility because of existing competition or were reluctant to make a midlife career change to a new field as an older worker. This could be a chance to try something you have always wanted to do. Since you are in a special category as an American abroad, your age is not your most conspicuous label.

4. You decide to pursue an entirely new field of interest after becoming familiar with the country and its business opportunities.

New Career Horizons

Ross Johnson came to Costa Rica eight years ago after a career in public relations. "I was run down physically and mentally. I didn't know what I was looking for, but I came to Costa Rica with a ticket to return in two weeks," explains Ross. At first he lodged, as would any tourist, at a resort hotel. But he extended his stay week after week and then finally rented a villa and remained another seven months. "Things started getting better and better. My health started to improve, and the first thing I knew I had met a woman, was married and settled down." Ross now owns a dairy farm, an established business with a capable staff and management. He decided to expand his business in a new direction. The idea occurred to him when a visitor from Belgium mentioned that the climate would be ideal for commercial flower cultivation. As of a few years ago, only one other small farm in the area had entered the commercial flower market.

His decision to enter this new business had a few snags, however. When he tried to procure the root stock necessary to start his business, California growers would not sell to him, Ross explains. When he found an alternative root stock source in Europe and began exporting to California, his shipments were hindered by high duty charges. But his business improved; he found other markets in Jamaica, Belgium and elsewhere. Subsequently, the California duty was relaxed and his business there began to flourish. "Europeans, Canadians and Americans in the Northeast just can't get enough of our roses," he says.

The roses grown on Ross Johnson's farm are deep red and salmon in color, are of a very high quality and command top prices at retail. He also grows a small white flower that is combined with roses in floral arrangements. Quality control is one of the reasons for his success. "I make videotapes of every step and hold training sessions," says Ross, explaining how new workers understand each delicate step in floral processing. As a former urbanite, Ross brought skills from his management and marketing background that have proven useful in a second—and entirely unexpected—career abroad.

Working for Improvement

Warren Downey spent more than two decades as a superintendent with the National Parks Service in Utah, with assignments at Bryce Canyon and Capitol Reef. When he was offered a chance for early retirement, Warren took the opportunity but knew that he needed to stay active; he wasn't ready for a steady diet of leisure-time activity.

Soon after moving to Spain, he had a chance to put his expertise to work. He made an initial contact with the Spanish interior department, a contact only intended as a goodwill gesture. But soon he was asked to consult with the government agency for a reforestation project. Although offered a fee, compensation wasn't his motive: it was the satisfaction of seeing hillsides full of beautiful trees when only a few years ago the same hills were barren.

American experience may be highly valued in other countries. Since the U.S. consulate has your profession on file as a resident, they may refer others to you. Veronice Alta, who retired from a career in gerontology in Philadelphia, was also invited to be a consultant. Even though she is a part-time resident in Spain, as she explains, "The University of Málaga was developing their curriculum in gerontology, but they had difficulty finding faculty with expertise in the subject. They asked the U.S. consulate, who referred them to me." Veronica receives a tax-free honorarium for her consulting.

Going Commercial

A hobby can be another source of income, and sometimes can expand so vigorously that either you must decide to limit it or turn commercial. Roy Teicher retired from law when he moved to Costa Rica in 1976, although he is a consulting lawyer for American residents and says, "I spend a lot of time saying 'No, no—take it slow,'" especially when clients want to rush into a business deal. He also has two greenhouses filled with exotic plants for export and loves to explore in the jungle for new species. "Hundreds are unclassified," he explains. It began as a hobby when he first started collecting orchids from the jungle. First he built a greenhouse, then had so many that he built a second—from his original 29 plants, he now has 10,000."I decided to go commercial to support my hobby. Once you collect orchids—each is a little different—the pleasure is right up there with sex." Noting that there are over 2,300 varieties in Costa Rica he adds: "They bite you. That's it."

Hobby Management

Len Kennebeck could turn his hobby into a business but prefers not to. "I'm doing it as a hobby that pays for itself," says Len, who has a professional carpentry shop in his home in Portugal. Although his career was in corporate management he explains, "I've always loved to work with woods." He does projects for American and European friends and could handle more, but has avoided expanding because he would need to hire employees and says, "I like to maintain it myself. I want to do the work, not turn it into a big business."

Another reason that he limits his hobby is because his wife's hobby has mushroomed: as word about Tanya's yoga classes spread, the demand grew until now it is a full program of courses called the School of Light. "Tanya teaches most of the foreign community here and has Portuguese students, too," comments Len, who notes that it provides the focus of their social life. He adds: "We don't suffer from lack of people."

To accommodate the School of Light's expanding enrollment, the Kennebecks first converted their two-car garage to a studio, but when classes continued to grow Len designed and built a circular structure. Its massive ceiling radiates toward the apex, and windows encircle the room, drawing in sunlight and creating a perfect setting for meditation. The Kennebecks also added two cottages to their property for overnight guests and have future plans to add a vegetarian restaurant (they grow their own organic produce). "If this is retirement," observes Len, "then there are times when I've never worked harder."

Real estate and construction attract many Americans who live abroad. By the time they learn what is needed to buy or build a home, some are eager to make further use of their expertise. Larraine Grey, an art teacher when in the U.S., says: "I'm not cut out for a life of leisure." When she moved to Portugal she learned new skills by following closely as construction proceeded on the remodeling of her home. With her art and design training, she applied her background in a new field—home remodeling.

Opportunities in Tourism

Barbara Moore made a career change after moving to Portugal. For 25 years, she was a real estate broker in Albany, New York, and her first impression of the Algarve, she recalls, was "Oh, I can make money here. I can do real estate." But she was discouraged by the aggressive development of the Algarve and didn't want to be part of the heated market. "I found something else, but it took a while," she explains. Barbara formed a business partnership to operate a pleasure boat on the Tagus River. In EC countries, Americans may be limited in the kinds of jobs they are allowed to hold—but even if it initially appears that there are working restrictions for you as a resident expatriate, it may be possible to structure your job or business to conform to a country's laws. Barbara's partner is Dutch (an EC member country); her position as publicity director is allowed for non-EC workers. They formed a Portuguese corporation, for which the Dutch captain needs a work permit, but for her position a permit is not necessary.

Mexico also affords opportunities for Americans who want an avocation or second career in tourism: the Feldmans in La Paz, Mexico, are helping to establish a La Paz visitors' bureau. Since they are interested in property, their efforts to promote tourism offer potential benefit for their own investments. Len Friedman, who was in the foundry industry in the U.S., found a service niche to fill for the American and Canadian expatriate community in Guadalajara. With a permit from the department of tourism, he and his wife established the American-Canadian Club, which provides services such as dining and travel tours as well as an orientation program for newly arrived *Norteamericanos*. "We make money, but we're not going to make big money—if we were, we'd come out of retirement and go back to the States," says Len.

In some cases, a technical background provides unique opportunities: Allie Yance and her husband were in their early 30s when they moved from New York to Costa Rica, with the intention of establishing a business. His training was in biological research (as a graduate student, he made his first trip to Costa Rica several years before). "We sat around brainstorming," says Allie. "and the idea came up of restoring a forest for use as a resort. We decided to buy land with these features: it had to have a waterfall, it had to border on a national park. That's how the idea was born." The land they found for purchase was even more than they had hoped for: not just one but two waterfalls of 160 and 120 feet; not one side bordering on a national park or protected zone, but both sides, since their property is corner acreage between the Barco Corregio national park and Zona Protectora de la Selva. Although Allie and her husband are now divorced, they are still friends and business partners in a 1,500-acre rustic resort that accommodates a maximum of 19 guests.

Business Planning

American resident Jim Fendell, who owns a newspaper distribution business in San José, Costa Rica, advises that whether your business is an avocation, an active business for income or an investment, "Use the same good caution you would use in the States. If it seems to good to be true, then it probably is. Check and double check the details." He suggests following these four rules: 1) Use an independent lawyer recommended by someone you know. 2) Use your own expertise, analyze what you can and would like to do, then find out if someone is already doing it. Don't assume that because you have managed a successful business in the U.S. that it will work the same way in another country. There is a lot of talent in most countries—don't assume that they are less sophisticated in business. 3) Take a close look at market niches—service industries or technical services may still be in a nascent stage in a developing country. 4) Be aware that if you go into the commercial field, there may be restrictions on wholesale and retail profits (in Costa Rica, for example, you are limited to 30% profit on both wholesale and retail items).

If you decide to start a business abroad, be prepared for frustration and potential strain on a marriage or friendship.

George Frank in Uruguay recounts the story of his retired stockbroker friend from the U.S. who saw an opportunity in manufacturing near Montevideo. "He wanted to start a furniture factory, but after six months his wife balked at the frustrations and insisted that they move back to the U.S."

You may find that many consumer services that thrive in the U.S. are not in great demand abroad. "A lot of people move here [Portugal] with dreams of living in the sun. They start a restaurant and run out of money," says Karen Knight. "Most service professions we are accustomed to in the U.S. are not in demand in the Algarve. On the other hand, technical skills are needed and there is lots of opportunity." Friends of the Knights began a computer business a few years ago and, adds Karen, "They can't begin to handle all the business."

SPAIN

From New York to Spain

Before Jack and Janice Baldridge retired from their advertising and teaching careers in New York, they started a travel/retirement plan by purchasing a three-bedroom ocean-view condominium in Fuengirola on Spain's Costa del Sol. For the next five years while they were still active in their jobs, they spent vacations in Spain before moving with resident status in 1979.

Their apartment, on the 11th floor of a 14-story building, "is 3 minutes from the shore and 20 minutes from the mountains," says Janice, who notes that the long months of warm weather from June to October enable them to enjoy an active outdoor life of tennis and swimming. As a year-round resident, Janice faces the hot summers stoically and says, "I used to die in New York's humid summers, but 100 degrees here is dry."

One of their criteria for a locale abroad was social opportunity. "We enjoy walking around town and meeting people. I think that's important when choosing a place to live abroad," Janice advises. "Here there is a village life, a town life." Another of Janice's criteria for choosing this area of Southern Spain was good transportation: "The transportation is excellent. I don't have a car. I don't bother. There are taxis, a bus every 15 minutes and the train is reliable."

The American Club is the focus of their social life and travel plans, since the club sponsors events and a lending library as well as local and distant trips. Each year Jack and Janice plan one local and one major vacation. In the past three years, they have traveled independently to Paris and Amsterdam, and joined the club on a journey down the Nile.

An adjunct to Janice's American Club activities is her volunteer work as a liaison with the police department, where she helps Americans who are in need of advice about documentation or insurance forms, or who require other kinds of paralegal assistance. Her volunteer work, consisting of what she describes as "in-depth interpretation," is provided at the police station for Americans referred to her by the American Club. "There is a shortage of people to do this. The Spanish would like to provide it, but they are short of funds," she notes, explaining how her role came about, "and it's very unusual to find a foreigner behind a desk in the police department."

For such community involvement, a good grasp of Spanish is essential. To become proficient, Janice studied both formally and informally, seeking opportunities to converse with Spanish-speaking residents. Now that she has become the linguist in the family, her husband largely relies on her to act as interpreter when the need arises.

For the cultural activities that are important to both Jack and Janice, Málaga is only a short distance away with its Teatro de Cervantes, which offers programs of opera and ballet. Since there are many retired theatrical expatriates in Fuengirola, the town boasts its own successful amateur theater group and also sponsors a variety of other performing-arts events. In 1989, for example, the American community in Fuengirola celebrated Irving Berlin's 101st birthday with a "101 Songs Marathon." With its sizable expatriate community, the Fuengirola-Málaga area offers an abundance of familiar tokens, from English-language books and the *New York Times* to good pizza, Chinese food and New York deli take-out, as well as a wide rental selection of American and European films on videocassette.

The Costa del Sol has experienced rapid development in recent years, but Janice has adapted to Fuengirola's evolving landscape, and offers this perspective: "When we first came here a decade ago we were near fields and goats, but I don't see the change as any reason to leave. Development is typical of any desirable area in the world. Costs are rising—but it's still much cheaper than living in Manhattan."

Chapter 7

Recreation and Entertainment

"When I moved to Mexico, I thought I was going to do a hobby of mine—copper enameling—but I've done everything else instead."
Peter Haddon
Guadalajara, Mexico

During the adjustment period you may be absorbed by daily tasks: preparing meals in new ways, writing letters to those who await accounts of your adventures (a one-fits-all newsletter is a time-saving way to keep in touch). However absorbing your everyday chores, you will want to provide for recreation and entertainment and should have a general plan before making the move.

The time to begin is when first exploring an area for living or retirement potential. List the activities you enjoy, ranking them in order of importance. Add those you would like to pursue but have not had the time. Will you be able to enjoy the things on your personal activity list in this country and region? Are the facilities or supplies you need available—if not in the region where you want to live, perhaps in the capital city? Which activities are most important to you and which can you live without?

If you don't find a match between your preferences and what a country offers then consider alternatives. Some recreational activities do not travel well. One retirement preplanner restores classic cars, but now that he has decided to live abroad he will need to find a substitute. Another collects rare books (American first editions), which is also difficult to pursue abroad. In fact, most avid collectors would be advised to start a new kind of collection and to see what is available in the country, although sometimes it is possible to acquire items from the U.S. and keep up your hobby or collection. You may want to try out an alternate activity while still living in the U.S., or take a few classes (landscape painting, chess or photography, for example) to develop your skill level before you go.

A new hobby could take you by surprise: George Frank started a collection of antique clocks after he retired in Montevideo, Uruguay. His collection was the result of an inconvenience: after electricity faltered a few times in his apartment building and his electric clocks had to be reset, George decided to find a wind-up clock. He found a handsome antique clock in need of repair and explains "I got parts in the U.S. and had a great time repairing it, so I started collecting them."

Sports and Outdoor Life

Golf is a favorite expatriate activity in resort areas and can be surprisingly affordable in some countries, but not a bargain in others. If you are a golfer with a modest recreation budget, find out about costs and membership availability for expatriates. On an exploratory trip you may see a beautiful golf course, but get the details from resident Americans: the club may be too expensive or may not encourage foreign memberships. Len Kennebeck in Almansil, Portugal, plays golf with a group of friends; George Frank, retired in Montevideo, is also an avid golfer and plays at two golf clubs near his home, where memberships for both he and his wife (i.e., four memberships) total only $60 U.S. per month.

Birdwatching is another popular activity for Americans who live in Costa Rica and Uruguay. Costa Rica offers abundant outdoor opportunities. The excellent fishing is a reason many Americans discover Costa Rica (and sometimes decide to move there). For those interested in natural history, few countries offer as many delights, especially for birders who have over 350 species of birds to stalk with binoculars and log on their life lists.

Peter Haddon is typical of many Americans abroad. His recreation and entertainment interests cover a broad range. "When I moved to Mexico I thought I was going to do a hobby of mine—copper enameling—but I've done everything else instead.

I spend a lot of time gardening—I have more opportunity here than on the East Coast because of the year-round climate. I also swim, read a lot and the golf course is right behind me." His golf dues are included as one of the amenities of his condominium, which also has tennis courts and a swimming pool. There is a soccer field nearby and he watches an occasional game. Since soccer is the most popular spectator sport in most countries outside the U.S., the baseball or football fan has a choice of watching American games televised on satellite or, like Peter, developing an interest in soccer.

A Taste for Culture

The Haddons also enjoy Guadalajara's Diego Yado theater, a beautiful structure built in Classical Greek style. "It has international programs. Folkloric ballet, on Sundays, visiting philharmonic and opera companies. There are a lot of cultural opportunities such as art exhibits and galleries throughout the city," says Peter.

The Erlands in Portugal's Algarve hold season tickets for a concert series in Lisbon and frequently visit the capital for other concerts, ballet and opera. Ruth Walkington finds that in San José, Costa Rica, "There is just about anything you would want to do. There are plays and wonderful, clean movie theaters. We have an English theater group that produces one musical and one play every year, and there are visiting cultural events from all over the world. I saw a visiting Soviet ballet company for $7—it would cost many times that for a ticket in the U.S."

For visual entertainment at home, English-language video rental is available in many resort areas with a sizable expatriate community. And for those outside such areas, there is always satellite TV, which brings in English-language channels. The Thalmeyers in Costa Rica receive six English-language channels on their television (satellite hookup was provided through their residential development). In Warsaw, Poland, Laine Arden installed a satellite dish and received an array of international channels, including CNN. She also found out that most films are shown in English with Polish subtitles.

Night Life

Pamela Winger found an unlikely "night club" near her vacation home in Ireland, a place where she and her husband feel welcome to drop in and have a good time. "There is a place called '4 P's' because it is at the intersection of four provinces. There's a live band and everyone learns Irish dances. So far, we seem to be the only people there who are foreign born. We've been twice so far and it's wonderful."

City night life usually means a special trip. Buenos Aires, Argentina, with its sophisticated restaurants, entertainment and theater, is a favorite getaway for Americans living in Montevideo who like to take an inexpensive flight for the weekend. (Such short trips to an adjacent country can be facilitated if you are a resident, since the "residents" line is usually processed at customs more quickly than the line of tourists holding different international passports.)

Arthur Loeb, near Blois, France, describes how he and his family combine country living and city pleasures: "It is one reason we chose this area. It is flat so we can bicycle. There are places to go, like spokes in a wheel, around our home—châteaux, small museums, beautiful countryside. And it's only two hours from Paris by train or car. If we're feeling ambitious we can go to Paris, see an exhibition, have dinner and be home the same day."

Not all areas offer diversity and your preferred activities could influence your choice of a region within a country. While Karen and Paul Knight were exploring different regions of the Algarve, says Karen, "We decided that the activities we like were mainly found in the central area. We were interested in horses and most of the riding activity goes on here."

Travel and Other Pleasures

Travel is one of the most frequently cited reasons for living abroad, one you can enjoy anywhere and even on a limited budget. The Grunings in Guadalajara like independent travel by bus. "One of the things we like about Mexico is that by living here inexpensively, we can get ahead on our budget and travel. We take a monthly bus trip on our own to different towns and stay a few days—longer if we feel like it. Buses are surprisingly inexpensive." The Grunings have tried both first- and second-class bus travel in Mexico, as Lauren explains: "The second-class bus has no bathroom, stops at every bend in the road and there is no guaranteed seating. The first-class bus, called the Royal Executive, is a bargain at $15 for a typical 350-mile trip, such as from Guadalajara to Aguascaliente in the north. The bus has a game room, snacks and restrooms." After completing one trip, they start planning another: "After every trip we flip through our guidebooks to see where we want to go next."

Dara Glass in Mexico City drives her Volkswagen to her favorite spots within an hour or two of the capital. Tepoztlan, not far from Cuernavaca, is "a little town in a beautiful area," Dara explains. "The mountains look like they were carved by ancient people." Another of her favorites is Tequisquiapan, with its hot springs and mineral baths ("a lovely place with good restaurants") and Ixtapan de la Sal, an inexpensive hotel/spa where lodging with three meals is only $15.

Arthur Secunda in Paris keeps a car, not primarily for use in the city (which has good public transportation) but because he likes to travel. His trips, as he describes them, are "just going to see something, it's not so much a tourist thing." It may be a photography festival in St. Remy de Provence in the south, or a music festival in the Netherlands, both reachable within a few hours by car. Secunda likes the combination of easy access yet a trip with a distinctly different national flavor, as does Veronica Alta.

One of Veronica's favorite short trips from her home in the Costa del Sol is to the British colony of Gibraltar. "I enjoy visiting Gibraltar—you know you've been somewhere different." For local travel, Veronica likes to book her trips through Spanish sources and remarks: "They are a quarter the price of U.S. tours and we go where tourists do not go." Another favorite getaway for the Altas is London. Other Americans report that they plan trips to different countries each year or two: George Frank lives in Uruguay eight months of the year. Since his cost of living is around 40% less than in the U.S., it enables him and his wife to travel the other four months. Recent trips include Spain and England, and next year the Franks are planning a trip to the Soviet Union. Barbara Moore in Portimao, Portugal, notes that one of the advantages of international friendships is invitations to visit other countries. It is more interesting to lodge with an insider than to stay in a hotel as a tourist, and it is much more economical.

You may not need to go far for travel adventures, which can save money on transportation and lodging costs. Ralph Breyer has traveled extensively to other countries since moving to the Algarve but he is now less interested in other countries and is concentrating on Portugal. "Portugal in the north is very different from Portugal in the south," he observes. Barbara Moore agrees: "You can travel so easily in this country. You can get in your car and in a half-hour you are in a different world. There are old castles only an hour or two away. and there is so much diversity."

Chapter 8

The Creative Life

"We just go in the project room, set up the easels and do our thing."

Beth Hartman
Algarve, Portugal

Among the hundreds of people who have previously taken the Lifestyle Values Inventory (offered in the appendix), creativity ranks as one of the most important criteria for those who plan to live or retire abroad—especially for men. At first, it may seem surprising that the creative factor is so important to many men, primarily those facing retirement, but a second glance reveals the reason: creative expression serves as an alternative to self-expression in a career.

Unlike the alternative leisure-time activities of entertainment and recreation, creativity offers psychological benefits that closely resemble the best qualities to be found in a satisfying career or profession, such as visible results from one's efforts and the experience of having personal control over a project. Creative projects travel well and offer other advantages over entertainment. Creativity doesn't rely on access to theater tickets, English-language films (or subtitles), a free tennis court, an open tee or a bridge partner. You can enjoy it any time you wish, independently.

Preplanner Hal Bennett owns a home on Long Island and is currently negotiating the purchase of property in Portugal. He is planning for several independent activities in his five-year plan and says, "I'm realistically aiming for retirement at 58" (he is now

53). He looks forward to enjoying two of his creative interests abroad: color photography and ornamental gardening with trees and shrubs.

In the Algarve, where prime land is coastal, he notes: "There is plenty of noncoastal land available because most people don't want to go back in the hills." He made two trips before finding an older house to refurbish and will add improvements so that when he is ready to retire, the house will be ready. He intends to have a darkroom, and since he plays tennis Hal is buying property with enough land to add a tennis court and swimming pool—and he will still have enough acreage to enjoy ornamental gardening. This combination of gardening and photographic activity is also part of Charles Yarby's plan for retirement abroad (although Charles's version includes black-and-white photography).

A change of scenery and culture is a stimulus for creative energy and is one reason many American writers, artists, musicians and actors have homes abroad. Ireland offers a special incentive for creative expatriates, a kind of "tax shelter" for income from creative work. As a resident of Ireland, you may qualify for this status under certain conditions if you have produced a book, play or professionally recognized painting, sculpture or other such work.

Even for the amateur, living or retiring abroad is a good chance to pursue a creative outlet, since by choosing this way of life you draw on your own resourcefulness and are primed for innovation.

Whatever the nature of your muse, you will probably find that she thrives on foreign soil. Music travels well: Don Hartman in the Eastern Algarve bought an organ after he moved to Portugal. "I can play the organ for hours and the time just disappears," says Don (who also does a lot of reading and likes to play billiards).

Art also travels well: "I used to do some oil painting in the States, and I took ceramics and china painting," says Beth Hartman. During her working years, she had little time for such pursuits but says, "I've started painting here again." Beth meets once a week with an English friend and has a room in her house for art projects: "We just go in the project room, set up the easels and do our thing." Some countries appear to have special qualities that enhance creative work. The celebrated light of

Greece has inspired many poets and artists, and Lily Cairns finds Mykonos an ideal place both to write and to paint, as well as a good place to forget the worries of her film production career.

Writing travels well: both Lauren and Ben Gruning are writing novels from their home base in Guadalajara, although painting is Ben's main interest. For Joan Feldman, who already had a writing career in the U.S., work continues with added energy in La Paz. Bob Martinelli decided, at the age of 51, to take up writing. He expects that the home he and Linda own in Italy will gradually become his writer's retreat. They have owned the home only a year, so at first their main interest (during the part of the year they spend in Italy) will be to take short exploratory trips. Bob has already finished his first novel and has begun a second. In the U.S., he uses a word processor and plans eventually to have one in his house in Italy, as he explains: "That will make it easy to write. I'll just take the floppy disks back and forth with me."

David Mead was 62 when he retired in Thailand. Decades ago in college, he intended to be a writer until his career took a different turn. After three years in Thailand, David began a long-delayed writing project using historical source material he had collected over the years. With his first book now completed and negotiation with New York publishers underway, David has begun a second book. His subject is a period of American history, which may seem a project rather "displaced" in Southeast Asia, but many well-known writers find that more can be accomplished when working at a distance from the actual locale about which they are writing. Gore Vidal, for example, has written his best-selling novels (many, such as *Lincoln*, on American historical themes) from his home in Rome. Distance or creative displacement sometimes frees the imagination to do its best work.

Trailblazing in Thailand

If you decide to break Country Criterion 9 (Availability of Familiar Tokens) by moving to a locale with few Americans in residence, you will need something special: fluency in the language, native friends in residence or both. It is also an advantage when moving to a more exotic destination to have some kind of expertise or interest that can serve as a bridge to establish new relationships.

David Mead never dreamed that he would live in Thailand. When the New York advertising executive had occasion to conduct business with a sophisticated, multi-lingual couple from Bangkok, he approached the situation like any other agency-client relationship. During the Thai couple's trips to New York several times a year, David escorted them to the theater and Manhattan's top restaurants—all part of an ad executive's routine. After a while, he found that what began as business was turning into a valued friendship.

When he was invited to spend a vacation in Thailand, David gratefully accepted the offer, since the chance to enjoy an insider's view of Thailand was a rare opportunity. He had been to Europe a number of times but never to Asia and looked forward to the trip. As their guest, David's vacation was both comfortable and rich with experiences. They included him in trips and activities that would not be experienced even by a seasoned traveler. For David, Thailand was like a fascinating puzzle; everything from the language and cuisine to rules of conduct were different, and to grasp this new culture was one of the greatest challenges he had faced in years.

For two years, David spent his vacations in Thailand as guest of his Thai friends, where he was introduced to their wide circle of acquaintances, most of whom spoke English as the *lingua franca* of international business. His knowledge of American marketing and advertising made him a sought-after guest among Thai businessmen and women who often asked his advice about projects.

On the third trip, one of his new friends suggested that David retire in Thailand, where he could live very comfortably on his Social Security and interest income—a near impossibility in Manhattan. The spark of an idea began to form. Accustomed to challenges in his fast-paced career, David was approaching retirement without a plan of action. He was divorced with a grown son, free to live anywhere and the idea appealed to him. In 1985, he retired and moved to Thailand.

At first David was a houseguest of the Thai couple. Soon he was offered more consulting work than he had time for, and since he didn't want to complicate his residency or pensioner's tax status by earning income abroad, he only accepted noncash honoraria for consulting—honoraria such as the use of a car and driver, or weekends at one company's condominium in the resort area of Pattaya. After a few months, he felt that he was able to navigate alone, so he thanked his friends for their hospitality and found a residence of his own. David's two-bedroom Bangkok apartment, in a four-story building with primarily European tenants, cost $350 per month in 1986. The apartment had two balconies draped with bougainvillea—*fueng fah*, "curtains of heaven."

After a year of exploring Thailand through short trips, he was ready to leave fascinating but congested Bangkok, which had served as a good urban transition after life in New York. His choice was the northern city of Chiang Mai. "I loved Chiang Mai since the first day I came here," says David, who repeated the process of adjustment by staying with friends for a few weeks until he found a place of his own: a large house with a beautiful garden and caretaker, all included for the same monthly rental price as his Bangkok apartment. The house was secluded and separated from one of Chiang Mai's major hotels by undeveloped land, or what David describes as "literally, full jungle."

David was managing well on his own by this time, learning the language and widening his circle of friends and acquaintances, which now included several Europeans and Americans who were affiliated with the United Nations or in foreign service posts. Then he met a British-educated Thai professor and together they began a new life in Chiang Mai.

"One day some people drove down our quiet street. We spoke with them and learned that they were soon to develop the land between the house and the hotel. The time had come to build a house of our own." David and Lakanna wanted a home for the same reason that many people do in the U.S., to have more control over their housing and for an investment. Since in

Thailand there are restrictions on ownership by foreign nationals, the purchase was negotiated with Lakanna as the principal.

In 1987, they paid a total of $40,000 for both a large lot and a custom-built home, including the cost of an architect. Within three years the value of their property had tripled. David points out that in the past three years the Thai economy has burgeoned, and although inflation hovers around 7% the dollar remains strong. Tourists are likely to feel the pinch of rising prices (although still a travel bargain), but as local residents, David and Lakanna are provided with 10%–20% discount cards offered to regular customers by hotels and restaurants. For an American in Chiang Mai, prices are very low by U.S. standards. David pays $8 to have a cavity filled; $4 per day for his gardener; under $2 per hour for a maid who comes six days a week.

With resident status, David is obligated to pay taxes on worldwide income in Thailand since the U.S. and Thailand do not have a reciprocal tax treaty. (In countries with a reciprocal agreement, you only pay tax in one country to avoid double taxation.) Says David: "If the tax rate were higher I'd resent it, but it's so low I don't." He pays around 12% on the pension and interest income that he imports for living expenses. "I have to report each year how much I've brought in," explains David, adding, "I don't have to bring in much money, so it's not that painful."

Compared with life in New York City, Chiang Mai does not offer abundant cultural events such as theater, ballet or music. "We have our own music at home, and we rent English-language videos," explains David. "If I had not had so many years of cultural events in New York—so many concerts and plays—I might miss it. But since I've had so much I don't need it now. I'm happy with this serene life."

Chapter 9

Lifetime Learning

"Without learning the language, you are always a foreigner."
Susan Broward
Lagoa, Portugal

A new culture provides rich material for lifetime learning, especially language skills and appreciation of history. The learning curve is steep when you move abroad and sometimes recalls memories of high school or college years when discoveries were abundant. To many of us, this was also a time of carefree travel and exploration before jobs and responsibilities limited vacations to a few weeks (preceded by complicated preparation and followed by an accumulated workload waiting on your desk).

It is almost impossible to live in another country without picking up some of the language. Most people approach the speech of their second home as a welcome challenge; others avoid learning a second language, or rely on a spouse to take charge of translation. Living abroad is the best possible language lab: daily interaction with neighbors and local merchants, an abundance of films and television programs and Europeans of different nationalities with holiday homes all provide a chance to use the high school or college German, French or Spanish that you thought you'd forgotten.

Peter Haddon says, "I confess I'm a poor linguist, but I get along." He took a few Spanish classes before (and one after) moving to Guadalajara. Rather than concentrating on the language, Peter is more interested in history and culture, as he explains: "We also took courses in cross-cultural differences offered by a professor in Guadalajara, and I took a course on the history of Mexico. I'm especially interested in archaeology—and there is plenty of chance to enjoy it here."

Speaking Out

Lauren Gruning offers: "I bumbled through Spanish in high school. When we moved to Mexico a year ago we first concentrated on three tenses. Now I'm working on pronouns, and we manage to make ourselves understood." Without formal classes in the country, your progress may be slow. Dara Glass took an intensive Spanish language course in Guadalajara before moving to Mexico City, then used this foundation to become more fluent by adding words and phrases in new situations.

Your activities shape language skills. "We don't have an awful lot of opportunity for conversation, mainly the market, fabric store, art supply store," says Lauren Gruning. "Your vocabulary becomes strange depending on your interests." The Grunings also have found that Spanish seems easier to understand when they are outside of Guadalajara, and Lauren suspects "perhaps it's the Guadalajara accent." She has also discovered that many everyday words vary from her Spanish-English dictionary, which is based on European rather than Mexican usage. "We used the word for 'stamps' in our dictionary, and no one knew what we were talking about. Then I pointed to one and was told 'Oh, *estampillas!*'"

No one keeps quiet until they have mastered a language. There are times when you must wing it, however ungrammatically, such as when you need auto repair while on the road, or when it's necessary to ask for directions. You'll get plenty of practice on short trips, using your home as a base of operation. Language skills are important if you plan to enjoy independent travel to out-of-the-way places. Larraine Grey in Almansil, Portugal, agrees: "You have to be willing to use the language as best you can. My verbs are terrible—my past and future are awful—but if you learn present tense and pronouns, you can get by."

Often Americans who move to Spain, Mexico, Costa Rica or other Latin American countries already have some familiarity with Spanish. Portuguese is more difficult. Bernice Gabler says, "I'm working on mastering enough of the language to get around more independently." One of Bernice's friends in New York reminded her that Portuguese is one of the most difficult languages, along with Korean and Dutch. "I don't know about the other two, but Portuguese is tough," she agrees.

You may confuse nouns, adjectives and verbs at first, but usually the mixup is more amusing than embarrassing. Bernice, who takes every opportunity to speak Portuguese with her maid, has had some odd conversations on the funny road to language fluency. Once Bernice tried to tell her maid that she was going to have tea at a friend's garden party. The maid look puzzled for a minute, then responded, "But why are you going to take your gardener to tea?"

The learning adventure sometimes extends to friends and family. Louise Harris's grandson, who vacations every summer in Costa Rica, now speaks the language more fluently than any of his fellow students in his college Spanish classes in the U.S. Children often learn a new language faster than adults, especially when they make friends abroad. Children learn while playing as there are few barriers when kids are having a good time, and if they attend school abroad they experience hours of intensive language exposure every day. Meanwhile, a parent faces more formal social obstacles to international friendships. But children can help bridge the social gap for parents, as Darren Thomas found out when he lived in Hamburg, Germany, for three years: "When local children play with your own children and visit your house, it's a natural step toward meeting other parents in the neighborhood."

When Language Is a Must

The French are obsessively proud of their language and you would never reach a comfort level in the country without passable French. Most Americans who live in France have prior language experience before making the move. Arthur Loeb worked in Paris for a few months after college, and says of his return three decades later, "I understand almost everything and I can make myself understood." Sally Barber assumes the role of public relations for the Barber family. Says John: "I read the newspaper every day, but I don't speak it. I had two years of high school French and two years in college, but it didn't take." Sally, on the other hand, had several years of French in school—and it took. When the Barbers are in the U.S. during the winter, she also attends conversational French class every week to maintain her fluency.

Joan Peters and Mel Waterhouse own a home in Southwest France near the historic Lascaux caves, which provides another chance for lifetime learning. Joan also speaks French and Mel is practicing. She advises, "If someone is serious about living in France, it helps to speak French. If you don't it can isolate you. If you do, the French really appreciate it."

The Language Bridge

Language fluency will set you apart, and it is a good way to meet friends—both native residents and visitors. "I love dealing with tourists and being the intermediary," says Allie Yance, who spoke no Spanish before moving to Costa Rica and now speaks fluently. Her goal, she says, "is to get to the point where people no longer say 'your Spanish is very good.'" Tanya Kennebeck in Portugal offers an example of the kind of independence that comes with learning the language: "I feel that you can negotiate better bargains." Similarly, with her fluent Spanish, Veronica Alta shops for bargains in the non-tourist areas of Málaga, Spain, and Len and Nellie Friedman in Guadalajara confirm the value of mastering a second language. He pays $235 per month for his apartment, while many Americans are paying $400 or more for similar housing. "We are both bilingual," says Len, "so we can compete with Mexicans in the rental market."

A combination of classes and informal "field study" is the usual approach. David Mead preceded his move with an informal study of Thai on language tapes. Since moving to Thailand, he practices with his multilingual Thai friends, whose command of English enables them to explain subtle shades of meaning to David. (He can say in English, "How do you say X" and immediately learn the exact word or phrase he needs.) During his everyday errands, local shopkeepers are eager to help him learn new words and correct his pronunciation. Since it is unusual for Thais to meet a foreigner who knows their language, they are surprised and delighted when he greets them and asks questions in Thai.

Susan Broward says it even helped to have some knowledge of Spanish before moving to the Algarve and learning Portuguese. "Without learning the language you are always a foreigner," comments Susan. "When I speak in Portuguese they are always surprised." She points out a drawback to learning only in the field. Since she first learned Portuguese by ear rather than by formal study, she picked up the local dialect. "When I go to Lisbon they say 'Oh, you are from the Algarve.'" Having a recognizable dialect isn't really a problem, but she adds, "If you start saying things wrong you have two jobs. You have to unlearn the bad habits. I started learning from the gardener, the maid and the builder, then I realized—as a former speech major in college— that I wanted to learn proper Portuguese, so I had to go back to class and study it over again. Now my maid wants me to teach her some of the fine points of her own language."

FRANCE

Chapter 10

Friends in a New Country

"It's a goal of mine to know more Costa Ricans—and to know them better."

Terry Lohman
San José, Costa Rica

What is the best way to meet native residents, Americans and other members of the international expatriate community—and how will you find friends who share common interests?

Don't worry. You will meet people easily, since Americans in another country naturally gravitate to each other, and soon you will find yourself in the middle of a round of introductions. Charles Yarby discovered this during his months of simulated living in St. Croix (U.S. Virgin Islands): "When I went to St. Croix I didn't know anyone, but soon I met people and they introduced me to other people." On the experience of leaving his old friends from Philadelphia behind when he moved abroad, he explains that this was an acceptable part of forging change in his life: "People's lives change. Friendships change—and our interests change, too."

Even a move to Florida means a change in relationships, as many retirees find. In the U.S., there isn't the magnet that draws Americans together abroad. The international equivalent of the Welcome Wagon is powered by the bond of expatriate friendship. Rose Leigh describes her move to Florida, where she spent two years: "It seemed like old friends would come down two weeks out of the year. The rest of the time the house was empty."

The "American community" abroad is not composed of expatriates who are next-door neighbors. Some neighborhoods, apartments or condominiums do have a concentration of Americans, but you will still be included in activities (if you wish) even if your residence is in a neighborhood with few expatriates. Some contact with Americans is advisable during the adjustment period. You may decide later to rent, buy or build farther away from the primary American community. By then you will be past the adjustment phase. A first-time move to a more remote area may satisfy your desire to be independent, but the hurdles could be discouraging. By starting where there are Americans, you can always make a second or third move later on. Some Americans, especially single women, choose to remain close to the American community, which provides their primary social contacts.

Not everyone wants to be social, whether living in the U.S. or abroad. You can be socially active, or live a very private life. Brian Jones, who is planning his retirement in Costa Rica, describes how he and his wife feel: "In some ways we're antisocial. That doesn't mean we don't like people. We like to talk and get to know them, and we might even join a group; it's just that we don't need a very active social life."

Socializing means activity. Although at first the resident Americans are likely to make a friendly overture, the rest is up to you. You will need to reach out. "Life is very pleasant here, but you have to do something to make it pleasant for yourself," says Elsa Van Dam in Málaga, Spain, who adds, "I do a lot of work for foundations and clubs—I am one of those people who are doers." She also belongs to a bridge club and gives a hand to friends who volunteer for church bazaars. "I am not a churchgoer myself," she adds, "but I give a hand."

Formal Clubs and Groups

Find out which organizations already exist and which you may want to join. It may be an American Club, a book club, a bridge, tennis, golf, photography or a garden club. In expatriate communities, larger organizations usually have subgroups for special interests, or you can start one. In some countries you will also find a Pensioners Association. Since this is usually a legal status of residency (you may also be allowed to join as an associate), it enables its members to stay informed of changes in policy as well as to enjoy membership for social functions. The *Pensionado Association* in Costa Rica, for example, has international members, as does the Foreign Homeowners Association in Portugal's Algarve. If such organizations do not already exist, you may want to find other interested parties and form a group. Some groups are privately sponsored, such as Guadalajara's American-Canadian Club, which offers orientation for newly arrived Americans and Canadians, as well as an ongoing program of events, trips and special interest activities, including an art fair, amateur theater, ballet, opera and symphony evenings.

One of the advantages of making your first move abroad within an organized American community is to establish a network for smoothing your adjustment. Whether the expat community fills your need for friendships depends on: a) what is available, and b) how willing you are to take the initiative. Portugal has fewer organized groups for Americans than does Costa Rica, Spain or Mexico. You will need to be a social self-starter in Portugal. Beth Hartman says it hasn't been easy for her to make new friends in Portugal, although she has a few. "I miss belonging to places like the Emerald Club at home," she says. Her husband offers: "I think she would like to get things started. Maybe have a Valentine's party or a Halloween party for the American community. She would also enjoy belonging to an art association but so far none has been formed in the area—although she is thinking of organizing one."

On the other hand, Ruth Walkington says her social life is more active in Costa Rica than it was in the U.S. "I joined a little theater group and the Costa Rica–American Women's Club. There are all kinds of special interest groups—art and music appreciation, stitchery, book, bridge and excursion clubs, and some have fund-raisers and an annual bazaar."

Veronica Alta is a member of the American Club, which has several chapters in Spain. "It is a social, civic and cultural club. When an American gets in any kind of trouble, we rally to help them. There is always someone to call in time of need," she explains.

The club was founded in 1974, is legally registered according to Spanish law and is modeled after the Professional Women's Club of Madrid. The Torremolinos chapter meets in the Flamingo Hotel, where the suite includes a lending library of American books. "We have visiting committees for those who are sick, and we go on trips," says Veronica, citing two of the club's many activities.

Nancy Thalmeyer notes that church activities are important for her social life in Costa Rica. "We attend a nondenominational English-speaking church." She explains that the ministers are not permanently appointed, but usually remain for one or two years. She also belongs to a book club and a garden club. On social choices she adds: "You can be perfectly anonymous here, or you can be so busy that you don't know what to choose."

Committees are another way to stay socially involved. Usually there are problems and issues that need airing, and interested parties work together for improvement. This is especially true in small communities. Louise Harris says that in the rain-forest community of Monteverde, Costa Rica, "There were so many committees that you could be busy all the time."

Cultural Barriers

Most Americans abroad note that their closest circle of friends includes few native residents, although many Americans say they value—and make an extra effort to cultivate—these friendships. "We have some Portuguese friends, an elderly couple in their seventies who like to come over and visit with us. They raise their own food and when they visit us, usually on Sundays, they'll bring a dozen eggs or figs," offers Beth Hartman.

Don't be disappointed if you don't make immediate inroads into the native community. It takes time. You may have international friends in the U.S., but they are in your country for business or a college education, or have relocated to join their families in the U.S. and may be your neighbors. The United States is a country founded on many nationalities. When you move to a traditional culture, native residents abroad are inclined to keep to themselves.

Language problems usually present an obstacle to American/native resident friendships. Veronica Alta explains that the American Club tried an exchange arrangement with the Spanish Women's Club, but most American women didn't act on the opportunity because of the language difficulty. "I wish more would come. It's an opportunity for intercultural exchange," she adds.

Terry Lohman in Costa Rica belongs to a little theater group, the women's club and also a walking group. "There are seven of us. We walk every day and have coffee afterward." She also belongs to a group that does "light exploration" once a month and says, "A lot of interesting people go on that—Costa Ricans, Europeans and Americans." She has recently joined another group consisting mainly of Costa Ricans. She points out that it takes an extra effort to make friends among native residents, since it is easier to spend time with Americans. "It's a goal of mine to know more Costa Ricans and to know them better. Usually they are inclined to be friendly only if you are related by blood or marriage; otherwise they tend not to get close." She adds that improving her language skills will help. "I speak Spanish, but not as well as I'd like. I can make myself understood, but I'd like to speak it as fluently as I speak English."

Take an Interest

One way to deprive yourself of friendships with native residents is to avoid opportunity for contact. Joan Peters was beginning to make friends in her French village, but then on her next trip she explains that she and Mel were "lazy" and spent the summer with expatriates. She is determined on their next visit to regain lost ground. "I want to keep mixing with the French. We just have to make the effort, improve our French and have people over." One gaffe caused a setback: they hired a British resident to repair their house. "I think our neighbors would have appreciated it if we had hired a French craftsman instead."

Nancy Stangos, who spends time in her family's home on Kalymnos every year, says, "Greeks appreciate it if you take an interest in their culture. If you do that, you will be easily accepted." Lily Cairns agrees, but points out that sometimes Greek friendships can be a bit overwhelming. "The Greeks are warm and friendly and *so* hospitable. I have to argue with my Greek friends in Athens every time I visit—they don't like it if I stay in a hotel, but I like to stay where I can walk to the Plaka," the cultural center of the city, quite a distance from her friend's residential neighborhood. "So they are always offended," she adds.

Sometimes you may think you are being considerate when you are not. In the U.S., it may be thoughtful to stay in a hotel rather than inconvenience a friend or relative by moving into their spare bedroom. In some other countries, however, such personal sacrifices (like giving up privacy for a visitor) may be a point of pride for a host. Laine Arden in Warsaw, Poland, found the Poles to be very friendly, but sometimes a bit "overwhelming" in their graciousness. As Laine explains: "They make you very welcome in their homes, but it embarrasses you. You think they've saved up all their meat ration and are serving it in your honor."

Other Expats

After Americans, Europeans are usually the second tier of friendships. Making friends in the international community is one of the benefits of living abroad in a resort area, says Barbara Moore. "I've made friends from all over Europe, and I've visited friends in Scotland, Holland, England—all of whom I met here in the Algarve. I never dreamed I'd have the wonderful extra of knowing a lot of Europeans." In a resort area—where many residents stay only part time—even European friendships may have to be scheduled, especially for a single person. Lily Cairns likes to be alone but she also enjoys her international friends, who like herself are part-time residents of Mykonos. One of her neighbors lives in Munich, one is Canadian, one is British. "I know when Manchester is coming and when Munich is coming. We'll all be there together part of the year."

On the other hand, you might not like all of your European neighbors, or find some to be standoffish. One resident in Portugal prefers the Portuguese (and cultivates these friendships) rather than the large number of British who live in the Algarve. "For some Americans it can be difficult to be around the British all the time. Americans are forthright. We say what's on our minds, but not so with the British. I actually find that the Portuguese are more like Americans than the British are." Karen Knight, another Algarve resident, says, "We know one French couple and have a few Portuguese friends, but the American and Portuguese communities don't mix, by and large. I find that the Dutch are easier to get along with than the British. The Germans, on the other hand, stay very much to themselves."

In some areas, your European friends may outnumber Americans. Dara Glass in Mexico City likes the cosmopolitan aspect of living in a city: "I have very good friends of different nationalities—American, French, Bulgarian, Cuban and Russian. You have a much greater exposure to different people than you do in many places in the U.S." She tells of standing in a bank line with a French and a Russian friend. She and the French woman were griping about the long line, while their Russian friend said, in their common language of Spanish, "But this is a *much* shorter line than I would have at home."

For younger expatriates, there are alternatives to traditional clubs or church groups. Allie Yance relies on two groups for her social life. One is regular but informal: "Gringo artists gravitate together for Sunday potluck. The musicians bring instruments and we have a jam session." In this group she met her current boyfriend, an American silk-screen artist. The other group is an international running organization called the Hash House Harriers, which began as a club for expatriates in Koala Lumpur, Malaysia, and now there are chapters all over the world. As Allie describes her Costa Rica chapter: "Members are from their 20s to their 70s. It's multinational, around half North American, also British, German, and around one-third are Costa Rican. Every Monday at 5:00 we meet at a different spot. It's always an adventure because you have to find the 'trail.' The 'hares' mark the trail, and the runners check for the three-dot sign. Some people get off work early to participate. There were 50 people at our last run." She adds that after each run, everyone gathers for beer and singing. It's one of the mainstays of her social life, or as she says, she is an avid "hasher"—and through this social network, she found her charming small house in San José.

Vacations in a French Village

For their vacation home abroad, John and Sally Barber chose a 300-year-old stone farmhouse on a narrow lane in Southwestern France. "There is a timeless charm about it," says John. "Sheep pass by in the morning, and in the afternoon cows file through the village on their way to be milked."

Their country hamlet—a group of homes related to a farm—is located halfway between Paris and Barcelona near the River Dordogne, far from the world of high technology. Dairy farmers in the region keep herds of eight or nine cows; villagers cultivate small vineyards to produce their own wine. "People in the village all help pick the grapes as a neighborly gesture," John explains, adding, "and no one expects to be paid."

As a food broker in the U.S., John praises the cuisine that he and Sally have sampled since purchasing the farm in 1973. "We love to enjoy French food and my wife prepares dishes from produce she buys in nearby villages like St. Cyprian." The Barbers dine out every other day and John estimates that "there are about 20 wonderful restaurants within a 30-minute drive." In 1985, they could enjoy a full-course dinner for $5, plus another dollar for wine. Today the same meal is $10 (and $2 for wine). "It's the kind of meal that on the San Francisco peninsula would be $35. At $10 it isn't cheap compared to earlier years, but it's wonderful and still a bargain."

The Barbers bought their farmhouse for $9,000 in 1973. After almost two decades, the Barbers are still the only non-French owners in their hamlet of 17 homes, although four urban French families now own vacation homes in the area. "This is happening a lot in France where homes are unoccupied. Local people die and city people find a vacation home in the country," says John. "Right now there are four empty homes here. Some of them will remain empty, some of them will become vacation homes, but it will be a pity if we lose all the full-time residents."

As part-time residents, the Barbers have worked out a schedule in which Sally arrives in June each year and John follows in August; together, they return to the Bay Area in October. With five grown children who visit almost every year, with

120

friends traveling from the U.S. plus visits from neighbors, Sally Barber has a full calendar until her husband arrives mid-summer.

They host up to 40 houseguests each season. "It's the kind of work she loves," says John. "We have two refrigerators, a washing machine and a young woman in a nearby village helps with the cleaning." It may sound like the Barbers' farmhouse has guest rooms aplenty, but it is actually a simple structure with three bedrooms and a large downstairs room that serves as living room, dining room and kitchen. The centerpiece is a large farm table that seats a dozen people; the floor of the main room is lined with small stones in the traditional style of the region.

After buying the farmhouse, the Barbers added another $15,000 in restoration and upgrading during the next two years. "We had to put in water, a bathroom and electricity, doors and windows and a new floor," John recalls. "It's a very comfortable house with a lovely barn, very pleasant grounds and a terrace—we can feed 20 people outdoors from our barbecue." The barn is their secret of houseguest success: John says, "I'd like to build guest rooms in the barn but no one listens to me. The young people prefer to sleep in the hay."

The villagers like the bustling activity of the Barbers' many guests and the young people who visit, especially since many of the villagers are elderly with grown children who have moved away to Paris and other cities. One of the lead cyclists in a recent Tour de France is a friend of one of the Barbers' sons. As John explains, "He came to the village to train for several days. During the Tour de France his wife and in-laws visited us while he was racing past our part of France—that adds a lot of spice to the village."

Sally speaks fluent French, a skill she has cultivated over the years; John, on the other hand, reads the French newspaper every day and although he understands the language somewhat he admits, "I don't speak it—I'm lazy." Sally has demonstrated to the village that she respects their language enough to master it and the rest of the family rides on her laurels. Yet sometimes language skill isn't necessary for communication. The Barbers' eldest son, who is a cabinetmaker, visited the village and was introduced to the local craftsman. "They don't speak the same language but they knew what they were discussing—the tools and the workshop," says John.

For independent living while abroad, the Barbers keep a car garaged in the barn on their property. "Sally just got a new used car," John explains. "She likes to go to Barcelona or Provence. Usually there will be a friend from the States with her, and often one of the neighbors comes along, too." When John arrives, they take an auto trip to a different area each year, but it isn't necessary for them to travel far for diversion. Besides the charming village and its surrounding pastoral landscape, the prehistoric caves of Lascaux are only eight miles away. "I had wondered if we would get tired of this life and want to visit other parts of the world, since the whole family loves to travel. But we haven't tired of it after all these years," says John, who observes that since he and Sally are getting older (although John has no intention of retiring from his business), they find that challenging travel is becoming more difficult. Sally was planning a trip to India, but as John explains, "Her knees are giving her trouble and we're not traveling like youthful people any more."

Friendships among the villagers will become even more important now that the Barbers are limiting their outside travel. One friendship dates back to when they bought their farmhouse: they first found their home by driving through the region where they wanted to buy property. The home was empty and had not been lived in for 40 years. After they located the owner and agreed on a price, the owner and the Barbers arranged for the transfer of property through the *notaire*, which John describes as "a combination of a title insurance official and a lawyer. He does everything." Since the transaction, the *notaire* has become a lifelong friend.

The friendship has provided many memorable experiences, as John recalls: "One day I was driving through the woods in our car and noticed that a little car was trying to catch me. I slowed down and saw that it was the son of the *notaire* who said, 'Stop, we want you to come to the *atelier* and play chess.' His brother brought wine and cheese, his parents joined us and we played chess and drank wine for hours. The village is extremely friendly, but in a very different way than what we are accustomed to in the States."

Chapter 11

Visitors from Home

"Young people love to sleep in the haymounds. Sometimes we'll have as many as 10 or 12 young people sleeping in the barn over the summer."

John Barber
Dordogne, France

Visits from family and friends may be most frequent while you are still in the adjustment phase. Your enthusiastic, detailed letters will naturally attract those who want to see what you are so excited about. It can be a good time to share that energy—although it can also lead to a tiring stream of house guests. You may also find yourself inviting too many visitors as an antidote to your own slight case of homesickness, since it is people you are most likely to miss.

Yet among the more than 50 people interviewed for *Adventures Abroad*, loneliness was rarely a complaint. New friends and visits from home add up to a satisfying social schedule for just about everyone, and visits from grandchildren can be especially gratifying. What might otherwise seem a routine visit to grandfather and grandmother, especially for teenagers, can turn into an adventure. Louise Harris has enjoyed summer visits from her grandson for years, and as a result of summers in Costa Rica he has made numerous Costa Rican friends. The friendships reinforce his desire to spend summers abroad with his grandparents, especially now that he is older and free to choose how he spends his vacation months. "I believe we are closer than we would be if we lived in the U.S.," says Louise.

College-age children seem to relish family vacation homes abroad. However, once they begin careers their vacation time becomes more scarce. Arlene and Paul Dexter's home in France has been a busy vacation spot for their sons (and their sons' friends) during college years. Now that the young men are starting their careers, the Dexters are watching their progress while deciding on their own retirement plan. As Arlene explains, "If our sons decide to work in the U.S., I think we would maintain something—maybe a condominium—in the States." But if they decide to work abroad, which sometimes occurs when children discover international living, then Arlene and Paul would not keep property in the U.S. and would retire as full-time residents abroad.

Not surprisingly, expatriates with large families report having the most visitors. Even if there is a lull after the first visitors, the stream may not stop as sons and daughters-in-law, nieces and nephews and your children's friends appear to liven things up again. College-age children with their friends are inclined to fill up the household during summer vacations, sometimes using your home as a base for their own explorations. John Barber's solution is to use the barn on the property of his farmhouse in France, where fresh hay is provided by a local dairy farmer as a neighborly gesture. Says John, "Young people love to sleep in the haymounds. Sometimes we'll have as many as 10 or 12 young people sleeping in the barn over the summer."

Len and Nellie Friedman in Guadalajara have a "large merged family"—this is a second marriage for both, and their 13 children and 14 grandchildren visit regularly, as does Len's 89-year-old father. The Friedmans visit the U.S. once a year for a brief visit. "Most people come down to visit us, and once someone comes down, they keep coming back. You can have more company than you want," says Len.

One way to manage visitors is to make a list of people you'd like to have visit, then suggest possible dates for visits—that is, if you want to avoid having too many guests in close succession. The task of host can be tiring and expensive, depending on how you arrange expenses for side trips and restaurant meals.

Trips Back Home

The frequency of your trips to the U.S., for those who choose to be year-round residents abroad, is an individual decision and one likely to change over time. Some Americans living abroad routinely visit the U.S. every year—others rarely return. One Costa Rica resident who lives in a remote coastal area with other expatriates says, "We went back to the U.S. in 1987. I couldn't wait to get back to my beach. You can have the rush-rush, buy-buy mentality, the fumes and all."

Your ties with the U.S. also depend on whether you arrange to keep a home or apartment in the States, or if you plan other accommodations with friends and family for your return trips. House- or apartment-sitting is an inexpensive way to visit, and it can be an equitable way for friends to return the favor after visiting you abroad. Lauren and Ben Gruning apartment-sit a friend's condominium in San Francisco every year, and this arrangement provides them with a way to fulfill the requirement to leave Mexico every six months, since they do not have resident status. In 1990, their apartment-sitting trip home provided a buffer between cities: they gave up their Guadalajara apartment, stored their belongings, and planned to make a move to San Miguel de Allende after their stay in San Francisco.

At first some people find that they want to visit the U.S. more frequently—within six months or a year. You should budget for this possibility as part of the adjustment period. But you may find, as others do, that you are so involved with life in a new country that years pass before you feel a need to return to the U.S. This is especially true if friends and family travel to visit you.

Don and Beth Hartman have seven children between them, a second marriage for both. In the past three years, two daughters have visited and they are expecting other family members to visit in the future. The first time they visited the U.S., two years after moving to Portugal, was a visit home to see their grandchildren.

When planning how frequently you may need to visit the U.S., consider the following possibilities and costs when budgeting for your move:

• The cost of a round trip to and from the United States (by air, car or other ground transportation) for each person, if you divide your year into six-month periods with tourist status. Your destination to fulfill the six-month exit requirement could either be a trip home, or just across the border. Since there are seasonal airfare changes, you might want to save money by planning your exits to coincide with good rates when possible.

• Anticipated trips for special occasions such as a wedding or the birth of a grandchild. Reservations may be booked in advance for economical airfares.

• Other visits home to see family. This is best handled with a coordinated timetable if you wish to see several family members; you might arrange a family reunion, or a trip with several stops to see friends and family.

• An unanticipated business trip to take care of property or other investment matters, although most business can be handled from abroad (see chapter 17).

• Family or personal illness or emergency, especially if you need specialized medical care outside the country. For illness or in case of the death of a family member, most airlines waive advance reservation requirements but require documentation from an attending physician.

Living abroad doesn't always provide an escape from family problems back home, but sometimes it can offer creative solutions. Terry Lohman was upset when her husband's family in the U.S. notified her that they were sending an 88-year-old aunt who needed care to Costa Rica. Terry was already expecting the arrival of her elderly mother, who was not in good health either. "My job right now is to look after the elderly," says Terry, who points out that with inexpensive home help at least the burden is lighter than it would be in the U.S.

For Larraine Grey, an unanticipated visit from a relative has turned out to be a happy addition to her Portugal family. Larraine moved to the Algarve as a single woman, then met and married her current husband. Her sister in Virginia asked Larraine if she would be willing to have her son visit Portugal for a year—now it has been three years and he is 15. Says Larraine, "He's a great kid and he loves it." Coincidentally, the boy had a Portuguese surname, which enabled him to make new friends more easily. Although the original reason for the one-year stay was the boy's problems with school, those problems disappeared when he came to Portugal. "He now goes to an English school where he makes straight A's, and he also studies Portuguese," explains Larraine.

Since almost all Americans living abroad have enjoyed international travel prior to moving, it's not surprising that their children like to travel or that some have strong ties with European family members. John Barber has a son who conducts international bicycling tours through Europe, which gives the family a chance to see him regularly when they are at their home in France. Arthur Secunda's son is a professional mountain climber. From Arthur's apartment in Paris it is an easy trip to Switzerland or Casis where father and son meet once or twice a year, or as Arthur sums it up: "He climbs and we visit."

For Americans with relatives abroad, living or sojourning abroad offers a way to maintain family ties—or to establish relationships that otherwise might remain a footnote on the family tree. Arlene Dexter and Susan Broward both have relatives in England. Their European home base provides a chance to see these relatives more often. "Now I have a base in Europe for my family to visit me," says Susan.

Taking the Children

Families whose careers require that they live abroad are accustomed to moving the entire family. For a stay of two or three years, the usual educational choice is an English-language school where the child will continue his or her studies and be prepared to re-enter the U.S. educational system.

Such schools are found in major cities around the world and are operated by British or American educators. Be prepared for tuition costs, as these English-language schools are privately run. If your choice (or your only option) is a British school, you should prepare your child to expect differences in attitude. Instructors will be more formal, classrooms and lessons more structured and even the children (if British expatriates) will be more formal and probably more class-conscious.

There may be a few other surprises: your child's performance may actually improve in a setting where discipline is emphasized and where academic goals are more clearly stated than in many American schools in the U.S. Your child will also be exposed to history from a different viewpoint, which can be an advantage for further development in critical judgment—obviously the American Revolution is presented differently in British schools. On the other hand, some remedial work may be necessary: a diplomat who lived in Edinburgh, Scotland, in the 1980s notes that he had to re-teach his son about the American Revolution.

The age of the child, and the duration of your sojourn abroad, makes a difference in the type of education needed. If you are thinking of a move abroad with a young child, then consider this

127

advice from Marion Baker, a teacher from Kansas who founded the Country Day School in San José, Costa Rica: "I believe that children should learn to read in their native language until the third grade; then they can start reading and writing in another language."

Other Americans abroad choose to send their children to college preparatory schools in the U.S. when they near college age. This was the eventual choice of John Nielson and his wife. Their daughter was 11 years old when they first moved to Costa Rica. Before the move, John arranged for Nancy to spend one month at the English-language Lincoln School in San José. When they moved, Nancy adjusted well and made new friends, but the Nielsons decided that when Nancy reached high-school age she should return to the U.S. and attend a prep school in the Northeast.

Older children may benefit from the educational experience of a native school. When Darren Thomas and his wife moved to Hamburg, Germany, in 1981, they had a choice of sending their son to the International School (where most students were children of diplomatic families, and where classes were taught in English), but they decided to send Glen to a German school.

At first the 13-year-old was disoriented, but he adjusted well and made many German friends. His popularity soared in English class, where all the German students wanted to learn "American English" (especially slang and current jargon). Although the headmaster tried to "correct" Glen's English, this was a minor drawback compared to the social advantages. Darren recalls that when boys from school would come to the Thomases' apartment, "At first they greeted me very formally, but soon they would say 'Hi'—they were learning Glen's American vocabulary and at the same time he was learning German."

It depends on the individual child's capacity for such cross-cultural challenges, but for those who are the right temperament, a few years of education abroad reaps lifelong benefits. "He came back with confidence and an experience that all his classmates envied," says Darren. "Glen had lived in Germany, he'd traveled around Europe before he was 16 and he spoke a second language."

Chapter 12

Helping the Community

*"I had always planned to do some kind of charity work, and I
found work to do here. At times my husband does more than I do."*
Debra Erland
Lagoa, Portugal

The most affordable countries are the most needy.
Whether at home or abroad, it is hard for us to ignore
those who have little to call their own. Americans living
abroad try to help in different ways, some through organizations such as the American Club, a church or social group, and
others through private projects. The business adage "find a
need and fill it" has a special application for helping others,
especially in developing countries, and there is always opportunity to help both needy residents and Americans who find
themselves in difficulty.

Retirees Matt and Joan Feldman in La Paz, Mexico, participate
in a fund-raising event that began a few years ago as a boating
auction. By selling old equipment, money was raised to buy gifts
for poor children in La Paz. Last year's auction bought presents
for 2,500 children. Ruth Walkington belongs to the Costa Rica–
American Women's Club, which holds fund-raising events and
an annual bazaar to provide money for different causes, including scholarships and contributions to an orphanage and to a
home for the elderly.

Informal groups often find projects of their own. Nancy Thalmeyer, who belongs to a group of retired American teachers in
Costa Rica, found a way to help residents by arranging for local
woodcarvers to produce dolls from coffee wood, with costumes

sewn by local women. The dolls are sold by the group, who only take out expenses and return all proceeds to the craftsmen and women, an enterprise that provides extra income for several families.

Expression of Gratitude

Clubs and organizations abroad frequently sponsor charitable projects. Elsa Van Dam in Spain belongs to a church group and a women's club that both raise money to help the needy. Her special project, along with her American friend Ann Lowry, provides a benefit for both Spanish residents and for Elsa and Ann's expatriate community.

The inspiration for their project occurred when Ann, who contracted typhus from a flea bite during a trip to Morocco, was so impressed by the excellent medical care she received in Spain that she and her husband decided to make a of contribution to the health care community. They established a foundation called FEE to encourage nurses in training to learn English (many doctors speak English, but few nurses do). Although there was a lot of red tape at first, in 1985 FEE awarded its first grant of $100 to the top student in each English class in the Nursing School of the University of Málaga. From three students in 1985, the course "English for Nurses" has grown to an annual enrollment of over 100 students. (FEE's list of essential medical terms appears in the appendix.)

There are also ways to help underprivileged individuals. Susan Broward sponsored a talented young man from Lagos, Portugal, to study in the U.S. She also writes letters for his uneducated parents so they can stay in touch with their son in the States. Susan is also active in animal protection projects. She both cares for many sick strays and tries to find adopted homes for unwanted pets—she also arranges to have stray animals spayed or neutered in an effort to help contain the large number of homeless animals in her area.

Stanley Walters in Montevideo, Uruguay, notes that there are many charitable opportunities for Americans living in the area—as there are in Portugal where Debra Erland says, "I had always planned to do some kind of charity work, and I found work to do here." Like many Americans, she found time for philanthropic work after her retirement, and so did her husband who works with her on many projects. Debra notes, "At times my husband does more than I do."

Another American in Portugal notes that much of the charitable work is done by expatriates. One recent example was a marathon run sponsored by an international running club, the Hash House Harriers. Each person who participated in the run was sponsored by a different American or British expatriate who pledged a certain amount for each kilometer completed by their runner. The marathon raised the equivalent of $17,000 and donated it to an association to aid the handicapped.

Working with an established group is a good way to meet other expatriates who care about the community, and by the time you are ready to try an independent charitable project you will be past the adjustment phase. That means you will be accustomed to the delays, frustrations and some language hurdles, and you will have a better idea of what kinds of projects are feasible. Alan Cox thought he could help the poor residents of Costa Rica by asking visiting American friends to bring along their unwanted but serviceable clothing. His friends and family were only too happy to provide clothing, but Alan found out that most Americans are much larger than Costa Ricans. Most of the adult clothing was too large or too heavy to be useful and some required dry cleaning, which low-income Costa Ricans cannot afford. Another of Alan's projects proved more successful. He now asks visitors to bring English-language books, which are enjoyed by both Americans and by Costa Ricans who are studying English.

The most effective efforts are those undertaken with an understanding of the community. Renee Wolpert has lived on and off in Mexico over the past 20 years, and when she resided in an upper-middle-class Mexican neighborhood of Guadalajara she learned how Mexican families express social responsibility. "You don't let a child die because your housekeeper doesn't have the money for medicine," explains Renee, recalling a time when her maid's little boy was hospitalized. Well-to-do Mexican families assume some of the responsibility of caring for their domestic help, but many Americans are not aware of this custom. Showing concern helps your relationship with domestic employees and establishes your reputation as a caring and favored employer. But few expatriates know to offer help, since it may not be requested directly.

If you show willingness to help, how can you prevent an employee from taking advantage of you? Renee found that when her household help faced a problem, the maid or gardener would usually ask for a salary advance or try to sell her something they had made to raise money. In one case, a maid asked Renee if she would buy one of her wedding presents. Renee explains how she responded to this: "I told her, 'If you need money I will give you some and subtract it gradually from your salary.'" She only withheld a few pesos every week, and adds, "I let them know they couldn't just ask for money, but at the same time they knew that I was concerned about them. And no one ever cheated me. I think one of the reasons I got along so well was that I followed the Mexican custom."

Plantation Life in Costa Rica

The Beckers' 13-acre *finca* or coffee plantation commands the rim of a hill near Grecia, less than an hour's drive outside San José, Costa Rica. A tile veranda borders the width of the one-story home, where a bright kitchen with traditional hand-painted woodwork and an adjacent book-lined den are the heart of activity. The veranda looks onto an unbroken horizon of green hills. On the rolling slopes that comprise the Becker's *finca*, rows of squat, leafy bushes produce some of the world's finest coffee.

In the late 1970s, the Beckers bought their plantation after two visits to Costa Rica, based on the recommendation of friends. "We liked what we saw and bought right away," recalls Cheryl, who notes that at the time, "people thought that we were going to Puerto Rico." Few people would confuse the two countries today since Costa Rica garnered international recognition for the Nobel Peace Prize awarded to its former president, Oscar Arias Sanchez, and for the country's efforts in rain-forest preservation.

For the past decade, Ed and Cheryl (who are now in their 70s) have divided the year between their home in San Diego, California, and their home in Grecia. In order to maintain *pensionado* status, the Beckers spend four to six months residing in the country each year, and many of their friends also divide the year between Costa Rica and a home in the U.S.

In 1979, the Beckers knew nothing about coffee cultivation, but they knew they wanted to retire abroad with an active plan. "You can't move here and not do something. You have to become involved with the country," advises Cheryl, adding, "and it's better if you come here with a purpose." They approached their project facing obstacles and challenges, "but Ed took an interest in the work," says Cheryl, "and now we have one of the finest coffee plantations in the area. You just learn how to do it—and then you do it." The income from their "hobby farm" covers the maintenance costs of the Beckers' home in Costa Rica. These days, Ed supervises the farm, which is worked during his six months in the U.S. by a reliable crew. During the first few years, though, he had a hand in every facet of the work, or as Cheryl explains, "Yes, he dug, too."

There are few American near their *finca*, "Just some of us diehards and several families scattered around who don't want to mingle," she says. Although many Americans like to live in San José with its urban conveniences and sizable American expatriate community, the Beckers prefer their rural location. When they want to visit San José, it's an inexpensive 35-mile trip that costs only 30 cents (U.S.) on a reliable, well-maintained bus with a stop in front of the Beckers' home.

Cheryl reports that it has not been difficult to establish friendships. "There is an informal kind of sociability out here that revolves around practical tasks. Four or five of us usually meet at the local coffee shop every morning. We visit and do our shopping, then it's time to go home and prepare lunch. We don't take a siesta anymore, but from noon to two businesses still close." The afternoon respite suggests a slow pace and hot afternoons. Yet the climate in Costa Rica is far from oppressive. The Beckers, like many Americans in residence, count the comfortable climate as one of the reasons they chose Costa Rica as a locale. The Beckers also wanted a country with a year-round climate, not limited to just one temperate season, so that they could visit any time of year. "The climate is basically the same in all seasons, so it doesn't matter when you go—it's like Hawaii," says Cheryl.

As the siesta tradition suggests, Costa Rica does have a slower pace than the U.S. "It's 20 years behind the times, as far as pace is concerned," she notes. "Costa Rica is progressing, but after six months when we return from the U.S., there isn't a new skyscraper or strip mall. It's like going home, in an old-fashioned way and that's a comfortable feeling." Life in Costa Rica isn't always slow-paced and leisurely, as Cheryl points out. "They scramble for shopping, especially every Christmas when employers pay a bonus—the *aguanalda*—and everyone receives it at the same time."

Costa Rica is an agricultural and family-oriented country, of which Cheryl observes, "I like the emphasis on family activities. There is a simplicity of life here." When Ed's mother became terminally ill a few years ago, the Beckers brought her to their home in Costa Rica where they could provide affordable home care. She passed away after some months, but at the funeral Cheryl recalls, "Everyone turned out in respect for our family. The young sons of the local department store owners carried the casket. There is a lot of love here, and they take the time to show it."

COSTA RICA

The Beckers intend to keep their home in the U.S., and says Cheryl: "We weren't going to burn our bridges." Her son visits Grecia occasionally, and friends come for visits, too, although houseguests were most frequent when they first bought their home. After a decade, there is still such a steady stream of guests that for a while Cheryl considered turning the *finca* into a bed-and-breakfast inn.

The Beckers say that if they had it to do over again, they would do it just the same way. They don't miss the U.S. during their six months in Costa Rica each year. Every time they change countries, it is "just a couple of days of culture shock, and then it's as though we've never left," says Cheryl. "It's amazing the way you adapt."

Chapter 13

International Banking, Investments and Taxes

"We can sometimes offer you a credit check on companies, but if you're burned we cannot act as a collection agency for bad deals."
Judith Henderson
Commercial Attaché, U.S. Embassy
San José, Costa Rica

Whether you live abroad year-round or part time, your primary banking relationship will be with a bank in the United States. For day-to-day operating expenses, you will want to establish a bank account abroad. But if you plan only to spend brief periods of time in another country and do not own property there, then you may not need a bank account outside the U.S. Your legal status affects your options: in some countries, with tourist status, you may not be allowed to have certain types of bank accounts (checking account, or a convertible dollar account, for example). Banking privileges are one reason some Americans choose to go through the paperwork required for resident or pensioner status.

The practice of maintaining only operating money abroad—especially if you are in a country with unstable currency—protects you against the possibility of local currency devaluation. With this safeguard in place, devaluation of local currency can actually stretch the purchasing power of your dollars. If you are uncomfortable about the prospect of devaluation, or the impact of a high inflation rate, then you might choose a country with a more stable currency—although the best cost of living bargains for U.S. dollars are found in the soft-currency countries. In developing countries, high street exchange rates can extend your purchasing power even further than the official exchange rate.

The Exchange-Rate Game

All currency fluctuates, but small variations in exchange rate will have little effect on your daily transactions abroad. The exchange rate does become important when making large purchases: Bob and Linda Martinelli watched the exchange rates expectantly when they had to transfer the purchase price of their house to Italy in lire. "We looked at the newspaper and tried to anticipate the exchange rate," Bob explains. "We would have been ahead if we had transferred in May, but we waited until October." When they chose a day for the transfer, the dollar had gone up somewhat against the lira; a few days later, the dollar dropped. They chose the right day.

When Pamela Winger bought her farmhouse in Ireland in 1990, she paid a deposit in August, then bought a futures contract (with a 10% deposit on amount) to lock in the exchange rate until the balance was due in March of 1991. Of course, if the dollar strengthens against the Irish pound, her locked-in rate could be a disadvantage. Pamela, who buys futures contracts in her travel business to guarantee the cost of tours, says: "Sometimes you win, sometimes you don't. In the past three years I have found that I usually win."

Fast Money

Wire deposit speeds the time necessary to transfer funds between banks in different countries, which can usually be completed in a day and provides more control over exchange rates. The Martinellis arranged to wire deposit with a bank branch in Verona, Italy, with which Bank of America has a correspondent relationship. The first bank you approach abroad may not be able to offer adequate expatriate services. Your current U.S. bank may not be prepared to do so, either. The Martinellis had conducted business with a different U.S. bank for years, but found it expedient to open an account with Bank of America when they bought their home abroad.

Access to Cash

The common vehicle for opening and closing an account abroad is a document of deposit. This proves that you legally imported a specific amount of money into the country; when you leave, you are entitled to convert this money back into dollars and take it with you—which is called "repatriation of funds."

Until you are ready to make a major purchase such as a home or car, you need only be concerned about everyday banking transactions, but you should provide enough liquidity in your expatriate account for some extras aside from basic living expenses. Your credit cards (Visa, MasterCard, American Express) are all you need for most unexpected expenses, such as airfare back to the U.S. in case of a family emergency, but unless you plan to live on traveler's checks (fine for short-term visits) or on credit card withdrawals (costly because of fees and lower exchange rates) you will need to do some research to assure that you have an accessible, safe bank account for most living expenses.

For banking and all money matters abroad, remember to assume that procedures are different than in the U.S.—then take steps to find out exactly how they differ. You'll discover that the variations are many: from irregular hours and unusual holiday closures to long bank lines and absence of the automatic teller machines so common in the U.S. There may even be restrictions on which days of the month you can withdraw from your account.

Now that you're prepared for obstacles, it's safe to add that banking abroad isn't too difficult. It's almost as easy to receive your Social Security check in Portugal as it is in Pennsylvania. Thousands of Americans receive their checks in Portugal and Spain, in Mexico and Costa Rica, and in almost every country on the globe. One service provided by the U.S. consular service abroad is distribution of Social Security checks to American residents, although an increasing number of expatriates prefer to arrange for automatic Social Security check deposit in their U.S. bank accounts, with a transfer arrangement to the foreign bank.

Your Financial Profile

To qualify for pensioner status, which in some countries affords such privileges as the right to import household items or to import or purchase a car duty free, it is necessary that you demonstrate a minimum guaranteed income. You must also meet financial qualifications as a non-pensioner resident, although in some countries a specific monthly or annual minimum is not set. In some countries, such as Costa Rica, an investment also qualifies you for resident status along with certain privileges (as detailed in chapter 17).

But no income guarantees are required in the early or "simulated living" stage during the months while you are a renter, and during this phase your banking vehicle will probably be a tourist checking account. This kind of account, permitted in most—but not all—countries is also known as a convertible account, because your deposit may be converted from the local currency back into home currency (i.e., dollars).

For an extended period of simulated living, or when you are ready to reside for six months or year-round abroad, you may want to arrange for deposits from your U.S. bank to a foreign bank account. When looking for a bank abroad, do some homework in the States first. Find out if your bank will wire transfer funds to your expatriate account, and also inquire about the cost of this service ($25 is typical) so that you can figure this in your budget plan. A check written on your U.S. bank will take around 3–4 weeks to clear, although you would thereby avoid the wire transfer charge. With planning, you can manage to stay ahead of your cash needs and avoid wire transfer costs except for special circumstances.

Writing checks abroad is another matter. Even if you become established in a community abroad where local merchants are willing to accept checks against your U.S. bank, the rules might change. Len and Tanya Kennebeck were able to write checks on their U.S. bank account for local shopping in Portugal with no problem; the merchants simply converted the check at the point of sale, as they would when accepting a traveler's check. Now the merchants refuse to take any foreign checks, because too many tourists were writing bad checks.

Alex Cox in Alajuela, Costa Rica, writes checks on his Costa Rica *colone* account, and says, "Once you're established, they will take your personal check." If that fails, you can always convert to local currency at the bank and practice cash-and-carry. Alan has arranged to have his pension wired from his Bank of America account to his bank in Costa Rica.

Finding a Bank

Few Americans report having any trouble with banking, although some recall that they had to shop around for a bank that offers what they needed—whether it was in Italy, Mexico, France or elsewhere. Lauren and Ben Gruning, who have tourist or visitor status, had to shop for a bank that would provide expatriate services to non-residents. "We opened a checking account where we could make deposits from our money market account in California to our checking account in Mexico," explains Lauren. "But the first bank we went to in Guadalajara said they didn't want foreign accounts. The next one only allowed us to deposit $200 at a time—that meant two deposits if you wanted to cover a rent check for $350." With a little more research, she could have found a bank with better services, but Lauren says, "We're now cashing checks at American Express. The main reason for the checking account was to pay rent, but now we'll just pay cash."

To prepare for banking abroad, consider the following:

• Before you move, research how payments are processed in the second country; much depends on the automation level of the foreign bank. Major banks abroad usually have agents or branches in the U.S. (New York, Los Angeles and some other cities) who can answer your questions. You can go to the Bank of Portugal offices in New York, for example, and ask: "What should I do to start the process of establishing my foreign account, and how do I arrange transfers between my U.S. and foreign account?"

• Electronic fund transfer is rapidly becoming a worldwide procedure. For the time being, however, your primary concern about banking abroad is gaining access to funds. Mail is time-consuming and unreliable. The more banking you can do by direct deposit and electronic transfer, the more convenient it will be for you.

• Establish relations with a bank abroad that will be able to negotiate your check, electronically or otherwise. Ideally, your U.S. bank has a relationship with your bank abroad.

• Arrange for your Social Security and other checks to be directly deposited. The government can send instructions to credit your U.S. account; you will know that it is received in your U.S. account on the third of each month. Many other kinds of income, such as dividends and veterans benefits, can also be deposited directly.

• Ask the foreign bank—either through its agent in the U.S. or by discussing this with the bank during one of your exploratory trips—what they will offer to someone planning to live or retire in that country. Will they cash a check from your U.S. bank? Is there a charge for this procedure? Must the account be maintained with a certain minimum amount? Are there other strings attached?

• Ask if, upon establishing an account with this foreign bank, your U.S. bank can wire transfer "by special instructions"—for example, you may want a set amount transferred (e.g. $2,000) on the third of each month. A U.S. bank will charge for this service; also find out if a fee is charged by the foreign bank.

• Although many kinds of payments are now deposited automatically, if some of your deposits (such as dividends) must be endorsed, you may wish to establish a power of attorney. If you are sick abroad and need funds, perhaps no one can gain access to your account because it has special instructions to transfer once a month. The bank will need a signature to change instructions and this requires time. With a power of attorney, a relative or trusted friend could instruct the bank directly to send money without having to wait for a signature. (If an attorney is used for this, a retainer can be costly, but anyone properly designated can act with power of attorney.)

• Another approach is to establish a joint account with a family member in the U.S. so that they can respond to a telephone request from you if an unusual amount of cash is needed for any reason.

• To keep your funds at work, while ensuring their security, you will probably want to maintain a money market or other interest-bearing but liquid account in the U.S.

• Your bank in the U.S. is also instrumental in establishing your financial-support documentation for residency abroad (although it cannot provide banking history for accounts you maintain in other banks). The bank verifies your deposits on a consular letter (for a fee of around $10), which may be included with your tax returns to show your financial picture. When researching requirements for residency, be sure to find out what the country will accept as financial documentation and how it should be certified.

Your Taxes Abroad

When you live abroad, you are potentially subject to income tax from the U.S. and the other country as well. If a country has a tax treaty with the U.S., you will not be double taxed. Only a few countries tax your Social Security or other annuity income, and usually at a low rate (see chart in appendix).

The U.S. claims tax dominance over U.S. citizens anywhere in the world. You will file your U.S. income tax return each year through the American Embassy in the capital city of the country; often the embassy sends a representative to an area where Americans are concentrated to help with their tax forms.

You must claim all income, but there is an allowable exception to income earned abroad (currently $70,000), as it is assumed that you will pay tax abroad on this earned income. Even if your income is not taxable in the U.S. (the exemption noted above), you are still required to report it on your U.S. income tax return. This applies to interest or dividends from foreign stocks as well as other income earned abroad.

It is suggested that you read the tax treaty between the U.S. and the country where you plan to reside to determine your income tax liability. You should also consult a lawyer or accountant who has some experience with this subject.

Abraham Badian, a senior executive with the New York accounting firm of Diamant, Katz & Kahn, has handled many American clients retired in Mexico. He offers the following advice on how to file your income tax returns:

• Filing your return: If you are moving to a foreign country as a retiree, you will probably have income from dividends, interest, Social Security or a pension. You are responsible for filing an income tax return and estimated tax payments. If you know you have an income tax obligation, you can usually arrange to have tax withheld from your pension and annuities thereby avoiding filing a declaration of estimated taxes.

• Automatic tax extension: An individual living in a foreign country who is out of the continental U.S. on the 15th of April is automatically granted a 60-day extension; that is, you must file your income tax by June 15.

• Retiree vs. worker: Tax liability differs for a retiree and for an individual who is working in a foreign country. As noted above, for an individual earning foreign income there is an exemption ($70,000) from U.S. tax, but you may still be subject to income tax in that country. The income received by a retiree in the form of pension, annuity, dividend and interest is not usually taxed in a foreign country, but there are some exceptions so you will need to find out about the taxation laws of any country in which you are considering resident status.

Offshore Corporations and Trusts

Some Americans live abroad expressly to shelter their money—legally or illegally—from the Internal Revenue Service. There are countries offering banking secrecy as a pillar of their national income—Andorra, Guernsey, the Isle of Man—and others known both for tourism and banking confidentiality, such as the Grand Caymans, the British Virgin Islands and the Bahamas.

This kind of tax haven opportunity may take the form of an offshore corporation or trust with a country that is not party to a tax treaty with the U.S. and does not exchange financial information. This level of tax haven is primarily for big-league players because of the costs involved in setting up and maintaining a trust or offshore corporation. Nor is banking confidentiality inviolable in certain cases of high visibility criminal intent: an example was disclosure of Panamanian chief Manuel Noriega's banking records in his "tax haven" accounts.

Offshore incorporation is not only for big players, however. It sometimes serves as a shield for substantial income earned outside the U.S., and some countries such as Costa Rica offer other tax-haven advantages. Alex Rosarian in Costa Rica says, "I live within a corporate shell—I use expenses out of the corporation to cover my living expenses, I entertain on the corporation, I drive on corporation gas." (Rosarian's status is that of investor-resident; with a minimum investment of $50,000, a foreigner may own and work in their own Costa Rican company.)

An offshore corporation may also provide a vehicle for insuring inheritance of property, since inheritance laws vary by country and can be complicated and sometimes costly: as shareholders in a corporation, family members may inherit without going through conventional red tape. If this is your goal, corporation details should be carefully verified and updated regularly to be sure it will accomplish what you intend.

Veronica and George Alta established an offshore corporation in Gibraltar, registered in the U.S., which holds title to their two condominiums in Torremolinos, Spain, for the purpose of assuring inheritance for a surviving spouse or for their children. Similarly, a couple in Costa Rica established a Costa Rica corporation as title holder for their home. "If anything happened to us, the shares would go to our heirs," explains Nancy Thalmeyer.

Some of the European Community countries have already introduced taxation provisions for offshore corporations, and other EC countries are expected to follow suit to harmonize the EC tax systems. This means that every few years, the capital growth of the assets of a company would be assessed for purposes of worldwide taxation of income. If you choose to establish an offshore corporation, setup costs can be steep and annual fees must be taken into account when planning costs. Consult an accountant with international experience before concluding that a foreign tax haven is for you.

Understanding Inheritance Laws

If you are thinking of owning property abroad, you should become familiar with local inheritance laws and how you should take title. Some Americans prefer to have their wills translated and on record in notarial books abroad, so that if any debate is necessary time need not be wasted in providing a translation. Susan Broward has two wills—one in the U.S., one (in Portuguese) in Portugal. Every few years when she visits the U.S. she reviews her will regarding any possible changes in inheritance laws that may have occurred either in the U.S. or in Portugal.

Inheritance laws vary in different countries. In the U.S., you may frame a will leaving property to the surviving spouse; in some countries, the surviving spouse pays tax on the value of half of the house and must raise that tax if the house is jointly held. If you know the law, you can prepare for inconvenience (or a cash squeeze), or find a way around the problem, perhaps in the way you take title. It is advisable to consider this before buying property.

Laws in Motion

When researching a country, if tax advantage is one of your motives be sure to acquire current information through the country's consulate and, if possible, speak with knowledgeable residents about possible pending changes in law. You can't count on law to remain on the books, especially in the changing EC countries. Portugal introduced a capital gains tax for the first time in 1989, for example. But even if you should lose a coveted tax advantage abroad, you are still likely to be in a country where rates are much lower than in the U.S. for taxes ranging from title transfer and property tax to income tax.

There is an international trend toward taxation on global income (with tax treaty exceptions). Although this will be difficult to implement, a number of European countries are beginning to cooperate to share financial information. Since the U.S. is not a member of the EC, as one British investment adviser remarks, "I think American citizens are a bit privileged—I don't think Uncle Sam is going to forward details of income in the same way we have recently seen happen with some of our European clients."

In any country, though, you may find yourself in a changing situation, so it is important to stay informed. And it is not advisable to choose a country only for its prevailing tax advantages (although you could always move if taxation laws not to your liking were passed).

Once you have relocated abroad, you can join (or if one does not exist, initiate) an association of American residents. One of the primary purposes of such a group, aside from social functions, is to serve as an information center for pending changes in laws and policies that may have an impact on its members.

Learning Tax Language

You should assume that everything pertaining to money matters abroad is different than in the U.S.—that means you should find out about other tax liabilities as a resident or property-owning non-resident. In Spain, for example, you must file what is called a *patrimonio* declaration of your net worth—that is, everything you own in Spain (property, bank account, car). The tax on this is minor (2.5%), but to anticipate it is to be prepared— even though some tax laws are clearly unenforceable. Technically, if you have resident status in Spain, you are required to declare your worldwide income. But as one American resident of the Costa del Sol says, pointing to enormous yachts in their moorings and Lamborghinis, Bentleys and Silver Clouds parked beside the marina: "Consider all the international millionaires in Marbella—they certainly don't declare their worldwide income."

For visible business transactions, such as buying or selling or renting property, you will have to pay tax (e.g., transfer tax, usually a type of capital gains tax, and in the case of rental property, income tax). Sometimes you will only pay capital gains tax abroad, not in the U.S. But you must declare sale of property abroad on your U.S. taxes. Incorporation may provide a way around this, but be sure to check with your attorney.

If you have a rental property, you must report that income in the country, although some people try to avoid it. You will find out what kind of local enforcement prevails, of course, but if your property is in a popular resort area, such as in the Algarve, rental property is often closely monitored—tax agents and cab drivers seem to share information about which houses have different sets of occupants.

Soft-currency countries usually encourage foreign visitors, and especially retirees with guaranteed incomes. Pensioners are offered incentives to become residents and import hard currency into the country. It is unlikely such countries will introduce restrictive taxation or discourage the infusion of foreign currency, although sometimes the pensioner privileges cause charges of unfairness by native citizens—if enough pressure occurs, it is possible that some privileges could be reduced. But in a hard-currency country, which is less interested in seeking hard currency (in some cases, U.S. dollars may be "softer" than that country's currency), incentives for foreign residents and pensioners will be rare. In these countries, your best advantage is property appreciation if you are in a position to buy.

Devaluation Worries

Peter Haddon in Guadalajara tells of his experience during the devaluation of 1982, when most Americans were caught unaware when the government confiscated all dollar accounts and converted them into devalued pesos. Haddon experienced only a slight loss because, as he explains, "I only keep an operating amount of money and advise other Americans to do the same."

Devaluation in Costa Rica over a decade ago had a minor impact on Americans living there—unless they had their money in colone accounts. One resident observes, "Actually, we're better off than before. Our gardener, for example, still charges us $1 per hour—although the number of colones I pay him has increased, I am paying the same dollar equivalent I did in 1975." For Allie

Yance, who was employed as a musician in San José at the time of the devaluation, the effect was more serious because her income was in local currency. "The colone dropped, all prices went up and my salary was the same—it was very difficult."

Investment Opportunities Abroad

There are many investment opportunities abroad, but you should be even more cautious than when investing in the U.S., primarily since language differences and terminology can lead to misunderstandings. Be sure that you clearly define terms, benefits and potential tax consequences.

Most Americans living abroad would agree with Alex Rosarian of Costa Rica who says, "When considering an investment, don't reach in your pocket for the first six months," until the honeymoon with a new country is over. Until then, everything seems new, possibilities unlimited—and some opportunities are too good to be true. As Judith Henderson, commercial attaché with the American Embassy in Costa Rica points out, "We can sometimes offer you a credit check on companies, but if you're burned we cannot act as a collection agency for bad deals."

Investments

Some American firms provide investment services abroad. The international division of Shearson Lehman Bros./American Express, for example, offers its clients opinions on investment offerings based on the principals' track record. It also provides investment vehicles that satisfy the requirement of some foreign countries that retirees with pensioner or renter status demonstrate a certain annual income.

Foreign Interest Income

It can be tempting to place some of your savings in a high-yield overseas bank account, such as in Mexico where a peso savings account offers as much as 40% interest. Since this type of account is in local currency, not only is there no guarantee against devaluation but you may find that your funds are only "liquid" at certain times, as Dara Glass found out when she was told that for her type of bank account, "You can only withdraw one day a month." A "savings account" may more closely resemble a U.S. Certificate of Deposit, so be sure you are aware of withdrawal limitations. For those who can afford to take a risk, there can be advantages. In Costa Rica, interest-bearing colone accounts are tax free. And developing countries offer other investment incentives to encourage foreign business and tourism—in Costa Rica, for example, investment in tourism earns a 12-year tax deferment.

You do not need to live abroad to invest abroad. An increasing number of financial advisers suggest a global approach to investing: by considering opportunities in all areas, including the U.S., you will avoid single-market dependency, especially in a time when the U.S. is not the brightest star on the investment horizon. The most cautious approach to investing abroad is international mutual funds, or a single country fund such as the Italy or Spanish Fund, both traded on the New York stock exchange—as in the U.S. stock market, you must stay informed about changes in the international picture.

Investing in Property

In most countries you can buy land for a residence or for investment without being a legal resident of the country. Usually the basic legal requirement is your certifiable identification. There are some restrictions, such as coastal property in Mexico or certain areas within the Greek Islands, where foreign nationals are not allowed to own land. Before considering a purchase, find out what the country's restrictions are; a real estate agent should point out the limitations, but if you know in advance you will avoid wasting time. Familiarize yourself with the real estate law of the region you are interested in.

The necessity of defining terms became apparent to a group of Americans visiting a new development in the Algarve. The condominium offered a program of ownership with a "leaseback" arrangement—but our usage of this term differs from the way it is used in some other countries. In this case, the owner purchases the property outright, then signs a contract to rent it out for five years at a net 7% of rental income—with no guarantee of occupancy, but also with no maintenance costs. The owner may use the condo for six weeks during the year and may take occupancy in five years. This is not a traditional leaseback arrangement, so define your terms (and theirs) before you become deeply involved in a transaction and find that you may need to back out—if it's not too late.

Most complaints by foreign property owners result when buyers take few precautions, even the simplest precautions that they would have taken at home. It may be the result of romantic enthusiasm about finding a property abroad, or wanting a dream to come true without asking very unromantic questions or doing research. Investing in property abroad can become a more subjective decision than an investment at home with a proposal grounded in estimates of profit and loss, so don't send your critical judgment on vacation. As Algarve real estate agent Bill Oddy suggests: "It's easy, with a beautiful sunset, to hear the seller say, 'Yes, you can build here.' But you have to be sensible and cautious." It is useful to listen to Americans abroad to better understand advantages and pitfalls, but when it comes to any legal matter or large investment, always consult reputable professionals before making your final decision.

Agricultural and Other Investments

If you study the market you may see a niche to fill, an item to export to the U.S., a crop or burgeoning industry to invest in or a service to provide. Agriculture takes understanding: some Americans have been burned, whereas others have enjoyed profits from small-scale investment, such as the Beckers' coffee *finca* in Costa Rica. Most "exotic agriculture" requires research and professional advice. Investment in an area with growing tourism, such as La Paz, Mexico, can provide opportunities for those who see a gap to fill, but plan on a long timetable before your plan comes to fruition. Tourist investment may run in the red for a long time, and require a lot of promotional seed money to boost visibility, before your inn, pleasure boat or other venture has a steady stream of paying customers.

A Greek Island Getaway

"The light in Greece is the most beautiful light I've seen anywhere in the world. It grabs you and you never get it out of your system," says Lily Cairns, a single woman originally from Pennsylvania who now resides in New York.

Lily has owned her home on the southern tip of the island of Mykonos since 1983. "Mykonos is a cosmopolitan island with a lot of expatriates and an art colony," she explains, noting that although the island is a famous destination for people "who like to dance all night," her life is tranquil and offers a respite from her high-pressure city career. "It's wonderful and very peaceful. After Manhattan, it's really nice to have a very different lifestyle to cool me out."

She paid $30,000 for her one-bedroom condominium in a French-built organized community. The cash transaction, which she describes as "relatively simple," was handled through a lawyer who also assisted with payment of Lily's one-time tax. "I bought it from a picture and a concept—that with a new house I knew I wouldn't walk into electrical and plumbing problems. And I knew that there would be someone living in the village, so I didn't have to worry whether, if I closed up the house, I would come back and find it vandalized."

The village is built in the traditional Niconian architectural style, which served as the inspiration for architect Le Corbusier's international cluster housing. Regulations on Mykonos prevent building over two stories in height; all homes are white, although owners take pride in their world-renowned colorful doors and window frames. Quality of life is enhanced by a ban against cars in Lily's village, which has beautiful walkways and landscaping. "I am only a 90-second walk to the beach," says Lily. "I need to be near the sea and in Mykonos it's just outside my window."

The house is built on rock in a rugged setting where the ochre color of the terrain complements the whitewashed homes and bright doors "After the rain there are thousands of wildflowers—it's fabulous in the spring," says Lily, who notes that although her village is modern in its amenities,"it is still rustic. I wake in the morning to the sound of sheep and birds and sometimes the wind." Picturesque windmills are one of the characteristic features of the island. "There are days when the wind is so strong that the ferry boat can't come in, so if you're trying to cross you just stay on the mainland, but there could be worse places to be stranded."

With a home base in New York, where there are frequent flights to Greece, Lily's airfare is relatively inexpensive, compared to someone who might have to travel from other U.S. cities. But it is not a direct flight to Mykonos. She flies to Athens, where she sometimes takes the ferry from the port of Piraeus. Or at other times, she takes a 40-minute flight from Athens to the island. Once on Mykonos, she could take a taxi or a five-minute bus ride between the town and her home in the organized community, but usually she manages the short distance on foot and explains: "I'm a New Yorker—I walk."

Describing her community, Lily says: "It's an entire village just outside of Mykonos town and has a pool and tennis courts." Her neighbors are Europeans who use their homes for holidays and well-to-do Athenians who often travel to the island for weekend visits. Lily avoids "high season" when the island is packed with tourists, but a sojourn off season doesn't mean isolation. In spring and fall, several of her European neighbors are likely to be in residence at any one time.

Lily enjoys cooking in Mykonos and finds this to be a good social bridge to her international neighbors. "I do an enormous amount of cooking when I'm there. I bring Bisquick and make a lot of chicken pot pie and strawberry shortcake because I like to feed crowds. Once I went through seven boxes in two months." On one such trip, Lily recalls with amusement, the customs official reached into her baggage and pulled out what seemed to be an endless supply of Bisquick and pans. She also brings along her cat (and plenty of Miao Mix). The cat is innoculated for rabies, but since it is an indoor cat both in New York and on Mykonos, she explains, "I have special screens so I can leave the windows open."

A few times each week, Lily shops in town with stops at the greengrocer, the butcher, the baker and perhaps at one of the small markets. "Last year they opened a supermarket by the airport," she reports. "I find it amazing, but now—because of the EC—there is a wonderful selection of products from other countries. You can buy German and Irish butter, Danish and Austrian cheeses and produce from many different countries. As

GREECE

an American I could say that a supermarket is the best way to shop easily, but it signals great change for Mykonos."

She notes that the fish enjoyed by most tourists on Mykonos is imported, but that as a resident she knows the local restaurants that serve the fresh local catch, so she can eat like a native (as an alternative to Bisquick suppers) when she wants. Mykonos has a large agricultural area. She buys fruit and vegetables from vendors who come to town on donkeys and sell produce picked fresh from their gardens. Local food doesn't always mean bargains, however. A high inflation rate has pushed up prices in recent months. But a real cost saving is gained by avoiding the high season when, for example, a container of yogurt priced at 75 drachmas off season will be at least 100 drachmas or more when throngs of tourists are on the island.

Lily has learned some of the Greek language during her six years as a homeowner by practicing while she spends a few weeks in residence each trip. "I'm very comfortable ordering food. Of course, the first thing you learn before you set foot in any country is 'please' and 'thank you,' whether you plan to stay 10 days or 10 years. So far I understand more than I can speak." She agrees with those who say that your activities shape your language skills. In her case, she notes, "I've learned some of the vocabulary of the carpenter shop since I have spent a lot of time at the hardware store."

An admitted perfectionist, Lily is constantly improving her home. She painted her door and shutters, then painted all of her furniture—first sanding and then finishing it in white. An annual project traditional to the area gives her another chance to wield her paintbrush, as Lily explains: "We have flagstone in the courtyard and it's traditional to apply fresh white paint between the stones—so I do it every year."

Chapter 14

Shopping for Basics, Luxuries and Services

"I hired a person who does the paperwork. He got twenty-one copies of various kinds of papers while I sat in a corner and sipped a Diet Coke."

Dara Glass
Mexico City

Shopping abroad is a blend of exciting discoveries and frustrating moments. You'll want to rethink your everyday shopping habits, from the list you keep magnetized on the refrigerator door to the number of stops you'll need to find those items. For the most part, you can put away your credit cards and checkbook: most shopping abroad, outside of shops that cater to tourists, is cash-and-carry, not only for groceries but for other items. As John Barber notes, "When shopping in Southwest France we buy sweaters at the local woolen mill, but you can't use Visa or a check."

Basic shopping needs should be reviewed during the planning stage. Before you make a final move, determine those items that you must have and find out which are not readily available. One way to prepare is to draft a list, dividing items into Necessary, Preferred and Extras. Necessities may include some items that you have to import, have friends send or, preferably, as there is no duty for a "housegift," have them bring with them—such as hard-to-get pharmacy supplies or, in some places, vitamins. On the preferred list may be a favorite brand of packaged goods, such as cereal or peanut butter. These may be available but only at a premium price.

When David Mead moved to Thailand, he couldn't find Kitty Litter or a commercial substitute for his pedigreed cat, since Thais do not keep indoor cats. David retrained his cat to use shredded paper, but it was a treat (and a good source of ongoing jokes) when friends from the U.S. brought along cat litter as a housegift.

Health supplies should be your first concern, then food and clothing, then hobby and other supplies. It is best not to take availability of any item for granted, although almost everything can be found in an alternative form and at a reasonable price. Plan on a period of experimentation with substitutes, then you will decide whether you want to ship in your favorite brands or use local alternatives. Some items might be found under another name, whether packaged goods or produce. If you are a gourmet cook and need cornstarch for a family recipe, you will find that it is called "corn flour" in some countries. In the tropics, you won't find celery, but there are good substitutes such as "snake root" or Chinese cabbage.

Americans living abroad agree that by using substitutes, low-cost living is indeed a reality. And sometimes the substitute is better. Dara Glass in Mexico City says, "I have dry skin and couldn't find anything like the cream I'd been using at home, so I went to a dermatologist who sent me to a special dermatological pharmacy. They prepared my own personal cream—you'd never find that in the U.S."

Some categories of food may seem like staples to you, but if they are not in demand locally then there will be little supply, high prices or poor quality. An example is alcoholic beverages. In Costa Rica, Mexico and Thailand, for example, since beer is the preferred popular beverage, wine may be expensive or of poor quality. If you live in France or Italy, on the other hand, you can drink some of the world's best wines at bargain prices.

Local Specialties

Ruth Walkington in Costa Rica advises, "If you live with the local economy in mind by shopping their wide selection of fruits, vegetables, meats and fish, then there is no reason anyone couldn't live well and pleasurably year-round." You will notice abroad that cuts of meat differ from your market at home (you will also find this occasionally in different regions of the U.S.). But soon you will figure out the cut nearest to what you are looking for and modify your favorite recipes to fit the selection. You'll also do much of your canned and packaged-goods shopping by perusing pictures on labels, especially if the language is difficult to decipher as in Greece or more exotic locations.

With an attitude of flexibility, shopping is fun; if not, you'll have to pay more in time or money, or wait for occasional shipments. "If you must have Skippy and don't have friends bringing it in to you," notes Ruth Walkington, "you'll find that imported items can be very expensive." Comparing food prices and quality to the U.S., she notes that in Costa Rica fruit and vegetables are a bargain year-round and offers a few examples: watermelon-sized papayas for $1 U.S.; pineapple with less acidity than is available at home; sweet juicy radishes—a favorite Costa Rican *boca* or hors d'oeuvre. She recalls a party where one of her American neighbors featured the latter as an edible centerpiece: "My friend had a huge radish arranged decoratively so that the juicy, sweet slices filled a meat platter."

Jim Erland in Portugal notes that shopping for fresh food is one of the enjoyments of expatriate living. "The bread tastes like bread, not like most of the squishy commercial bread at home. You have a choice of maybe 10 different home-style breads in the market. And the fruit tastes like fruit because it is picked fresh daily, rather than being picked green and then stored and shipped around the U.S. The food spoils more quickly, so you go shopping almost every day."

David Mead occasionally buys Western food and finds it not terribly unreasonable when he wants a taste of home. A small can of baked beans, for example, is $1.60. But usually he prepares Western dishes with Thai ingredients. Most Thai dishes are too spicy for his restricted diet, and when he does splurge, as he explains, it is usually for a social occasion: "For two people, Thai cuisine isn't as much fun—you need a lot of people. The fun of a Thai meal is 10 dishes served simultaneously."

A Range of Shops

Shopping venues are a factor when you choose an area for your home or apartment. Cities offer the best opportunity for convenience shopping, often in a one-stop centrally located market, such as the *Gigante* chain found in Guadalajara. Arthur

157

Secunda loves the outstanding variety of foods available in Paris: "The food is different and more elaborate than in the U.S. More food, more spices, more of everything." Allie Yance lives in a central location in San José, Costa Rica. Within two blocks of her house is a fish market, two pastry shops, a supermarket, a 24-hour convenience store, a dry cleaner and a number of restaurants. "I'm a natural-food person," says Allie. "It's wonderful here because you can get whole wheat bread, rice and natural grains."

In some cities, supermarkets are well stocked and managed; in others, you will find better alternatives. Dara Glass avoids the supermarkets in Mexico City, regarding them as "dirty and over-priced." She enjoys shopping the street markets that roll (on wheeled carts) around her neighborhood each day. There are also street markets in different sections of the city on designated days. "There is a street market not far from my apartment that has the most beautiful produce—you don't eat before you shop because they give samples," says Dara.

Convenient markets are often found near apartment buildings where the concentration of shoppers enables such a business to thrive. Even if you have a house, if there are apartments nearby there is a good chance that you will have convenient shopping, as do the Hartmans in the Algarve: their home is near an apartment complex with its own *minimercado* so that they can easily walk to the market. If your home has a yard, you can also grow some of your own produce; the Hartmans raise carrots and tomatoes. After they purchased their apartment in Spain, Veronica Alta found that her husband—who resisted shopping in the U.S.—now likes to shop for fresh food. They have a small refrigerator and buy their fresh fruit, fish and vegetables every few days. As Veronica points out, unlike much of U.S. produce, which is grown on huge commercial farms, her produce is from nearby farms. "There are no chemicals used—it's healthier," says Veronica. Buying like a native requires some adjustment. Be prepared to find an occasional weevil in the rice—just pick it out and appreciate the proof that you are buying natural food. Access to shopping is a consideration when considering a home outside a city or town. One American, whose custom-built home is in a planned residential community outside San José, chose the area in part for its shopping services. It is a mile from a small town with a post office, two gas stations, two restaurants, a bank, two good markets and a hardware store, as well as a Red Cross agency and a fire station.

Food at Hand

Variety and frequent, leisurely shopping is part of the charm of living abroad and leaving old habits behind. If you decide to live in a smaller village or rural area, you may need to plan occasional shopping trips to the nearest town to stock up on some packaged items, but you can always count on even the smallest town to provide colorful markets with inexpensive produce brought in fresh from the countryside. In many areas of the U.S., there is a trend toward a few discount supermarkets in place of neighborhood markets. Prices are good but you have to drive farther, and if you don't drive you may have to depend on a combination of convenience store items (offering little or no fresh food) and reliance on others to transport you to the supermarket.

In other countries, residents do not travel far for their food. The neighborhood market, butcher shop, fish market and pastry shop are a self-contained way of life. Besides a reliable supply of and staples—rice and beans, bread, pasta or potatoes, depending on the country—neighborhood markets may have different fresh produce every day: carrots one day, green beans the next.

Availability or quality can vary, even in different regions of a country. Nancy Stangos in Greece says, "There is wonderful seafood on Kalymnos." She notes that although durable goods are quite expensive on the island, "once your car and appliances are purchased, the cost of living is modest. Day-to-day expenses are minimal. There is a lot of fresh fruit, wonderful seafood, meats are not bad either. And there are a lot of convenient foodstuffs and wonderful pastries both abundant and of good quality—better than at home." Lily Cairns, on the other hand, says of her island Mykonos, "People may find it surprising that most of the fish here is imported." The best prices for produce, she notes, are from vendors who come to town with baskets on donkeys and sell fruits and vegetables fresh from their gardens.

In Arlene Dexter's village in France, the baker comes around with his mobile bakery truck twice a day, blowing his horn to let everyone know that fresh *baguettes* have arrived, along with the latest news about what's happening around town. The butcher and grocer also offer their meat and produce, driving from house to house once each week. The Dexters especially love the outdoor markets and visit two or three times a week. Their favorite market is 5 minutes away by bicycle; another market is 20 minutes away, with two more outdoor markets a half-hour away by bike.

Tanya Kennebeck reports that when she first moved to Portugal in 1983, "the cow used to hang in the window. They'd take a piece off and that was it. Now they have different cuts with labels and prices. Before, you never knew just what you were buying." She and her husband like seafood, so the Algarve's selection of fresh fish makes her shopping a constant adventure. "For me, the fish here is an absolute marvel. I go to the fish market and stand in front of the huge array and ask, 'What's this? What's that?' I have a wonderful time buying fish and they tell me how to cook it. The Portuguese are the most helpful people." To really enjoy this kind of shopping adventure, whether it is learning a new recipe in the fish market or bargaining in an out-of-the-way shop, you'll want to develop some language skills. These shopkeepers are less likely to speak English, unlike their younger counterparts who cater to tourists.

Major Purchases Abroad

Your legal status can have an impact on importing items from home. One of the advantages of residency or pensioner status is the privilege of importing goods for personal use with little or no duty cost. However, most major purchases are easier to make once you are in the country, rather than having large items shipped. Appliances are especially tricky because of voltage variances. One drawback of shipping is the wait: the inspection and clearance can be a tedious business, often requiring several trips to the official agency before your goods clear inspection. Some countries are easier for clearing customs than others; one of the best sources of information is an American who recently made the move (since procedures change, recent information is best). On your exploratory trips, seek out current inside information about which items cause problems, as well as who (if anyone) and how much you may need to "tip" to assure that your goods will proceed smoothly through the legal channels.

To arrange for shipping household items, you should contact the consulate of that country and state that you plan to reside (or purchase property) in that country. Usually you have six months from the time that you officially declare your intention to live abroad to have your goods shipped. But there are exceptions: Larraine Grey, who has resident status in Portugal, was able to ship her furniture eight years later without duty charges.

There are loopholes, laws change—and loopholes may close; so if you are mapping out future plans, find out from the consulate if any policy change is pending regarding the importing of personal goods. For items you may discover you need after the move, remember that small items may be brought in by friends and family as gifts. But when you request an item from home by mail, or if well-meaning friends decide to send you a gift, these items are subject to tax—which can be as high as the value of the item.

Finding Treasures

Most Americans living abroad prefer to furnish their homes abroad with items purchased locally. Alan Cox bought everything he needed in Costa Rica. "I suggest that you sell your stuff—give it to your children," he advises. If you wish to buy custom-made furniture, the cost probably will be far less than in the U.S. If you like to search for antiques and treasures, there can be good hunting abroad. One couple in Spain enjoys finding choice items for their home this way. One of Veronica Alta's pet finds was a handsome antique table that she purchased for a few dollars and refinished herself. "It would easily have cost $500 or more at home," she says.

David Mead collects antique Thai furniture. "I was taken by *lanna*—Northern Thai—furniture, and am very interested in its history and lore," David explains. "Lanna was an independent kingdom until 1923. Its style was largely influenced by Burma, and in Burma by English colonials. We have some pieces that are 80 years old."

Uruguay and Argentina offer abundant opportunities for finding European antiques, because of the large number of immigrants who flocked to South America in the early 1900s. Surprisingly, it is a treasure trove of vintage American cars, especially of models manufactured in the 1920s, a boom time in South America when many cars were imported from the U.S. Mechanics in major cities are also experienced in servicing such collector's items.

Behind the Wheel

When planning your shopping needs, an important consideration is transportation: do you plan to walk, bicycle and use public transportation or taxis, or to drive your own car? No doubt you have purchased several cars in your adult life, but the purchase of a car abroad is a different kind of experience, from the time you purchase it to the time you sell it—and perhaps, to your surprise, you may find that when you sell abroad you may receive the same price you originally paid or even realize a profit!

Most people prefer to purchase a car abroad rather than to import one. Although at first glance this may not seem necessary, it is often a good idea. In Costa Rica, for example, you will see familiar models of Hondas, Mercedes-Benzes and Nissans on the road, but it turns out that these are different from their counterparts in the U.S. For one thing, they have heavy-duty suspension, designed for some of Costa Rica's more adventurous roads. And they do not have catalytic converters and they run on regular rather than unleaded gasoline. An imported car with a catalytic converter may not be serviced properly, since mechanics are not accustomed to repairing them.

Privilege and Profit

Your status as resident, pensioner or tourist makes a difference when purchasing a car in many countries. As a pensioner in Costa Rica, you are issued *pensionado* license plates, which have a very low renewal tax. After five years, you may exchange these for standard license plates and sell the car to a resident. Pensioner status may enable you to realize a profit, since as a *pensionado* you bought it with a low tax added to the cost. For a Costa Rican, on the other hand, the tax would have raised the price of the car as much as 300%. When you decide to sell, the resident gets a pass-along bargain and you still come out ahead. Plus you are free to buy another car as a pensioner and then repeat the process another five years later (assuming, of course, that the law does not change).

Although cars can be more expensive in many countries than in the U.S., in some places you can find bargains. Americans in Costa Rica, for example, report that new car prices are slightly lower than in the U.S., and if you don't want to purchase a new car you can purchase a used vehicle with the advantage that your license plate will not indicate PEN (for *pensionado*) and you will blend in with other residents.

Elsa Van Dam in Spain buys a new car every four years and has become a used-car source for her friends. When she bought a new Spanish Fiat in 1985, she sold her four-year-old model to another American, who then sold it to another friend four years later. It is common for the expat community to buy and sell cars among themselves because it is easy for the seller to advertise by word of mouth, and the buyer benefits by knowing something about the car's history.

The Hartmans in Portugal bought their used car locally from a Budget rental agency and report that they have been very satisfied. "We still have the Budget rental sticker on the car. When we go by the police, they think we're tourists and we've never been stopped," jokes Beth. Knowing value and recognizing an opportunity to buy a good used car can be important where car prices are at a premium. Dara Glass in Mexico City bought a Volkswagen from another American and calls her purchase a bargain. "Cars are much more expensive here, but the seller spent so much time out of the country that he didn't know what it was worth. I paid $800—I could sell it for $2000 today." Len Friedman in Guadalajara bought a new compact Mexican car and says of prices, "If you buy a subcompact or compact, you can find one at close to American prices." The luxury cars carry the highest prices in comparison with U.S. cars, he notes.

Expensive Bargains

The Knights in Portugal found it easy to buy a car, since they knew the car's owner. They used an agency that specializes in car-ownership transfer, but Karen found that buying a used car in Portugal was more expensive than buying a used car in the U.S. Since residents pay a steep tax when purchasing a new car, that cost is passed along to the resale market. At first, the cost differences when purchasing abroad can be discouraging, until you realize that a "bargain" is relative to that country.

Once you are living in another economic structure, you will view a good buy (and a good investment) differently. Larraine Grey sold her car in Kentucky and planned to buy an inexpensive car when she moved to Portugal in 1980. "I thought I'd get a MiniMorris," she says, "then I found out that it was $2000 for a 10-year-old Mini." Peter Knight paid almost as much for his used jeep as the owner had paid for it new—but by then, the new car price for this model had increased dramatically and his purchase still had strong resale value.

When viewed as market value, although the entry cost may be higher in cases like these, the car is likely to remain a good investment once you have overcome your initial surprise at costs relative to the U.S. The same adjustment is necessary for the cost of gasoline, which is higher in most countries outside the U.S. However, the initial price of a car—particularly in Southern Europe—is expected to decrease after 1992, since cars are available in some EC countries—for example in Germany and Holland—more inexpensively than in other EC countries. When the border duty is eliminated, auto prices overall are expected to come down, or Euromarket share will be captured by the countries offering the best prices.

Your Car Is Waiting

One arrangement for Americans with vacation homes abroad is to rent a car during their stay, but some prefer to buy and store the car between visits. The Dexters decided to ship a car overseas to use during their month-long sojourns in France. "We were going to rent, but we found that it wasn't that expensive to ship one. We found an old, reliable car and shipped it over," says Arlene. Since U.S. emission standards are higher than in most countries, the Dexter's car exceeded French requirements, although they had to change their headlights to meet local standards. Now they have a car waiting when they arrive for their two-or-three-times-yearly visits. Arlene cautions that "it took a lot of calls to work it out, but since it was a one-time complication with long-term benefits, it has turned out to be well worth the trouble."

Part-time residents John and Sally Barber also keep a car at their home in rural France. Sally Barber and her son went car shopping and finally found just what they were looking for at a Renault dealer 30 miles away. She bought a diesel-powered station wagon. France has one of the highest costs-per-gallon for gasoline. "Diesel costs two-thirds the price of gasoline," notes John, who adds, "and Sally wanted a station wagon because she is always hauling guests and luggage." Another American in France tells his story of car shopping: In a rural area, an expatriate benefits from friendships with local residents. "In a neighboring town there is a wonderful winery," explains Arthur Loeb. "It turned out that the old father was retiring and wanted to sell his car. His great pleasure was to drive within a few kilometer radius of his home, so it had very low mileage. I found out about it from one of my neighbors, a notary—notaries know everything."

Utilities and Services

If you move to a country with a temperate climate, your utility costs may be far lower than you are now paying. As part of your exploratory trips and simulated living, you will face different kinds of weather conditions and should estimate your needs for heating or cooling a residence. You will need to understand what utilities are used for basic needs, such as cooking and heating water for a shower. In some countries, a conventional water heater is less common than a per-use water heater. These economical units are designed to heat just enough for a specific use; a small water heater is installed in a bathroom for showers, or in the kitchen for washing dishes or use in a washing machine. After activating the unit, hot water is soon ready to use. This type of unit is found around the world, from Hong Kong to San José, Costa Rica.

Before you move, you will want to know what method of electrical and gas supply is typical for residential use in your country, since it could affect your plans for purchasing or shipping appliances. Utilities can be quirky. One resident of Ajijic, Mexico, notes that gas cylinders, providing energy to heat water, are replaced at intervals. She always keeps a spare, and when the current cylinder is empty she uses the backup and immediately orders another. When a cylinder needs replacing, she arranges with a neighbor to be home for a delivery (the day will be specified but not the time). With this arrangement, the two neighbors share the delivery waiting game. No one wants to run out of fuel. She recalls the time she forgot to reorder a replacement and she had to endure a day without using her stove or taking a hot shower until the cylinder arrived the next day.

John Barber in France does not have to rely on delivery: he picks up a gas cylinder at the supermarket or gas station. Electricity is a public utility and he pays his bills automatically through the bank. "We are never aware of the electric bill. The telephone is handled the same way." The Barbers made this convenient arrangement through their bank, since such a procedure is not usual for French residents. Other assumptions about utility services in the U.S. should be set aside. Another resident of Mexico had the experience of not receiving a cut-off notice. She had forgotten to pay her bill on time and found out that the utility company literally cut her utility cable—she had to pay a repair and reinstallation charge.

Power supplies may be under par, by U.S. standards. If you rely on an electronic device, such as a computer or word processor, you would need to take this into account when looking for a residence. Power reliability can vary by country, city and dwelling. One American living abroad notes this peculiarity in her apartment building: "Every time someone turns on the hot water, which is pumped up from the street by an electrically-powered pump, the lights get dim." She uses a word processor and has to guard against computer crash with "a big surge protector"—and has learned to back up copies more often than she ordinarily would in the U.S.

The Value of Service

Labor can be one of the best values abroad, and in most countries—depending on where you choose to reside—you will find people who are willing to work for reasonable hourly rates compared with the U.S. It is very difficult to find domestic help in many regions of the U.S.; don't assume that labor abroad is cheap, however, because there are exceptions. Obviously if you decide to move or buy a vacation home in a country with a high standard of living, labor is not likely to be a bargain. And if you move to an inexpensive country but reside in an area with burgeoning tourism, the hotels, restaurants and other businesses may drive up hourly rates as they compete for workers from the available labor pool.

Household help, such as a maid or gardener, is easy to arrange in many countries—Mexico, Costa Rica, Thailand, Uruguay, Portugal, Greece, Spain and rural France, for example. Not only is household help relatively easy to find, but you will also discover that most other services are inexpensive. In the U.S., when you need to call a plumber or electrician, steep hourly rates make the clock seem to race forward. Americans living abroad often express amazement over incidents when, after painstaking work requiring hours of labor, the final charge turns out to be surprisingly low, whether for appliance repair, a tailor or a contractor. The Thalmeyers were astonished when their architect, after hours of labor and several trips to the job site, handed them a bill for only $78.

Aside from household help, it is not uncommon to hire help to run errands. In Mexico and Costa Rica, for example, some people hire "stand-ins" to hold a place in line at the bank, to shop for food or to do certain kinds of official business that often require a wait until your turn is called. For a type of official document, Dara Glass in Mexico City needed several copies from different offices at an agency. She hired a "person who does the paperwork. He got 21 copies of various kinds of papers while I sat in a corner and sipped a Diet Coke."

Household Help

One of the top-ranked advantages of living abroad is inexpensive household help—especially with food preparation. You'll find that shopping for ingredients and cooking and serving both breakfast and a multi-course midday meal are customary tasks for a maid-housekeeper.

Household help is usually a bargain abroad, but when hiring such services it is essential to have information about labor laws. Here is an example of how it works in Costa Rica, which has one of the more formally regulated systems among the several countries discussed in this book:

Nancy Thalmeyer notes that good household help is easy to find and that labor laws "once understood, don't really amount to a drawback." When hiring a maid on a temporary or day-to-day basis, you do not have to pay Social Security, but you should be prepared to offer extra compensation such as for birthdays, an occasional paid day off or some kind of bonus to assure continued good service. Nancy has help three days per week, three hours per day. But her reason is not to avoid Social Security payments; rather, she says, "I just don't want someone around all the time."

In Costa Rica, if you hire full-time help, as the employer you are required to make a Social Security contribution as well as provide a paid vacation. The employer must make a 28% Social Security contribution over the basic salary, and there are published minimum rates for different jobs. Vacation is calculated on the length of service; for example, a full-time employee who works from May through December is entitled to a two-week vacation or receives a one-month vacation per year. Often this is called "a thirteenth month of wages." There is also a traditional Christmas bonus, intended to serve as a savings plan for the employee.

If the household employee's work is not satisfactory, you must have cause for termination. The vacation and bonus requirements still apply and must be paid for the time accrued. If there is not justifiable cause for termination, then the employee is to receive severance (for example, two weeks' pay for six months of employment). So if you plan to use household help, laws concerning part-time or full-time help could make a difference in your budget plan. When researching costs, don't just ask Americans in residence about the current hourly rate for household help; also inquire about the official labor laws for domestic help and find out the customary expectations for bonuses and other benefits.

Supply and Demand

Tanya Kennebeck in the Algarve notes that the price of household help varies by community. To maintain a large home with her busy Yoga-class schedule, she has a maid for four hours daily and a gardener a half-day each week. She points out that labor costs have risen in the Algarve recently because it is an increasingly popular tourist area—whereas prices for household help in Lisbon have remained low. Eight years ago, Tanya paid $1.50 (U.S.) per hour; now she pays twice as much, but it is still a bargain by U.S. standards.

Elsa Van Dam in the Costa del Sol also notes that the cost of household help has increased since she moved to Spain over a decade ago, but observes that it is still very inexpensive compared to the U.S. For 10 years, she has had the same housekeeper, who comes four days a week. "I leave the house to her—she is the expert. She cleans everything very thoroughly when I am away," says Elsa, who keeps a very busy schedule and likes to have housework done while she is running errands or out for one of her social activities.

The best bargains in household help are found off the beaten path, such as in Uruguay where Stanley Walters pays $1 per hour for heavy housecleaning. David Mead pays less than $2 per hour in Thailand. If you live in a rural area, even in a country with a fairly high cost of living, you may also find household help at good rates. As Arlene Dexter says of France's Dordogne region,

"It's easy enough to find home help because there is little employment in rural areas, so there are people available to do housecleaning, gardening and painting."

As in the U.S., one of the best ways to find household help is through referral. Not only through your friends and neighbors who recommend an individual, but also through your own network of hired help. If you have a good gardener, ask if he has a relative who might like to do housework. Or if your neighbor is satisfied with his or her employee, perhaps the employee has a sister or cousin who might like to work for you. There is often more family pressure to provide good work when another member is already on your payroll. But it works both ways: unfair treatment by an employer could result in a family walkout.

Changing Prices, Relative Values

Prices have increased since the Walkingtons first moved to Costa Rica in 1980, but prices have also increased in the U.S. A decade ago, admission to a film was 50 cents, now it is $1.50 or more. But as Ruth Walkington explains, "Some things have gone up, others have not." The Altas note that prices in Spain have risen since they bought their apartment in 1985, but Spain is still a bargain. "When we first moved, it was 80% cheaper to live here than in the U.S., but now it's still 60% cheaper," says Veronica, who keeps prices low by shopping in her Spanish neighborhood rather than where expatriates are clustered.

For major purchases, it pays to watch the market. Thailand's growing economy points toward price increases, or as David Mead offers: "Since 1988, the economy has burgeoned and more people have been able to afford cars. We saw this and bought ours just before prices went up." Sometimes prices come down, as a market watcher will find. Says Len Friedman, who rents his home in Guadalajara but plans to buy property when he reaches pension eligibility: "Guadalajara is becoming more expensive and Lake Chapala is becoming less expensive. The Lake was seriously overbuilt around four years ago. You can buy lovely homes for between $60,000 and $150,000. The same homes would cost four times as much in California."

A Shorter Shopping List

Will you miss the shopping mall? If you must have your fix at the mall you'll find them in unlikely places: In the Pocitos district of Montevideo, Uruguay, where it is not uncommon to find a chamber music group playing for the enjoyment of upscale shoppers; or in Bangkok, which has one of the most sophisticated shopping malls in the world. Guadalajara has a plethora of American-style malls and they are beginning to sprout in other Mexican cities. But in most areas where Americans choose to live economically abroad, you will not find shopping malls. You may miss them at first, but after a while you will probably agree with many Americans who say that after living abroad, your needs are not as great as at home. One reason is the lack of marketing hype evident in the U.S., or as a resident of Portugal says, "Your desire for things is reduced dramatically. You don't need what we all thought we needed in the States."

Chapter 15

Security Concerns

"You get the feeling very quickly that everyone watches out for everyone else."

Arlene Dexter
Dordogne, France

Guadalajara is much safer than San Francisco, according to Lauren Gruning, who feels safe walking around the city—even at night. She adds: "Guadalajara is probably safer than any city in the U.S." Americans living abroad often feel safer than at home, and many cite rising crime in the U.S. as one reason they chose to move to a different country.

Ruth Walkington in San José, Costa Rica, points out that although petty theft seems to be on the rise, "Even today, I can go downtown alone and return to my car in the evening without being afraid. I can't say that about most cities in the U.S." And Ralph Breyer, who lives in the Algarve, concurs: "There is far, far less concern about crime here than at home."

The questions of crime and security arise wherever you choose to live, however. There are few locales at home or abroad so free of crime that you can leave doors unlocked at night or take an extended journey without wondering if your home and personal property will be intact when you return.

Assess Your Needs

If you are very concerned about security, two factors are especially important: first, the economic and political climate of the country; second, your chosen type of residence and its location. Is the crime rate rising or relatively stable in the country you are considering? A high inflation rate, unemployment or immigration from troubled neighboring countries all could signal trouble. But usually, the same precautions you would use in the U.S. are sufficient to ensure safety.

Allie Yance, a former New Yorker, says she goes everywhere in Costa Rica; when she is downtown in San José she walks with confidence because studies of urban crime have determined that a confident, purposeful stride is one of the best deterrents. "I walk with confidence and maintain my New York sense of caution. If I see a dangerous situation, I get out of the vicinity right away, even if it means jumping into a cab." But this doesn't limit her life or her activities. She even wears gold chains without worry. In recent years, she has added a precaution: she doesn't walk alone late at night but now takes a cab instead. The neighborhood where she rents her small home is one of the wealthiest areas in San José, and since many of the homes have extra security it gives her an added sense of protection as a woman living alone.

In Southern Europe, the increasing influx of vacationers of all ages and socioeconomic levels attracts petty criminals. In Spain's Costa del Sol, for example, it is necessary to take precautions, especially regarding property (such as not leaving suitcases or other objects of value in an unattended car). Elsa Van Dam in Málaga, Spain, has been the victim of a purse snatcher and once a necklace was grabbed from her neck. Her apartment is on the third floor and as she explains, "I have a door with a combination lock."

Crime appears in many guises abroad, but usually is not personally threatening and is sometimes rather exotic: One of Elsa's neighbors, on the ground level, was taking a nap one day when gypsies broke through his window and helped themselves to a few items of little value.

In most countries, amateur thieves are your main concern. In Spanish-speaking countries, the perpetrators are called *ladrones* (petty thieves), who look for items such as small appliances, which they can turn into cash at a pawn shop. This type of burglar is far from bold, will flee at the slightest noise and is unlikely to be armed, unlike many burglars in the U.S.

Security Strategies

To protect yourself from burglary abroad, there are several recommended strategies. One is to install decorative wrought-iron window bars commonly found in most Latin countries. The traditional use of such bars is largely decorative; often they are only installed on front windows (so a burglar could enter with less hindrance through the side or rear). In France, heavy wooden shutters are a traditional exterior window treatment that provides protection from summer sun and winter winds, as well as deterring any would-be burglar who would have to attract the attention of neighbors to gain access.

An apartment or condominium complex designed for security, with a combination of secured access, intercom or central reception area to identify visitors (or even security guards), is the most comprehensive and expensive way to assure the safety of your property. But if your lifestyle requires expensive art objects or costly electronic equipment, no doubt you are already accustomed to paying for extra security. High-visibility wealth may attract trouble at home or abroad. One couple, now living in a security complex in San José, were satisfied that they had covered their security needs abroad. Ironically, when they returned to Florida to visit friends, they were accosted on the street outside their Boca Raton luxury hotel. The hotel and the couple's attire were magnets for trouble at home, and although they have not had any problems while living abroad since moving in 1987, the robbery in Florida has made them more cautious about display.

You will also find that police are more helpful in some countries than in others. According to some residents, one reason Spain tends to have a higher crime rate than surrounding countries is that the police focus more attention on traffic control than tracking stolen property.

In the opinion of Dara Glass, Mexico City police are not very trustworthy. She advises caution and notes that sometimes you cannot even be sure whether an officer is bona fide or is an impersonator. Outside of the capital, she adds, this is not as serious a problem. In Portugal, on the other hand, the police seem to make more effort to recover stolen property. The difference is due in part to Mexico City's economic and social conditions; in part, the attitude in Portugal is traditional.

Portugal has traditionally emphasized the values of truth and honesty, as symbolized by the motif of the rooster, which appears again and again as a reminder of one of Portugal's enduring legends: The rooster is the symbol of the peasant who was wrongly accused of stealing. The accused vowed that if he were innocent, the roasted poultry on the police magistrate's dinner table would rise up and crow his innocence. As the tale goes, the rooster crowed and the wrongly accused man was set free.

But as Portugal's tourism has grown, so has the influx of people heading south to the Algarve for work and play, along with a fringe group who prey on tourists. American residents observe that often it is outsiders who are the perpetrators, and your Portuguese neighbors will be just as suspicious as you are about transients. As Susan Broward advises, if you make an effort to know your neighbors, they will help keep an eye on your property and you will do the same for them.

Neighborhood Watch

When selecting a residence, the neighborhood makes a difference, just as it does in the U.S. (where some of the best neighborhoods are "red-lined" by insurers because of the high rate of car and property theft). A neighborhood with many expatriates is often more prone to burglary than one with mainly native residents because burglars assume that expatriates are wealthy. In Costa Rica, the Thalmeyers, whose neighbors are all Costa Rican, have not had a burglary problem, nor has Veronica Alta who lives in a Spanish neighborhood in Torremolinos.

The type of dwelling you choose can afford varying degrees of security. A condominium or attached villa is more secure than a freestanding house. Many Americans living abroad have obtained homes that provide special security advantages. The Grunings in Guadalajara found an apartment with a special security arrangement: the landlord's family occupies the lower floor of a three-unit apartment building, and some members of the large family are always at home.

In Italy, Bob and Linda Martinelli bought their property from a builder whose own home is across the street. Their relationship assures that a concerned individual will keep a protective eye on the property when the Martinellis are in the U.S. part of the year. Personal connections, even if only through a business transaction, add to your peace of mind. In this case, the seller built the property on a lot he had owned for many years; his personal involvement with the design and construction of the home makes the seller even more concerned for the safety of the property than if it had only been a resale transaction.

The old shepherd's house now owned by Joan Carver and Mel Waterhouse in rural France has a special security advantage: their small home is adjacent to a farm, where they enjoy the vista of many acres of surrounding land—which makes their own acre seem many times larger. And since their property appears to be part of the larger working farm, the constant presence of the farm family means that no harm is likely to come to their shepherd's cottage.

A family area, where neighbors are likely to be home during the day, is a good precaution against burglary, especially if you have outside commitments such as work or social activities. You are likely to find that people watch out for each other even more than they do in most cities and suburbs in the U.S. The two-career family, which means an empty house during predictable hours, still is not common in most countries abroad.

"You get the feeling very quickly that everyone watches out for everyone else," says Arlene Dexter, referring to the French village where she and Paul own a home. Another American suggests: "Your best defense is a nosy neighbor." Sometimes a casual attitude can clash with security-conscious residents: "Our neighbor is an older widow who is very concerned about our security," says John Barber, whose vacation home is in rural France. "We're fairly free about inviting friends to stop in—we tell them to just make themselves at home if we're out. But if someone comes, she'll call our caretaker who drives over even late at night to be sure everything is all right. He doesn't seem to mind—but the neighbor really gets irritated."

Live-in Security

Live-in help, or arranging to have housekeeping done on the days you plan your outside activities, is another hedge on property crime. As Lon Temple, a long-time resident of Costa Rica, says: "The first line of defense is a live-in maid" (at a cost of $150–$200 per month). The low cost of domestic help is one of the advantages of living abroad in less-developed countries, especially when it enables you to have someone in your home when you are away for a trip or a return visit to the U.S.

175

Even if you don't have live-in help, usually you can arrange to have your part-time housekeeper or gardener stay at your home during a journey. A gardener also provides highly visible activity around the home when you are not in residence, and if you do not live in the home part of the year, you might want to arrange for regular gardening to avoid the appearance of an empty house. Ruth Walkington's gardener, for example, sleeps in the house when the family is on an extended trip. There are lights at night providing a lived-in appearance, and he enjoys the use of the residence. She notes that he is also careful not to abuse this perquisite, knowing that others would like the job.

There is always some risk of theft by household help no matter where you live. Fair treatment of employees, as well as fair wages and personal appreciation expressed through occasional gifts and favors, is the best way to assure loyalty and honesty. It's best to have a home safe for irreplaceable items such as heirlooms, and you should avoid leaving valuable objects such as jewelry and cash lying around to tempt someone whose standard of living is far below your own.

One American in Costa Rica notes that more than one of her housekeepers seemed to think it was acceptable to take something she had left lying around carelessly, as if the owner didn't care about it. "If you're not using it, they seem to think it is all right to take it. When I confronted the woman, she simply said, 'But I needed it and you weren't using it.'"

Even though the help may be loyal to you, their friends can pose a security problem. Renee Wolpert in Guadalajara recalls an incident when her family planned a trip to London. She offered her maid a paid vacation during the same time (Renee points out that she had close neighbors who kept an eye on each other's property). Instead of being pleased at the offer of paid time off, the maid was disappointed. "She was crushed—she had planned on having her new boyfriend over. I didn't mind that she had the run of the house, but I was worried about him, since his interest in her seemed to flower just before our planned vacation. I was quite sure he was interested in gaining access to the house." Renee's neighbor, an upper-middle-class Mexican woman, advised her to be cautious—and not to leave a key behind for the housekeeper.

Leisure activities also affect security decisions, if you plan to travel extensively or participate in a number of outdoor activities that mean many days each year spent away from your home. The more time you plan to spend at home, the less you need extra security measures. Just as in the U.S., you don't want to signal the fact that you are absent, especially if you have outside activities at predictable times. One way to cover your absence during trips is to offer your home for a friend from the U.S. to "house sit." This means a vacation with no lodging costs for the friend, you are covered and you might want to overlap their visit a few days to see each other.

Safety on the Road

Highway security is another concern of many seasoned travelers who have found during trips abroad that roads often seem more perilous than in the U.S. In most countries, highways are improving: In Southern Europe, such improvements are prompted by the European Community requirements for higher standards. In Costa Rica and Mexico, many highways are being improved with the addition of lanes, better marking, signs and signals. An American in Costa Rica comments, "Driving is less hazardous than it was a dozen years ago. One reason is the driver's education courses now offered in the schools."

Even driver's education, lanes and signs won't entirely offset cultural attitudes, however. Especially in Latin countries, red lights and caution signs are often disregarded, as though observing the rules is somehow not *macho*. When you are a pedestrian, you have to be wary—a red light might not stop a driver intent on running the intersection (as any New Yorker already knows). When driving abroad, as one American advises, "You have to drive defensively." John Nielson in Costa Rica notes that if he sees a risk-taking driver in a long line of two-lane traffic, he just slows down until the passing lead car has maneuvered into a safe position. When a traffic accident does occur and the other party is at fault, even though your insurance company will cover damages, you may not receive the legal satisfaction you would expect in the U.S. The party at fault—even for an offense as serious as vehicular manslaughter—may actually avoid penalty.

Cautious Cuisine

With regard to food and hygiene, most Americans living abroad observe the same safety precautions as when traveling anywhere in the world: fresh food is best when you buy it whole and prepare it yourself; prepared food from vendors may be questionable if you don't know how long it has remained without refrigeration; bottled water, soda and beer are safer than water or beverages served from bulk containers; hotels and good restaurants—or moderate but very popular restaurants with high turnover—are generally more reliable than out-of-the-way places where supplies may not be as fresh as you would like. Wherever you are, seafood should be questioned, especially shellfish in areas where water is polluted. With seafood, you want to be sure that "today's catch" isn't left over from last Tuesday.

Owning a Bit of Ireland

Travel agent Pamela Winger had a chance to scout areas in Ireland before she and her husband decided to buy a charming farm for a good price: their 130-year-old stone farmhouse, with 13 acres and two barns on the property, cost $34,000 in the summer of 1990.

The nearby village of Kerry-on-Shannon, Pamela notes, "has all the modern conveniences—shopping, grocery stores and about 300 pubs. Everything you would need." There are good restaurants, and tea shops. A tasty three-course dinner in one of the better restaurants costs around $10 "and everyone has Guinness in the pubs," adds Pamela.

The farm has ample living space but needs upgrading, and consists of five rooms: two bedrooms, a small room that could convert to a bedroom, a living room/kitchen area and a sitting room. It has electricity, telephone and district water piped in (plus a well on the property), but as Pamela explains, "Like a lot of farmhouses in the area it doesn't have a bathroom. We'll add a bath and master suite with a fireplace." She estimates remodeling will cost another $12,000–$15,000, but adds, "we'll end up with a very nice property one mile outside of the village."

Since Kerry-on-Shannon is in a mid-Ireland agricultural region, the Wingers enjoy Saturday open-air markets and visit the Tuesday cattle mart and weekly sheep market held on Thursdays. "Tom would love to be a gentleman farmer. We call him Farmer Tom," says Pamela, whose husband is a naval architect. Since they became interested in rural Irish property, he has been reading up on agricultural uses of land.

She finds the weather pleasant but there is no mistaking it for a sunny Southern European setting. "It rains in spurts, but there is sunshine every day. It's cool and moist, and in summer it can even get very hot. Summers are comparable to England, but it's not as cold or as rainy as Scotland." Although the popular Southwest Coast is warmer, Pamela explains: "I wanted to stay away from tourism, which is mainly in the Southwest or Cork area and is where most Americans buy. We wanted to be in the lake district where there is more to offer in hiking, fishing and historical sites. Of course, there is the famous Blarney Castle in the South, but we have castles here too. One is the beautiful castle at Roscommon where there is no toll gate, you can just walk through. And this area has the best trout and salmon fishing in Ireland." The Irish also love to play golf, and there are six golf courses within a 20-mile radius of the village.

The area is popular with French vacationers as well as with Germans and British. The Wingers were the first Americans to buy in their area. "They like Americans very much and regard us as though we're all their children who have emigrated," says Pamela. One of the reasons property in Ireland is attractive to Europeans and Americans is the absence of property tax.

With an MBA in marketing and finance, Pamela approached her vacation-home investment with a sharp business eye. "I buy antiques," explains Pamela. "We knew from our antique shopping that antiques reflect prices in an area. We did some further research and found out there were two counties in Ireland where property prices were low."

The Wingers were surprised to find that although antique prices were an indicator of prices in an area, the real economic factor was the price of beef. "Two years ago in this same area, when beef prices were high, the price was 2,500 to 3,000 Irish pounds per acre. Now beef is down—and an acre is available for 1,000 to 1,500 Irish pounds. " An American wishing to purchase property abroad would be similarly advised to determine local economic factors; by following such market indicators you might be able to buy property in a low market, as did the Wingers.

The farm is located between the two major cities of Dublin and Shannon, and is two hours by train or less by car from either of them. Once they had identified the county where they wanted to buy, the Wingers drove around 100 miles per day during their property search. "Buying property was simple," says Pamela. "We sent a deposit, bought futures to secure the exchange rate and we will pay the balance in March of 1991—although we were allowed to take possession in October." When buying futures, one deposits 10% of value and pays the balance on an agreed date based on the exchange rate of the original transaction day. "Sometimes you win, sometimes you don't. In the past three years, I have found that I usually win," explains Pamela, who buys futures to lock in prices for the corporate tours she books at her travel agency.

She did a lot of homework to make her vacation-home investment as profitable as possible. Her research showed that there are

IRELAND

farms with "good" land and "bad" land. Since her farm has good land, she now leases out the acreage for cattle grazing. (On good land grass grows quickly, providing forage for younger cows that bring better prices.) One of the advantages of buying property in a European Community country such as Ireland, Pamela notes, is that there are several kinds of subsidies available. The EC provides a grant to add a bathroom to a home or farmhouse; or if land is bad, the EC will subsidize the cost of planting land for reforestation; even if land is waterlogged, the EC will pay most of the cost of planting trees on the land.

The Wingers intend to use their Irish farmhouse partly as a business expense ("as a perquisite for clients") but hadn't thought about renting it out until a neighbor suggested that they use it as a "self-catering" cottage. The Winger's typical tenant, for a week or two, might be a French fisherman on holiday. For a small fee, one of the neighbors would keep an eye on the property and assure that the farmhouse was in order both before and after the each vacationer's visit.

The neighborly advice is typical of the friendly way Irish villagers conduct business. When the Wingers bought their farmhouse, the signing of the contract included a ritual in the Irish tradition. "We signed papers in the solicitor's office at 10:30 on a Saturday morning," explains Pamela. "Besides the solicitor there was the son of the owner and the auctioneer who handled the sale. We signed the papers, then the three gentlemen invited us to go next door to the pub—at 11:30 a.m.!" Pamela decided it was too early for her to join in, so the men went off for the ritual toast. "They each had to buy a round. Tom was two sheets to the wind when he got back, but it seemed very natural because that's how they sign a contract in Kerry-on-Shannon. It's a friendly way to get business done. In the meantime," Pamela adds, "I went shopping."

Chapter 16

Health Care Abroad

"My doctor provides not only inexpensive but very professional care—although the surroundings are not as elegant as you would find in New York."

David Mead
Chiang Mai, Thailand

When you are ready to seriously consider living or sojourning abroad, you will have many questions about health care: Does your current insurance cover overseas treatment? If not, what alternative insurance is available and at what cost? What is the level of health care in this country—how well-trained are physicians, specialists and nurses? Do medical staff speak sufficient English for you to communicate your needs? Are hospital facilities sanitary and well-equipped, and do they have an adequate number of beds per capita?

Accessible, high quality, affordable medical care and health services—with provision for emergency treatment—should be one of your priorities when choosing a locale abroad. Even if you are young and in good health, you may still need emergency treatment in case of accident or unexpected illness. For an older person, health care is even more important to maintain continued health or to monitor any chronic problems.

Access. If you become enamored of a scenic homesite a long ride by unreliable transportation from the nearest medical facility, then you (and your partner) should be favored with very good health. More likely, you will choose a town or village near amenities and not far from a hospital or clinic. Access is not just geography, but also communication. You should find English-speaking doctors able to adequately explain to you a diagnosis and proposed treatment—doctors to whom you can pose questions that concern you. This is not as difficult as it may seem: a high percentage of physicians in other countries are multilingual, and often English is their second language.

Quality professionals and health facilities. Recommendation is the most reliable way to find a good physician; that is, through referral from American and British residents. If you require the care of a specialist, be sure there is one in or near the area you are considering for your home abroad. In many countries, health care is two-tiered: public clinics and private-physician care.

Medical costs. Chances are you will find medical costs very inexpensive in most countries outside the U.S. The cost of health care in the U.S. is growing at an alarming rate, but quality medical care abroad is usually far less expensive. One reason for rising costs in the U.S. is malpractice insurance. Since other countries are far less litigious, you will enjoy lower costs but your chances of winning a hefty malpractice settlement would be slim.

Another reason for lower costs is that medical facilities in the U.S. invest in costly advanced-technology equipment. Abroad, you may find that several hospitals in an area share one expensive CAT scanner. In the U.S., facilities in the same town may all have the gamut of expensive diagnostic equipment. Outside the U.S., you may need to travel farther to a hospital possessing the technology you need.

As a result, you may find that medical treatment abroad turns out to cost little more (or even less) than your usual deductible. Because of lower medical costs abroad, you will find that local and European insurance policies with coverage in your chosen country can also be a bargain: since their costs are lower, this saving is passed on to the consumer.

In Uruguay, two levels of medical care are appropriate for a foreign resident. The most popular type of coverage is a health maintenance arrangement with a monthly fee of around $25. The other option is private care, where although an individual pays the entire amount, costs are very affordable compared with the U.S. George Frank, who uses the British hospital in Montevideo, recently had a minor physical where the doctor's fee was only $12, and, notes George, "Uruguay has a high level of medical professionalism." British hospitals are found in many areas with a large number of British expatriates; often Americans in residence choose this hospital, and its affiliated physicians, for health care.

In Costa Rica, there are three levels of medical care: public facilities, private clinics and private practice care. Nancy Thalmeyer—who worked in hospitals before her retirement to Costa Rica—is pleased with the health services in that country. She feels that it is not necessary to seek out the more expensive type of care. Even members of Costa Rica's wealthier class often use public facilities, she notes. Recently she visited a friend who had surgery in the Social Security hospital and the president's sister was hospitalized in the adjacent room.

Shopping for Health Insurance

You will need to reconsider your insurance options. Most conventional policies do not cover expatriates. Some offer supplemental coverage to evacuate you for treatment in the U.S., but at a high premium. More widely available are short-term policies intended for the traveler. There are many other options, however, including European health plans with worldwide coverage, most of which are available to American expatriates, such as Extra Sure (British), Sanitas (Spanish), Bravamerica (Spanish), Dinamarca (Danish), Exeter Hospital Aid (British) and Bupa (British).

When looking for an insurance policy, you should seek extra coverage that might not be necessary for someone living in the U.S. Karen Knight in Portugal advises, "I would not have health insurance that didn't provide evacuation coverage, or one that wouldn't cover me in a number of different countries." She notes that some kinds of Blue Cross policies only provide coverage if you return to the U.S. Karen and her husband now have Extra Sure, a British health plan. "There are a number of international carriers—English, Danish, German—who sell expatriate health insurance. And it's cheaper than American health insurance," she observes.

There may be local health-care programs offered to residents, pensioners or members of expatriate organizations. Diane and Hal Oster in Costa Rica have insurance coverage through the *pensionado* (retiree) association for a fee of $25 per month. As she explains: "This entitles us to medical care at the public clinic, or we could go to a private clinic for a small extra charge."

Some Americans abroad—in countries with very low cost medical care—decide to self-insure, often using CDs or other investment vehicles to cover the possibility of health care costs. The Thalmeyers in Costa Rica have Blue Cross and pay a monthly insurance premium of $182. They are thinking of self-insuring, and plan to deposit the $182 per month in an interest-bearing colone account (paying 18%-24%). Over the dozen years that they have been paying Blue Cross, says Nancy, "We've paid out more in premiums than we'd ever get back."

Before you rush to change insurance programs, remember that during your exploratory or simulated-living phase, short-term traveler's coverage will meet your needs while you are deciding on the next step. During that time, you may explore alternatives to U.S. insurers. Two considerations when looking for coverage abroad (especially for older retirees) are provisions for evacuation if special treatment is needed and expatriation in case of death.

When considering expatriate insurance coverage, bear in mind such factors as direct payment vs. reimbursement, outpatient care, air ambulance coverage and the required waiting period for eligibility as well as preexisting condition exclusions. Ralph Breyer in Portugal advises: "The time to look into insurance and medical care is when you don't need it."

Adjusting to International Care

If you are reluctant to relinquish the assurance of your family doctor, this could become important in your adjustment process. U.S. health care is rapidly becoming an international business. If you are a member of a health maintenance organization, the fastest-growing segment of the U.S. health-care industry, then you probably have already made some adjustment and are accustomed to international physicians trained at medical schools around the globe.

When you consider living abroad, you should evaluate your current and anticipated health needs. If you are in good health or have minor complaints, you will find that health care ranges from adequate to excellent, depending on whether you opt to use the least expensive facilities (a public clinic) or more expensive private care. But even the best health care abroad usually costs far less than in the U.S. Says an American diplomat in Portugal (where an X-ray costs around $15 and an office visit to a specialist approximately $28), "The embassy personnel have minor surgery here and we deem it adequate—with a private clinic it is more than adequate." When he broke his leg, the cost of treatment for doctor, hospital and physical therapy, "didn't even come up to my deductible." He adds: "I didn't turn around and go to a private doctor to save Aetna (his insurance carrier) money, but because public treatment was adequate."

Adjusting to international health care is best accomplished by suspending your medical expectations. Elsa Van Dam in Spain (who has European health insurance through the Bravamerica insurance program) reports that compared with the U.S., where a visit to an efficiently run doctor's office may mean a short wait and a short consultation, "In Spain, sometimes you have to wait an hour to see the doctor, but once you are with him he gives you very good attention and really takes his time."

Another American in Spain, Janice Baldridge, had Blue Cross/Blue Shield pension insurance when she moved abroad 10 years ago (Blue Cross/Blue Shield coverage may be an option if you are insured through your employer during your pre-retirement job, and may be part of your retirement package). Janice and her husband have switched to Sanitas. The advantage, she points out, is that if you are in an accident, with Blue Cross/Blue Shield you must initially pay for the treatment and then file for reimbursement from your insurer. Sanitas offers 100% coverage with no out-of-pocket expenses, an important consideration if, like most Americans abroad, you arrange to have a fixed amount of living money transferred to your overseas account each month.

Peter Haddon in Guadalajara also had Blue Cross and notes that the premiums were quite high, but that when he and his first wife moved to Mexico 15 years ago she had a chronic health problem and the Haddons felt that they needed this type of coverage. "She had a physician in Guadalajara, but when she needed a major checkup we went to a specialist in Arizona or Boston, so actually we used a combination of local and U.S. doctors," he explains.

When his wife died, Peter switched to Mexican social security insurance, which is available on a limited basis for foreign residents over the age of 65. The procedure for enrollment is somewhat unusual by our standards, as Peter points out: "The government opens its membership on occasion—it is announced in the newspaper—and foreign residents are allowed to join at that time." Peter's second wife is an American who has lived in Mexico longer than he has. One of the reasons he changed to the Mexican insurance program is that she had used it for years, and has had all her medical care, including surgery, covered through this program.

Modest Facilities

With many international insurance companies to choose from, health-care coverage rarely poses a problem once you have done your homework. But you may need to shop for a physician or specialty treatment with more diligence than in the U.S. Also, you may miss American hygienic standards—or the apparent lack of such standards, for sometimes it is merely the lack of office decor that causes some dismay for a first-time patient abroad. Dara Glass in Mexico City (who has Blue Shield) has been hospitalized more than once. She agrees that "finding a reliable doctor can be hard. You do it through word of mouth." She also found that hospitals in Mexico City appear to be below U.S. standards.

It took David Mead in Thailand two years to find his current physician, after being dissatisfied with others. Now David says, "He is the best and brightest doctor I've had in my life. He's in his late 30s and his English is fluent, even though he has never been abroad." David had bypass surgery in the U.S. a few years before retiring in Thailand and he has to closely monitor his blood pressure, so his search for a good specialist was very important during the adjustment period. He reports that office visits are $4–$8 including medicine and adds, "It's not only inexpensive but it is very professional care, although the surroundings are not as elegant as you would find in New York." David further notes that when his doctor takes an EKG reading, "it is totally computerized and it prints out the EKG diagnosis in English."

For routine care, including procedures such as hip surgery, cardiac care and even most types of cancer treatment, you will find satisfactory—or even excellent—physicians in most countries cited in this book. Nancy Thalmeyer had hip surgery abroad and praises her orthopedic surgeon. She also notes that medicine is an international community of professionals. Her orthopedist is a visiting lecturer at universities in the U.S. each summer. She is confident about medical care in Costa Rica for most types of illness, but adds: "The only thing I would be concerned about would be very unusual types of cancer treatment or very complex surgery."

An Emergency Plan

Emergencies and unusual illness are another matter. When deciding on a locale, it is a good idea to draft a plan in case of both minor and major emergencies. For a minor emergency, you would want to know clinic hours and alternatives; for a serious emergency, if you do not live near a large hospital, then you will need to consider transportation—and remember that you are not likely to find the equivalent of U.S. paramedics who arrive minutes after you call 911 in the U.S. But when you find a good general physician near where you live, he or she will be prepared to arrange for specialty treatment and even transportation if you need it. Since telephone communication may not be as sophisticated as in the U.S., with our round-the-clock physician answering services, you may want to inquire of your doctor how to handle an emergency if one should arise late at night, on weekends or during holidays.

Portugal resident Len Kennebeck offers one of his positive experiences with medical care, but he also points out a possible disadvantage of medical care in Portugal. Len had been doing metalwork around the house but didn't realize that he had a small splinter in his eye. When the eye became painfully inflamed, he didn't think of the metalwork as a possible cause of the eye problem. "I went to my local Portuguese doctor who said, 'I can see that you have two splinters next to your pupil. If I had the right equipment I would remove them, but I am going to send you to an eye specialist.'"

Len describes the specialist's office as a modest building "very simple and unimpressive. But when I got into the office and looked around, the whole room was filled with the most sophisticated equipment I've seen anywhere." Len adds that although his own experiences have been good, the biggest complaint throughout Portugal is emergency treatment. "Once you get into the hospital the treatment is great. It's that damned emergency room. They don't have that organized properly."

Another Algarve resident, Susan Broward, reports that she has had good experiences with emergency treatment. When a visiting friend received a deep cut in her hand, recalls Susan, "We took her to the *clinica* and they took her right away, put in the stitches and we walked out. You can't get better emergency treatment than that."

Some Americans living abroad are skeptical about local doctors. Harold Parr is not too confident about diagnosis for unusual problems in Málaga on Spain's Costa del Sol. Harold's son was visiting his family in Connecticut a few years ago when he began to have severe headaches. When an examination determined that he had a brain tumor, he was taken to the medical center at Yale University where it was established that the tumor was benign. Yet Harold ventures: "If he had been living here in Spain at the time, the doctor might have just given him an aspirin. Of course," Harold adds, "Yale has one of most advanced facilities for neurosurgery in the world." His son was lucky in his location, since even an average physician in the U.S. also might have prescribed only an aspirin.

One occasionally hears accounts of laboratory errors both in the U.S. and abroad. Karen Knight had a disturbing experience in Portugal, as she explains: "I had a biopsy of a lump that was misdiagnosed as tuberculosis. After having the skin test, which came out negative, I suspect that they mixed up the slides."

Depending on which Americans you speak with about local care, you may hear complaints or compliments. Another American on the Costa del Sol was impressed with the diagnostic skill of her Spanish physician. When she told him of her lingering flu-like symptoms, he gave her a thorough examination and began to question her intensely about her habits and routine. By reconstructing her activities over a period of several weeks, he concluded that the illness could be traced to a trip to Morocco that for her was only a memory with no apparent connection to her illness. He correctly diagnosed her illness, which resulted from a flea bite during the trip. Just as Harold Parr looks at the incident with his son as evidence that the boy was lucky to be in the U.S. for a tricky diagnosis, Ann Lowry gives her Spanish physician full credit for a diagnosis that probably saved her life. Emergencies, accidents, contracting a rare disease—if you are the patient, the "best treatment" under the circumstances partly depends on an element of luck and timing, whether you are abroad or in the U.S. But for medical care you can anticipate, or for elective surgery, you have a choice—based on research and referral.

Although there are mixed opinions about medical care abroad for critical problems, local routine care often receives praise: Ruth Walkington, who has lived in Costa Rica since 1983, reports that "health services and dental care are excellent." So is cosmetic surgery, and at prices only a fraction of those in the U.S. Another Costa Rica resident, Cheryl Becker, agrees that the facilities are "excellent," but she points out that medication can be more expensive than in the U.S. if prescribed by your doctor at home rather than a brand prescribed by a local doctor.

Bedside Manners

Another difference between medical care in the U.S. and that of countries abroad is the personal touch. Many Americans cite the high level of concern and attention shown by doctors and nurses. Beth and Don Hartman were sick with the flu when they arrived in Portugal five years ago. Don's flu became serious, as Beth recalls: "I called a neighbor who called a doctor. He was wonderful—he came to the house on a Sunday and drove me to a pharmacy." The doctor cautioned Beth that if the medication did not work then Don would have to be hospitalized. The flu turned into bronchitis, but the doctor arranged for home care; for four days, a nurse visited their home twice daily. The entire treatment, including three doctor's visits and the nursing care, came to a total of $29. This plus the care and concern were a pleasant surprise for two Americans accustomed to less personal medical attention at home.

The strong family tradition in many countries means a different kind of hospital experience for an American living abroad. In some countries it is customary for a family member to remain with the patient. Louise Harris in Costa Rica says that when her husband was treated for a bleeding ulcer, the cost—including doctor, hospital room, meals and all treatment—came to $350 for five days. She adds: "They like to have a family member stay with the patient. The hospital here is far more sensitive and warm than it is in the States. And you don't have to go to a four- or six-bed ward as we chose to do. You can elect to be in a private room for an extra charge of around $70 per day."

The other side of the family-care tradition is that the family may be expected to offer support and even some of the nonmedical attention that would be provided by the nursing staff in the U.S. Lily Cairns says of medical care on the island of Mykonos in

191

Greece: "I don't think I'd want to be sick here." One reason is the likelihood that she would need to travel to the mainland for treatment. Lily points out that in the hospitals in Athens, the family is, by tradition, expected to help with the patient's hospital care. Cots are provided for family members. But if you don't have loved ones abroad (or if they do not understand this custom) then you may not receive as much attention as other patients in the hospital.

If hospital procedures are different, so are those for home care—and the latter is a decided advantage in many countries. Len Friedman in Guadalajara notes that not only are medical costs low in Mexico but you can afford to have home care. A staff of two to help care for a sick or elderly family member costs around $200 per month. Nursing homes for the elderly run $400–$700 per month, and notes Len: "Some of my friends have parents in nursing homes here." Ruth Walkington agrees: "I feel that in the event I become disabled, in the U.S. it is so expensive to go into a care center, but in Costa Rica I could hire a couple to do the cleaning, cooking and to care for me for far less than I would need to pay in the States—and I could still live in my own home and see my friends."

Since few nurses are likely to speak English as a second language, some language skills will make you more comfortable should you need to be hospitalized for any reason. Yet even with a general command of the language, you are not likely to know terminology useful for medical care. A list of common medical terms is provided in the appendix; you should have this list translated into the local language in advance for use in emergencies or as a bedside reference when communicating with non-English-speaking medical staff.

When rating medical care, be sure to weigh opinions from several Americans in residence since one person's bad experience may be linked to a particular instance, or to one in which the patient perhaps had overly high expectations. By listening to opinions and hearing about both positive and negative experiences, you can plan your medical strategy rather than have to seek care randomly when need arises.

Starting Over in Portugal

When Karen Knight departed to Greece for a vacation in 1984, she only expected a few weeks of sunshine far from the congestion and winter sleet of Manhattan's concrete canyons. She had no idea that within two years she would move to Portugal, leave behind her satisfying but high-pressure career as a psychologist and launch a new avocation as a restaurant critic and editor for an English-language magazine in the Algarve.

The getaway to Greece turned out to be more than a vacation. In fact, it turned into a vacation romance with Paul Knight, a British citizen who had also chosen Greece for a respite from his job in Saudi Arabia. After many long-distance telephone calls, Paul traveled to New York for a purposeful visit, or as Karen tells it: "He came to New York, said 'Let's get married,' and I said yes."

One of the big questions faced by Karen and Paul was where to live. For over a dozen years, he had worked in the construction industry in the Middle East and now Paul was ready for a change but did not want to return to England. Karen recalls her own decision to move abroad: "I was at the stage of my life and career where I said to myself, 'This is fine, but do I want to stay in New York and do this for the rest of my life?' I always thought that living in Europe would be wonderful. We were young—that is, youngish, in our 40s—and we could do it. I could see that if we didn't do it now, then in another 30 years I would still be a psychologist in New York and never have tried anything different."

Paul was more experienced in international living, so he drafted a checklist of what he wanted in a country: a European location, a country that was safe and politically stable and one that had a reasonable cost of living. Starting a new life together in a different country meant a career change for both. One strategy they discussed was pooling their assets to start a business venture. Like many Americans, Karen assumed that she and Paul could easily establish a business that catered to travelers and expatriates with sophisticated taste. "We thought of opening a restaurant, but we saw that Portugal was much more developed than we had imagined. Finally, when we started to think about the life that went with it, we realized that neither of us wanted the lifestyle that goes with running a restaurant," says Karen.

They found out that Paul's expertise in a technical aspect of construction was in demand. "Paul decided to start a business importing plumbing products," explains Karen. "We wanted to be perfectly legal with this. Some people come here and start illegal businesses, but we both felt that if this were something that grew, it must be legal so that we could either sell it or keep it—a business that we could live with."

Paul's business thrived, and at the same time the Knights built a residence, drawing on his understanding of construction and her experience with property renovation in New York. They carefully researched legal aspects of real estate and development before purchasing two lots. The parcel, on which they planned to build their home, was a half-hour drive from the beach just outside the tourist area. "We fell in love with the location, liked the idea of living in Portugal but not in an English colony," recalls Karen. The second piece of property had investment potential, with an existing farmhouse that could be renovated and with enough land (with the right zoning) to build a second home for resale.

Paul's background provided a bridge to their new life. "If you have an expertise that is needed in a developing country, then there is an enormous amount of opportunity," Karen advises. At first, however, it seemed as though Karen had burned her own bridges. Sometimes the adjustment is easier for one person than the other when a couple moves abroad. Karen kept busy working with Paul in the establishment of his business, but she missed having her own career. "I found out that there was very little I could do to use my skills, so I just found bits and pieces of things."

Those "bits and pieces" began to add up to a new career, although it took some time before the fragments became a whole. One way, Karen discovered, was to link her past and present. She had enjoyed horses during her childhood in Illinois, but hadn't ridden regularly since she was a teenager. Returning to pleasures of childhood is a way to recapture the best of your past. Karen now owns a Monterrey (Paul's horse is a Portuguese Crusado) and says, "It takes us 20 minutes to gallop to the beach, or we can ride through the woods—we can ride outdoors all year long." The Knights stable their horses at a riding center in the area, as do many expatriates in the Central Algarve where jumping is a popular equestrian activity. "I'd never jumped a horse in my life," says Karen. "Now we're in

PORTUGAL

competitions virtually every weekend and this is a major part of our social life."

Karen also had a chance to contribute articles for the glossy, English-language *Algarve Magazine* when the editor found out about her interest in gourmet food. As a food critic, Karen writes restaurant reviews and also does interviews, each accompanied by a detailed recipe of a noted chef. This pursuit also drew on Karen's past, as she explains: "I am fascinated by food and I've always loved to cook, but I didn't have much time when I was working in New York." From her interviews with chefs, she started branching out to interview other personalities in the Algarve. At first, her unexpected writing career seemed like a complete departure from her first profession, then she realized that she was drawing on her background after all, or as she explains, "I've spent my whole professional life talking to people—you could call it interviewing people."

For anyone moving abroad, Karen advises that it may take a while before new friendships and interests develop. She cautions against a simple expectation of paradise in the sun, an endless vacation of passive enjoyment. No matter how strongly you are attracted to a country abroad, you will need to find activities to provide a sense of belonging. "It seems to be a matter of engagement—and engagement seems to be related to how well it works out, since when we move to a new country we are naturally alienated from the culture around us." Those bits and pieces need cultivation if they are to turn into satisfying activities, and as Karen adds, "It is also a matter of determination."

For her, the best feature of living abroad is "the adventure—the chance to do things I never had the time or opportunity to do, and the chance to meet entirely different kinds of people than I would have met." The Knights did not choose Portugal with a retirement plan in mind, but only as a midlife experience and a new start for both of them. They might move back to the U.S. some day. If they do it would not be to New York, as much as Karen loved it during one period of her life. "I don't think I could live full time in New York again, but I'd probably like to visit regularly," she explains, adding, "I have a profession that I love. I needed a break, but I can always go back to it. I'm having a great time. I'm a food critic, among other things. Where would I have had the chance to be a food critic in the U.S.?"

Chapter 17

Legal Matters

"When a lawyer says 'no problem,' assume that there could be problems and have him go through the details with you—don't sidestep involvement just because it looks unfamiliar."

Barbara Moore
Portimao, Portugal

How do tourist, resident and pensioner status differ? What are the advantages and disadvantages of each—and what are your legal options? In most countries, the answer depends on whether you plan to spend more or less than six months in residence. Usually, you have several options as a U.S. citizen living abroad, and none of these choices requires relinquishing your U.S. citizenship.

Citizenship is a privilege of birth. Of the more than 56 Americans interviewed in *Adventures Abroad*, only one chose to relinquish his citizenship: Roy Teicher, a self-styled expatriate who is the only American in his edge-of-the-jungle community in Costa Rica. Roy says that relinquishing his citizenship has not changed his life or affected his mobility, and he claims that "you can go to your hometown in the U.S. as often and for as long as you want."

One of the benefits (and perhaps there are others that Roy does not want to discuss) is the change in attitude of U.S. officials when Roy travels back and forth to the U.S. "As a citizen they would say suspiciously, 'You're a California lawyer but you don't speak Spanish. Who are your clients?' Now they say, 'You speak good English for a Costa Rican. How long are you going to stay in the States?'"

197

The word *expatriate* simply means "one who leaves the homeland," so that even a traveler becomes an expatriate for a short time, although the term is usually applied to those who reside rather than simply journey abroad. *Expatriate* is a handy way of referring to non-native residents. Whether you choose to live abroad for 2 months or 20 years, you are automatically a member of the U.S. expatriate community as well as of the international expatriate community in your chosen country. In Portugal's Algarve, for example, the Foreign Property Owners Association includes members from a dozen countries.

As a U.S. citizen residing abroad, your passport must be renewed at the current legal interval of 10 years like any other traveler. But it isn't necessary to return to the States for renewal; once you reside in another country, your passport may be renewed through the U.S. Embassy. Americans abroad vote by absentee ballot, so your vote still counts—although it is difficult to have as active a role in the political process when you live far from grass-roots activities. To some extent this is changing, however. U.S. expatriates around the world are becoming a more significant political factor. In a decade of rising global business and communications, there is a strong movement toward establishment of congressional representation for U.S. "expats." This means that in coming years expats will have a more unified and stronger voice in molding policy and supporting representatives who understand the international point of view.

From Tourist to Resident

Your residency status could change over time, since you may begin with an annual vacation of two weeks, expand your sojourn a few years later and perhaps become what is popularly known as a *snowbird*—a North American resident who migrates to a sunny country for a few weeks or months each year. Later on you may buy or build a home. If you spend at least six months in the country each year (in Costa Rica, four months or more) you may apply for resident status.

In some countries (including Mexico and Costa Rica), when you retire you are eligible to apply for pensioner status. This means privileges, such as tax abatement when purchasing a car. Such incentives are offered to attract expatriate pensioners, who not only bring in hard currency but whose income is (more or less) guaranteed. Pensioner incentives are most frequently offered by developing countries.

On the other hand, you may decide to move your retirement timetable forward and become a resident (or resident-worker) before you reach the age of Social Security benefits or pension eligibility. One of the main criteria for either pensioner or resident status is proof of income or assets.

Why do some Americans opt for residency status while others do not? After you consider the following points you will have a better idea of what seems best for you. If your lifestyle changes, you may find that a different status is more beneficial. Remember that laws can change; incentives offered today may be reduced or eliminated—or new incentives may be added. It is important to update your information using the worksheet in the appendix, and to stay informed of changes once you have begun to formulate your plan.

Among the interviewees living in a dozen different countries, those who reside abroad all year usually have resident status, although there are a few exceptions. Some full-time residents in Mexico retain tourist status by exiting the country every six months. Expats who divide their year between another country and the U.S. usually do not seek resident status, although these individuals would meet the six-month criterion and have the option of applying for residency in most countries (see chart in the appendix).

Those who travel back and forth for weeks or a few months at a time do not meet the six-month residency requirement and only have visitor or tourist status. Sometimes this can be an advantage: if a country does not have a taxation agreement with the U.S., a resident's Social Security or other imported income may be taxed, although usually at a very low rate.

Some Americans have special work-related status. Dara Glass, a journalist in Mexico City, has a resident permit with certain privileges such as priority processing when crossing the border. "If all journalists had to go through the usual red tape, the story would be dead," she observes. Arthur Secunda, who lives in Paris, has a 10-year artist's work permit. If he were a resident, he notes, he would receive such privileges as subsidies for medical care, but he would also be subject to French taxation. As a non-resident he is still allowed to buy property, as is the case in most countries. (If you rent out your property, you are subject to income tax.) Arthur finds that his status as a nonresident does not cause any inconvenience when crossing the borders. "Today, with the European Community, almost no one wants to see your passport—you have to beg them to stamp it," says Secunda.

For any status other than tourist or visitor, you will want to know approximately what it will cost to have your documents processed. Americans in residence are the best source of current information; chances are they can also tell you if a change of law is pending, such as an increase in income requirement. Alan Cox in Heredia, Costa Rica, notes that it currently costs around $400–$600 to process *pensionado* or *rentista* ("renter status" in Spanish-speaking countries) papers, and for the necessary government stamp. But he advises that some unwary Americans who did not do their referral homework have been charged as much as $800–$1500. In some cases, you may choose to pay a premium to expedite the processing. But before you start the process, which means hiring a lawyer to help you, find out the current average processing cost so that you will recognize an unfairly high fee.

The Explorer Abroad

If you are in the exploratory stage, you will have tourist or visitor status. In most countries, this allows you to remain for three months, but usually you may have your visa renewed for an additional 90 days and be permitted to extend your sojourn. In these countries you are required to exit the country within 180 days (six months) for a specific period of time, such as 48 hours. Technically, all you must do is remain out of the country for the prescribed time; you could stay at a hotel and return, or as some Americans do, use this six-month timetable to plan trips to the U.S. or to visit other countries. Since you may remain a tourist/visitor as long as you renew your visa (up to the allowable renewal limits) and as long as you leave the country within the legal time frame, you may decide residency isn't necessary.

For longer sojourns, you may want to apply for *rentista* status, which enables you to remain in the country longer than three months without renewing documentation or crossing the border. Time is not the only criterion, however. If you seek renter status in most countries, you must show a certain level of income. In Costa Rica, for example, you must have proof of at least $1,000 in monthly income.

Residency Status

As a resident, you usually live in the country a minimum of six months in each calendar year, and you are not required to exit every six months. On the other hand, residency application involves red tape, document costs and usually a lawyer's fee, but there are advantages:

• You will save on lodging and travel costs. If you do not plan to travel frequently outside the country, or if you live far from the border, residency obviates the need for a six-month exit. David Mead in the northern Thai city of Chiang Mai is a resident. His nearest borders are inconvenient, so as a resident he doesn't need to spend time and money to maintain his visitor status. He is, however, subject to taxation (at a very low rate) on money he brings into the country.

• Residency status usually allows you to import personal items such as household furnishings without duty or at a greatly reduced duty, although many Americans abroad advise purchasing furnishings locally to avoid the complications and expense of shipping.

• Residency may enable you to enjoy low-cost health-care. Peter Haddon in Guadalajara, for example, subscribes to a public health- care program.

• Another benefit of residency is that it can simplify travel to neighboring countries: since you are an official resident of country A, which borders on country B, your travel between the two will be eased by the fact that you are included in the processing of those who regularly travel across the border for business and family visits. Your research will determine if this is an advantage, should you want to plan frequent short trips to nearby countries.

• Under certain circumstances, residency may allow you to work or own a business. As long as your job or business meets certain requirements, as discussed in chapter 6, you may work with a resident status or special resident-worker permit, whereas this is not permitted if you have only visitor status.

Residency is not a requirement for property ownership in most countries, although if you desire residency status, in some countries it may be approved more quickly than for an applicant who is not buying property. (In Portugal, for example, as soon as you sign a promissory contract for purchase of property, you may start your application for residence in motion.)

Documentation

Most countries require several documents for a residency application: birth certificate, often a marriage certificate or divorce decree (when applicable), a financial statement, certification of a clean police record and usually a medical report. The financial statement or proof of income and assets may be supported by tax and banking records, proof of pension, property title, proof of rental income, investments or other income. The host country wants to be sure that you are financially sound and that you do not have a criminal record. Medical requirements vary in stringency and are often very lenient. Canada, on the other hand, has more stringent medical requirements as it does not want pensioners and non-native residents to be a burden on its national medical program.

Each country has its own criteria for residency documents, which are available from that country's embassy or consular office in the U.S. (see addresses in the appendix). Often basic information is available through the country's tourist offices in major U.S. cities. It is not difficult to fulfill these requirements, but be prepared for paperwork. In most cases, people choose to work with a lawyer in the host country to be sure that they have obtained the proper information and that it is in the correct format. An expenditure of a few hundred dollars in lawyer's fees can save you money in the long run. On your exploratory trips, ask Americans in residence for the name of a reliable local lawyer for this purpose.

Another residency status offered by some countries in that of "investor-resident." In Costa Rica, for example, the requirement for this status is an investment of $50,000 or more. In countries where this status is offered, it is usually the easiest kind of residency to acquire. The reason: investments, especially in the tourism industry in developing countries, help the country's gross national product, so red tape is simplified to encourage investment. Another privilege of residency in some countries is tax-haven advantages: residents Lon Temple and Alex Rosarian in Costa Rica live "in the shell of the corporation," with virtually all of their living expenses—both business and daily living costs—qualifying as a tax write-off under the corporate laws of that country.

Pensioner Status

In developing countries, pensioner or retiree status brings benefits to the country and the individual. The country gains hard currency and, in exchange, extends certain privileges. Even in some countries with a higher standard of living, pensioner status may be offered as a category of residency. In both cases, the stability of guaranteed income for an individual or a couple, combined with age requirement, define pensioner status.

Among the benefits are usually the waiver of import duty or tax on purchase of a car. This can result in a savings of as much as 50% on the purchase price in some countries. The alternative—importing your own car—is usually a privilege of pensioner or resident status also, but because of differences in automotive specifications (e.g., emission control devices) you may find that it is difficult to find parts or a mechanic who knows how to properly service your imported car, so it is often advisable to purchase locally. As a non-resident, usually you may import a car (or buy one) but must pay duty.

Renter Status

Renter status, in some countries where this status is offered, requires a higher monthly income level than for a pensioner, since this income is not as reliable as pension income, but there is no age requirement. To renew your status, once a year you will be required to show proof of income. One way to meet the requirement is by using CDs (certificates of deposit) as documentation. Since the country wants assurance that you have brought dollars into the country, for both pensioner and renter status you must show documentation that the minimum monthly income level (e.g., $600 or $1,000) was converted into local currency. In other words, be prepared to keep records.

Although the required financial levels are subject to change and invariably increase, the higher requirements are "grandfathered," that is, applicable only to new residents. There seems to be little risk, once you are admitted to resident or pensioner status at one level, that you would be required to increase your monthly income level. When a country increases its minimum annual level for a renter or pensioner, this does not necessarily mean that your dollars won't stretch as far. Often it only signals the fact that a lower dollar requirement attracts more expatriates. When recruitment is less aggressive, which may be influenced by a change in political leader or party, requirements may rise to stem the flow of applicants. Your cost of living in that country may not change, or could even decrease relative to the exchange of the dollar and local currency.

Insurance Abroad

The United States is probably the most insured—and the most litigious—country in the world. You will find that some of the policies you routinely carry in the U.S. are unnecessary or unavailable abroad. Insurance abroad ranges from slightly less expensive than the U.S. to surprisingly cheap. A closer look at the reasons for such bargains shows, for example, that personal injury insurance (as a feature of auto or homeowner's policy) is uncommon. In Costa Rica, for example, there is no personal injury law, so personal-injury lawsuits are uncommon.

On the other hand, if you are inclined to sue, you will find that there are slim pickings abroad compared with the U.S. And you may not have the satisfaction of seeing the party at fault pay for his or her malfeasance. Harold Parr in Spain notes that auto insurance is inexpensive but that indemnification and settlements are low compared with the U.S. Prosecution for fault is not strictly enforced, reducing the deterrence factor. Harold, who is a lawyer, offers as an example the following case: An American woman's husband was killed in an accident with a reckless driver. The wife received little legal consolation—or compensation—since sentencing did not occur for months, and when it did the driver only received a fine.

A resident of Portugal reports that she has found claims procedures to be very frustrating and recounts an incident in which her husband's car was hit by another driver. "It happened in a small village. Everyone gathered around and someone called the police who came and breathalized the other driver—he was way over the limit. But they handed him his keys and he drove off. Despite documentation of the other driver's alcohol level, we had to pay the deductible and there was no way to prove that it was the other driver's fault without going to court and spending months or years in litigation."

Barbara Moore notes that although you may choose to carry insurance even when it is not mandatory, you should expect to rely on your ingenuity more than you would in the U.S., where insurance settlements are a matter of course. A little ingenuity can save time and money. Barbara, who drives frequently throughout Europe, believes that "you should cover yourself for any country you are in"—as Californians do when driving to Baja for the weekend.

If you are involved in an auto accident abroad, she notes, everyone in the village may gather around. "It's the custom, but it does make you feel rather funny." Like many expatriates, she advises learning enough of the language to manage independently ("even if your verb tenses are wrong") especially if you plan to make frequent driving trips. "I had a minor accident with a market truck that had a wooden railing on the back," recalls Barbara. "We collided and—it was probably my fault—a piece of wood snapped off the back. The driver got out, pointed to it and said he wanted damages. He suggested a high figure. I said, in Portuguese, 'Let's go to the carpenter,' so instead I just paid a fair price to fix the piece of wood. Making a little settlement is often the best thing."

Whether to insure against theft is also a matter of understanding local conditions. Auto theft can be a problem in some urban areas. Dara Glass in Mexico City, who does not carry collision coverage (nor is it mandatory), owns an old Volkswagen. Her best insurance is a strategy: although auto theft is high in this city, her low-profile car is a model not likely to be stolen. Automobile insurance is quite inexpensive in many countries outside the U.S. because labor is inexpensive. You might be required to carry a minimum level of liability insurance (or collision coverage for a new car, if bought on credit), but many Americans abroad choose to "self-insure" since a banged fender costs little to repair. Often the parties in a minor accident settle at curbside. In countries with a higher standard of living, such as France, plan on carrying insurance. The Barbers carry both auto and homeowner's insurance. Says John, "We recently transferred from one agent to another because we thought we weren't getting enough attention."

John notes that with a stone house fire is not a concern and that vandalism in his village is unheard of. You may choose to carry insurance out of habit, but when living abroad you should weigh your usual insurance requirements against local customs and the likelihood of a need to make claims. (Homeowner insurance abroad is likely to differ from the kind of coverage you would have in the U.S. Insurance for flood, earthquake and other natural disasters is not generally available.)

Karen Knight in Portugal notes that her husband had difficulty acquiring auto insurance for their new car until he realized that insurance agents prefer to sell an auto-homeowner's package. The Knights carry collision insurance on their new Renault and Karen says, "We're keeping the insurance while it is still new, but at a point it's cheaper to self-insure." She notes that although her auto insurance is less expensive than in New York, and probably in most regions of the U.S., it is "not particularly cheap." Insurance in Portugal is still a bargain but it is possible that after 1992, as a member of the EC and with an anticipated rise in labor costs for the less-developed member countries, insurance rates could become higher. In less developed countries, or those with a lower standard of living, collision insurance is very low—again, because of cheaper labor for repair and the unlikelihood of liability lawsuits.

In Uruguay, Stanley Walters pays $600 per year for auto insurance ($100 for registration) and Diane and Hal Oster in Costa Rica pay a total of $800 per year for two cars (including $100 each for registration). Similarly, David Mead in Thailand only pays $400 in insurance per year for his new car. Insurance is not mandatory, he explains, "and my rate was recently reduced for having a good driving record." Len Friedman's auto coverage in Guadalajara, Mexico, costs only $257 per year—and he also notes that with his Mexican license plates when he travels to Texas he has no trouble when crossing the border.

Legal Assistance Abroad

When you decide to live abroad, you should set aside your assumptions about the way legal channels operate in the U.S. The experiences of Americans in residence offer the best reorientation, especially if you are the type who frets over legalities.

Law in the U.S. is based on the British legal system, but in countries such as Mexico, Costa Rica, Portugal and Spain, law is based on Roman law. A precedent does not have the importance that it carries in the U.S. By law in Costa Rica, for example, you cannot give up your rights—even if you write a clause in a contract to that effect, it may be superseded by a point of law. So it is important not to rely on contractual "clauses." Notes Jim Fendell, a long-time resident of Costa Rica: "Even if you have reached agreement with another party on a point, it may be invalid because a party cannot give up his rights." A lawyer is necessary for framing any agreement, since you do not know what your rights or those of the other party are.

As explained in preceding chapters, you conduct business differently with a notary abroad than you would in the U.S. The notary in many countries abroad is empowered with a high level of legal authorization, one recognized in other countries as well. Susan Broward and her husband own property in Portugal and in the U.S. At home, they have an appointed power of attorney. Their Portuguese notary enables them to conduct business abroad. Susan explains, "In Portugal, you go to a notary and they have your signature on file. You can take any official document there. They will sign, stamp it and acknowledge that they recognize your official signature as of a certain page in their book. That authorization is acceptable in the U.S. until our next trip, when we will have the document notarized again."

Some documents do require a trip to the U.S. Consulate, however. If you live away from the capital where the consular offices are located, this means planning a trip (expatriates often make this the occasion for a special dinner, shopping or theater). For residents in the Algarve, however, several times each year the U.S. consul visits the expatriate community to provide services such as tax advice.

Because of the high cost of legal fees in the U.S., most of us wouldn't think of retaining a lawyer for everyday business matters such as paying property taxes or utility bills. But in many countries, lawyers perform a wide range of convenient services and for a far lower cost than their U.S. counterparts.

In most countries, the bureaucracy—which translates into standing in long lines and filling out forms—can be quite daunting. Nancy Thalmeyer says she pays $50 per month to avoid such inconveniences and advises, "If you have a good relationship with an attorney, put them on retainer." She recommends this for older retirees, who benefit from not having to run their own legal errands or having to stand in lines. The Thalmeyers also pay extra for preparation of some documents, but the time saving is worth it to them and, says Nancy, "our attorney just calls us in for the signature."

For more complex legal matters, you may feel uncomfortable with the prospect of legal representation by someone whose native language is not English. But you will find that many lawyers abroad have an excellent command of English and, in fact, specialize in working with English-speaking clients. You may also find an expatriate legal "liaison," an American lawyer who is not permitted to practice but who may offer consulting services through a relationship with a local law firm. In most countries you will find that this adage applies: you need a good lawyer, a good doctor and a good auto mechanic. You will find all three if you shop by reputation. Usually you may choose your lawyer—but sometimes you don't have a choice. That doesn't necessarily mean a disaster: Lily Cairns was pleased with the lawyer who helped her purchase her home on the island of Mykonos, and explains: "He handled all the houses in the village."

When you have a choice among English-speaking lawyers (usually you will), you may need to ask several people to determine the kind of lawyer who is right for you. One resident of Portugal's Algarve took a recommendation for a lawyer to help with the purchase of her villa. The lawyer was good, but she believed that after he added on miscellaneous expenses his total fee seemed too high. She learned, however, that changing lawyers didn't solve the problem. She describes her second lawyer: "I got another lawyer who was recommended as being extremely honest. He is extremely honest—but he is also very slow. So I had to look for someone who was both efficient and honest." Her current lawyer lives a few towns away, but the distance is worth it: "She came so highly recommended and by so many different people that I finally decided that she was the person I wanted to use."

Barbara Moore in Portugal advises Americans to become involved in their legal transactions, rather than looking for someone who says "I'll do it all for you." From her experience, and that of her friends abroad, Barbara concludes that the best approach is to ask questions. "When a lawyer says 'no problem,' assume that there could be problems and have him go through the details with you—don't sidestep involvement just because it looks unfamiliar."

The need for legal advice is essential so that you may keep abreast of changes in law. As Nancy Thalmeyer in Costa Rica observes: "Laws are enacted and rescinded. It's a pattern in Latin America"—and in many other countries too, as anyone in the

U.S. knows who has experienced the many changes in tax laws in recent years. Keeping up with change doesn't have to be an isolated task. One of the functions of organizations such as a foreign property owners association, American club or pensioners association is to provide up-to-date information about changing laws and policies. As a group it is possible to organize regular seminars on taxes, documentation and other topics of interest to both new and long-time residents. One of the advantages of this group approach is that the cost of legal counsel to keep members up-to-date is shared by the group.

MEXICO

Chapter 18

Traditions: Exploring Your Heritage

"When I retire, I can see myself spending a large part of the year in Greece. I'm really glad the family home is there."

Nancy Stangos
New York City

This kind of adventure abroad has deep roots in stories and heirlooms and holiday recipes handed down for generations, sepia photographs from another time and place. The country of your grandparents or great-grandparents may hold a strong emotional appeal—Ireland, Italy, Greece, Poland or just about anywhere on the globe that your forebears called home. If you lived abroad as a child, memories could evoke the desire for more than just a vacation: you may choose to live again in your childhood home, if only for a brief time during the middle or later years of your life.

The opening of Eastern Europe is expected to attract an increasing number of retired Americans who recall a childhood abroad and still have old friends and family members in Poland, Hungary and other countries—and whose pension or Social Security dollars will stretch further than in the U.S. Anticipating such a market, Poland is developing retirement housing: new condominiums in Warsaw are currently offered for sale, with the price stated in dollars primarily to attract American buyers.

Cost savings and family ties must be strong for a retiree to choose a country with inclement weather and fewer everyday conveniences than in the U.S. But other countries with favorable weather also attract American expatriates who want to experience their heritage as a returning son or daughter.

Portugal Revisited

Sandra Orgell, who lives in Los Angeles, is in the process of planning a retirement in Portugal—her mother's home, where Sandra lived as a child in 1938. "The last time I returned to Portugal was in 1966—I loved it," says Sandra. "The language came right back to me. I felt a kinship with the area, because my mother was very proud of her heritage and she instilled that in me. I felt very comfortable in Portugal—I also have a capacity for adjusting to different environments."

Sandra, who is in her early 60s and divorced, returned again in 1989. The idea of living in Portugal was rekindled and she began to formulate a plan. When she retires, Sandra will live on her pension and Social Security supplemented by interest income on savings. For her U.S. base, although she plans to sell her home in Los Angeles, she may buy a condominium in Florida. She intends to rent (not buy) an apartment in Portugal where Lisbon is her preferred locale, as she explains: "There are many beautiful condominiums and apartments in the Algarve, but I prefer Lisbon because I would like to be able to go to an opera or play whenever I want, and I love museums and old churches." For Sandra, the outdoor pleasures of the Algarve are less essential than the cultural advantages of Lisbon: "I like to golf and I can probably do that around Lisbon, but I can also take trips to the Algarve for a week or weekend."

Sandra has no family members in Portugal, but she does have a childhood friend who lives in Lisbon, and as she explains: "My friend paints and is quite musical. I think that through her I would meet new friends with the same interests." In Los Angeles, Sandra sometimes attends performances at the Music Center alone, and she is aware that this may not be looked upon favorably abroad. With her friend (and new acquaintances) she expects to find others who will share an afternoon or evening at the theater.

Sandra explains that she is close to her two stepchildren. "They say that if I move to Portugal, it will give them a chance to see me and see Europe, too." She (and her stepchildren) consider Portugal as a convenient home base for travel, especially to London and Paris. To establish her residence, Sandra (like many people with family or friends abroad) has an advantage: her childhood friend, who owns an apartment building, has offered her a place to stay until she decides where she would like to live. Says Sandra: "I don't have any expectations, really. I will just find out how it works out when I get there. I might decide to stay a few months—or a few years."

The Lure of the Emerald Isle

One of the better property bargains in Europe is Ireland, where a sizable number of Americans own holiday and retirement homes. Since Ireland is far from a warm-weather retirement locale, most choose to buy in the relatively hospitable climate of the Southwest coast. Lily Cairns, who owns a home in Greece (and reports that she has no intention of selling it), is thinking of buying a second vacation/investment home in Ireland, where a friend of hers recently bought a home. Good prices are one reason Lily is considering this investment, but she also has a personal reason for choosing Ireland: her grandfather was Irish, and she is therefore entitled to carry an EC passport. Her first choice of an area is Dublin, both for easy airport access and because, as she explains, "I love cities."

Pamela Winger, who recently bought a farmhouse in central Ireland, spent her childhood in London and explains that although she has lived for most of her life in the U.S. she still feels a strong affinity for the British Isles. Her work in the travel industry brings her to Europe frequently. For this reason, she wanted to fulfill a dream of owning a farmhouse in Ireland—one that she could enjoy on stopovers during her business trips, as well as for longer holidays and as a possible retirement home.

The Career Experience

Retirement is the usual time for relocation to the land of one's forefathers, but some people make a midlife move. Unless you can afford an early retirement, however, this probably means seeking employment abroad. If you have supportive friends or family in another country, it may be possible to make an international career change.

Kay and Darren Thomas made such a midlife career change to experience life in Germany for three years. The move was facilitated by Kay's German family and friends in Hamburg, who enabled her to make a transition from a career in banking in the U.S. to a position with a German magazine where a relative was employed.

Like any American seeking employment abroad, Kay had to obtain a special worker's visa that stipulated that her bilingual position did not displace a German worker.

For Darren, the move proved beneficial to his career as an artist. His specialty—landscapes of the American Southwest—was a novelty in the German art market, and so was the artist. He received far more media attention abroad than he ever had at home. "As an American you stand out, no matter what you do," observes Darren, who was interviewed on television programs and also invited to speak on the cultural lecture circuit. On one occasion, he was invited to speak on a program sponsored by the U.S. Consulate, where the other speaker was novelist and poet Charles Bukowski (whose work was popularized in the film *Barfly*). "That was a hard act to follow," says Darren. "After the lecture, I took him on a tour around Hamburg, since I'd learned to find my way around by then."

The Citizenship Factor

Friends and family abroad can be the key to a smooth relocation, and your parentage can also provide other advantages as an expatriate. If you are thinking of relocating "to the old country," or if you anticipate an inheritance, there are steps you should take to assure that an opportunity doesn't become a legal tangle. The questions you need to ask include: as a son/daughter or a grandson/granddaughter of a citizen of this country, am I entitled to an EC passport? If I inherit property, what steps must I take to claim my inheritance? Are there costs such as inheritance tax involved?

For several years, Nancy Stangos has spent her vacations on the Greek island of Kalymnos, from which her parents emigrated 30 years ago. When her parents inherited property, they decided to develop the land and build a home for their retirement. In 1989, Nancy helped her parents make the move "back home."

Her father has American citizenship, but her mother does not. This split arrangement offered several advantages: her mother's Greek citizenship, Nancy explains, "made it easier for her to conduct business with Greece. She maintained her citizenship solely for that purpose—the property is in her name." Although

214

Americans may own property on many of the Greek islands, there are certain restrictions; for example, a foreign national may not own property on a border island as a matter of national security although (as in Mexico) there are ways of arranging a bank trust to own property.

As an American citizen, Nancy's father was able to purchase durable goods in the U.S. such as a washing machine and other appliances. Nancy explains: "This enabled him to have better quality at half the price," since the same items in Greece would be much more expensive. Nancy notes that with a number of Greek-Americans returning to Greece for retirement, businesses have evolved to serve the relocation market. "Through the America-Greece connection you can both purchase and ship items, and they also pick up any furniture you need to ship. If anything goes wrong, there is a representative in Greece to help out."

To make their move—and receive their household items duty free—her parents had to file papers with the Greek Consulate stating that they planned to live in Greece permanently; they were required to list anything they planned to import during a one-year period. "People tend to list anything that comes to mind, and some people take things along and sell them there—it's a one-shot opportunity to do this," explains Nancy.

The only snag in their plans was banking: "They didn't do their homework. Their pension checks were deposited directly into an account in New Jersey. They didn't know they would have a problem accessing their funds in Greece, but now they are clearing it up—changing banks—and soon everything should be okay."

Once major expenses, such as housing and durable goods, are out of the way, day-to-day expenses on Kalymnos are what Nancy describes as "minimal," despite the fact that this island has a wealthier and better-educated population than many of the islands. With their pension and rental income, her parents now have "around twice what they need to live comfortably."

The retirement home cost around $100,000 to build, but Nancy explains: "It is large by Greek standards. It has nine rooms and overlooks a bay, with a terraced garden and 400 square meters of terrace. Six months of the year, you spend a lot of time outdoors." Nancy notes that the architectural style is unusual, and one approved before style restrictions were imposed. The home is of modern Italian design, modified to meet their needs.

There is also a fruit orchard on the property, and the family pays a caretaker to manage the mandarin orange and lemon groves.

The land inherited by the Stangos family was large enough to build three homes. Initially, they built a one-bedroom home (at a cost of around $13,000 in the 1970s), which the family used for holidays and now rents out as a holiday home for $250 per month. The second home they built on the property has two bedrooms and rents for $550 per month. Construction of the two smaller homes was uncomplicated since the structures were relatively simple. Custom work causes more problems, however, and the construction of the Stangos's architect-designed retirement home took five years, many trips across the Atlantic and (as is often the case with absentee owners) "the building was a lot of hassle," says Nancy, "in a lot of cases things had to be redone and people didn't keep their word."

Now that the home is complete, Nancy's parents are enjoying their retirement—their terraces, the blossoming fruit trees, the half-dozen beaches close to their home. Rental income supplements their pension and Social Security income. To inherit, Nancy (an only child) will need to go through legal registration procedures, but for now she enjoys vacationing in Greece, as she has for many years. For the future, Nancy says: "When I retire, I can see myself spending a large part of the year in Greece. I'm really glad the family home is there," and she adds: "Kalymnians come back—even if they have lived in the U.S., France or elsewhere for generations."

A Sojourn in Poland

Laine Arden, who worked as a teacher in Warsaw from 1987 through the summer of 1990, found that the quality of life was far better than she expected to find in an Eastern European country. She notes that a large number of Polish-Americans have chosen to retire in Poland, especially in the smaller towns of the Northeast, where they find they can live very well on pension or Social Security income. "There are people living in Poland from all over the world attracted by a low living cost—Americans, Germans, Scandinavians, Cubans and a lot of foreign students."

A Polish heritage is the main reason most Americans retire in Poland since, as Laine points out, "the weather is miserable. It has the winters of New England or Canada, lots of snow and ice. But the summers are warm and mild, and spring and fall are beautiful." However, fuel costs during the cold winters are far lower than New England or Canada, says Laine: "There is never a lack of electricity or heat. Heat costs the same whether it is off or on. It's charged by the square meter of floor space in your apartment or home."

Housing is still scarce, although this may be changing (as far as American expatriates are concerned) since new apartments are now being built to meet the demand of Polish-American retirees. Prices of the new apartments are advertised in U.S. dollars and range from $60,000 for a two-bedroom apartment upward to $90,000 for a three-bedroom, two-bath penthouse (prices as of mid-1990). As Laine explains: "The Poles are building apartments and condominiums in the international style, and there are also very nice houses on the outskirts of the city, all built within the last 10 years."

Americans envision supply shortages and long lines in Eastern European countries, but as Laine points out, the strength of hard currency makes a big difference in access to goods. She found no lack of imported items. "They were reasonable for me because I paid in dollars. Fancier markets can get anything you might want. I could get avocados, Kiwi fruit, just about anything." Frozen foods are increasingly appearing in the markets, along with all kinds of fresh vegetables and delicacies such as year-round berries in the better markets. In the regular markets, she notes, there is always plenty of standard fare.

Nevertheless, premium market or plain, waiting in line is part of the system. "It is a type of crowd control," Laine explains, "because shops are so tiny that if everyone went in at once they wouldn't fit. In department stores, individual departments have baskets. You first have to stand in line for a basket, then you can enter the department. I had to stand in line just to look at house slippers. Bakeries have lines, too—either you send the maid out early, or you plan to go early yourself."

The lines may eventually become shorter because of retail expansion as Western companies reach for new markets in Poland. Sales commissions have recently been introduced for salesclerks, improving the level of service. "Now they take an interest in whether you buy something, rather than turning their backs and drinking tea," says Laine, who notes that Western companies are introducing everything from restaurants and hotels to specialty shops. "There is a beautiful new Marriott Hotel in Warsaw, more beautiful than any I've seen. It certainly matches any other hotel in cuisine, rooms and service."

Western sources of supply should also bring improvements in medical care, along with cost increases. Laine didn't require medical care during her three years in Warsaw, but she reports that, "In Warsaw there are very well-trained doctors along with a lack of medicine and materials. I had a Polish dentist who only charged $5 for dental work, anaesthetic and materials. And that was high—Poles pay less." Since all medical care is subsidized by the government, in the future prices could rise but would still be very low by U.S. standards.

During the three years that Laine lived in Warsaw, she found no lack of diversions and pleasures. Many films are shown in English with Polish subtitles. "There is great TV reception if you put in a satellite dish. I had Astro, Murdoch's British channels, CNN, IntelSat, Spanish, Italian, French and Soviet channels." Laine's satelite dish took one day to install at a cost of around $800.

Equestrian activities are a favorite with Poles. "There is swimming, tennis, horseback riding. Poland has beautiful horses. People who have never tried it take up horseback riding. There are wonderful trails within 10 minutes in either direction outside

Warsaw. There is also picnicking, camping and skiing—very good skiing in the South," says Laine.

One of her favorite pastimes was to travel throughout Poland. "There is so much of historic interest with castles, palaces and museums—although there is a modest number of great masters. Visiting castles was one of my favorite sports, along with attending concerts." The government subsidy of the arts meant that she could buy the best seats in the concert house for 25 cents. Although these inexpensive seats are still offered, such subsidies will probably be reduced or eliminated in the future, pushed aside by competitive and market-driven business practices.

For years, Poland has enjoyed more freedom of personal expression, commerce and travel than most Eastern European countries. "Poland was always very different from Eastern Europe. They didn't change their way of life very much," Laine observes, noting that Western values are causing change in Poland. Laine notes that unemployment and costs were rising by the time she moved back to the U.S. in August of 1990. "The cost of living until now was cheap relative to the U.S. But prices are going up and there is almost no black market any longer. Things are in flux. There is a lot of anxiety about loss of security, subsidized medical care and education—everything that was provided from cradle to grave."

With the prospect of a short-term increase in unemployment, household help will probably continue to be an advantage for American expatriates. "Household help is inexpensive, plentiful and reliable," says Laine. "The people who do housework usually do it part time, such as housewives or wives of professionals or those who have other jobs and want hard currency." Her household help received $1 per hour, plus Social Security and insurance payment (an additional 30%). Laine's favorite domestic employee worked for the dollar-per-hour rate and didn't need benefits, since her husband's work already covered both husband and wife. "She cleaned floors and windows, played with the cat to keep it from getting lonely and had dinner ready for me when I came home. I wish I could have brought her home to the U.S. with me."

When Laine moved back to the U.S., she traveled light after three years of living abroad, bringing only 2,000 pounds of personal effects (her teaching contract with the foreign service allowed her to move as much as 18,000 pounds). Among the

219

treasures she brought home were paintings and crystal. "The shopping was very good—oil paintings, down comforters, watercolors, wood carvings, embroidered tablecloths, coats and jackets. I brought home lots of crystal and recently saw an imported bowl in a California shop priced at $42—I paid $4 in Poland for one just like it."

Chapter 19

Retirement Preplanners

"I think we all want to try something new. What the hell, we can always go back."

Nathan Barsely
Greenwich, Connecticut

Whether you are 35 or over 65, a future plan to retire abroad is shaped by several factors: age, income/investments, family visits and career commitments. If you are married, or single and in a long-term relationship, another important part of your plan is making couple-based decisions. Some couples can communicate and define their needs, while this is more difficult for others. A tool, such as the Lifestyle Values Inventory (see appendix), can help to define both an individual's and a couple's needs.

In the following profiles of individuals and couples who are in the planning stage, you may recognize dreams, plans and even worries that are similar to your own. These are experienced "preplanners" who have gathered much of the research that leads toward a personally satisfying decision. All have made one or several exploratory trips, and some have already experienced simulated living in another country.

Ages of these advanced retirement planners range from the mid-40s to those who are already retired and looking for an alternative lifestyle to Florida or the Sun Belt. Their families may be grown or still living at home. All have some equity and savings, yet some are assured of a company pension while others are not. Some of the retirement preplanners are years away from retirement, for others it is imminent—but all want a retirement with variety and stimulation, a retirement to look forward to.

Early Retirement by Choice or Chance

Bob Slater faced early retirement at age 58 when his employer, a banking institution, merged with a larger corporation. "I think it's too early to retire, but should I have to—if another offer does not come along—I want to see what is available abroad on my retirement budget," explains Bob.

Ann Slater recalls the night Bob came home with news of the merger. The focus of their discussion quickly shifted from the shock of early retirement when Bob asked Ann: "So—where would you like to retire?" To the Slaters, this question turned unwelcome news into a potential opportunity. Earlier in Bob's career the Slaters lived in Japan and Hong Kong and enjoyed international living; they continued to travel extensively after Bob's work brought him back to the U.S.

The Slaters have discussed what is most important to them as a couple—and individually—and have defined what they are seeking in a retirement location abroad. Bob likes sports and reading; Ann enjoys music and cultural experiences. Of prime importance to both of them is ease of access for visitors. With two grown children in their 20s, they want easy travel for family visits and for their trips back home, since the Slaters plan to divide their year between a home abroad and one in the U.S.

Bob Slater points out that his retirement plan is based on a simple formula: "Given a certain amount of income, how much do you need to live in an alternative location? Ultimately the choice of how and where I retire will be an economic decision." The Slaters love to travel, so their retirement formula includes the estimated cost of maintaining two residences (one in the U.S., one abroad) plus travel. "That adds up to X dollars—that's the formula," says Bob, who notes that the "X" will become a quantifiable cost when they apply it to a specific country.

Bob favors international investments and owning property in more than one country, and for several years has invested in the Spanish Fund with good results. (With any investment, you must observe fluctuations and know when to sell.) Regarding real estate abroad, Bob notes that ownership of international property has long been used as a hedge against the uncertainties of changing economic climates: "When you are bicultural, economically you have two choices. Many foreign nationals have property—and even sons or daughters—in different countries. They spread their bets. I'll wager that Americans will become more that way over time."

After outlining their criteria for a location abroad, a process of elimination began. The Slaters explored countries with good retirement potential, including Portugal, Spain, France, Mexico and Costa Rica. They found several to be appealing. "Costa Rica is economically very attractive," says Bob. "It's easy to buy a home or a lot to build on. But transportation was a problem for us—there wasn't easy access from Dallas, since we would have to go through Miami." In this case, a better connection—if offered by an air carrier—would make Costa Rica more viable for the Slaters.

Another of their criteria was a very warm climate. "I was favorably impressed by Portugal and enjoyed the Algarve, but I found it a bit chilly," remarks Bob. Spain offered a warmer climate, but he and Ann wanted coastal or lakeside property and found that coastal property in Spain was too costly for their budget.

France was another country on their list, one with high marks for the cultural opportunities so important to Ann, but they decided that the more affordable areas did not meet their criteria for year-round warmth. The Slaters' European research turned up an interesting warm-weather alternative, however: the area around Algeciras, Spain, which offers the advantage of warm weather, a coastal location, cost savings (since it is not a highly developed tourist area) and good travel opportunities with proximity to Portugal and Tangier—plus an airport in nearby Gibraltar. The traveling distance from the U.S., though, caused them to eliminate it from their site list.

After exploring several countries, the Slaters now feel that Guadalajara, Mexico, and nearby Lake Chapala offer the best access to and from their home base in Dallas. A plus, says Bob, is that the distance can be managed by car in a fairly comfortable four-day drive, with the added benefit of saving on airline costs.

With his banker's eye for value, Slater found real estate to be attractive in Ajijic, Mexico, near Guadalajara, where a two-bedroom, two-bath, 1,800-square-foot home with a lake view was priced at $75,000 during their trip in 1989. Despite tempting real estate buys, Bob and Ann would plan on renting for at least six months, although he adds, "We may fall in love with a property and buy it."

Although common sense dictates that an American abroad should rent before buying, Bob observes that there is a strong desire to own property—as though somehow it makes you more deeply a part of the country. As Ann points out, there is another appeal to property ownership for those who divide their year: when renting, you must either leave the property unoccupied (while paying rent) or give up the rental, store your belongings and establish a new address when you return six months later. This is one of the primary reasons why most people who divide their year eventually purchase a home or condominium.

Bob offers another approach to owning a part-time property: that is, if the Slaters rent out their home to snowbirds during the winter, it could enhance their budget plans. "The area around Guadalajara has a fairly even temperature all year. Summer is the rainy season, but it's not unpleasant. It would be an interesting trade-off to spend winters in Dallas and summers in Mexico—and it could be very economical because it is not the high season."

Recreation for Two

High on Ann's list of values is cultural stimulation. She plays violin with a chamber group in Dallas but is confident that she would be able to join a musical group (or form one) abroad—that is, as long as the area offers a certain level of cultural interest and attracts expatriates who share her taste for music. Nor does she need American expatriates to enjoy this pursuit. "The wonderful thing about the violin is that you don't need to speak the language. You just put music in front of us and we play," she explains. Her plan is to first approach the U.S. Consulate and find out who in the American community has musical interests, then take her lead from this information to find other musical friends. Another advantage of the Guadalajara area, she points out, is the availability of an English-language newspaper, another good way to reach people with common interests. "The culture in Guadalajara is very attractive, and there are a lot of alternatives," says Bob, who is weighing the urban advantages of Guadalajara against the lakeside setting of Ajijic.

Ann's interests—in music and volunteer activities—are more well defined than Bob's, who admits that it will be easier for her to adjust to retirement than it will be for him. Like many men, career has occupied Bob for so many years that he has given little time or thought to retirement activities, and he is now facing retirement almost a decade before he anticipated.

Bob's first response, when asked about his intended activities abroad, is: "I am sports-oriented; add a good library and I'll get along just fine." Sports events are accessible via satellite broadcast, so that shouldn't pose a problem. He realizes that finding "a good library" might take more effort than in the U.S. But Bob's preference for spectator sports and reading are both passive activities, and he knows he will need some active or creative pursuits.

To this end, Bob is thinking of resuming an old avocation. Ann reminds him that many years ago, early in their marriage, Bob showed considerable skill with portrait painting. "He painted portraits of the family—and he was very good," says Ann. Bob's subject matter may change when he lives abroad; instead of family (who will visit and "sit" for him occasionally), he may try portraits capturing the spirit of a place and its people. The idea appeals to Bob: "I think that painting would be one of my first alternatives—I'd be intrigued by trying it again and I might take more formal training."

Early Retirement by Choice

Charles Yarby recalls that he was vacationing in the Bahamas in 1984—just after his 50th birthday—when "all of a sudden I realized that the opportunity for retirement was imminent—and the Bahamas seemed like a good place to retire."

As a real estate appraiser for the city of Philadelphia, Charles had the option of early retirement at age 55. He considered his assets and decided that he could afford to move his retirement plan forward by 10 years. The mortgage was fully paid on his elegant, restored townhouse (built in the late 1800s), which had greatly increased in value since he purchased it two decades ago. Charles says of the equity in his home: "It gave me the bonus of being able to have a second life."

Divorced, with elderly parents and a daughter just starting college, he knew his plan required regular visits to Philadelphia. He decided to sell the home, purchase a small condominium for a home base, and look for a country abroad where he would spend an increasing amount of time in coming years.

Charles was clear about some of the values he was looking for in a location abroad, although other details emerged after his first experience of simulated living. He wanted an active social life and entertainment with a certain amount of sophistication; he wanted a place where he could enjoy his hobbies—gardening and plant propagation, as evident in the lush terrace and garden of his Philadelphia townhouse, and the black-and-white photography which had been featured in several one-man shows. After three decades in the bureaucracy of civil service, he looked forward to leading what he describes as "a nice, unstructured life."

"I need an active and varied social life. I guess I'm looking for the lifestyle of a person who is not really retired," he says, summing up his idea of "typical retirement" as an endless round of bridge and golf games. "I think I'm in an awkward age group—I don't really identify with the typical retiree." Nor did he want a sedentary life in an American expatriate colony; he hoped to make international friends, travel and mix with the native resident community.

He began by exploring South America, with an eye to duplicating his urban enjoyment of art and architecture while reducing his cost of living. Rio de Janeiro satisfied some of his criteria: "There was a sense of liveliness there, nice restaurants and the style is expressive and I found the women to be stunning." But he decided that relocating to Brazil would be too difficult; the country's problems seemed overwhelming. By comparison with Rio's *favelas*, Philadelphia's poorest districts seemed almost desirable.

He then added further criteria to his search for a home abroad: "I want a place that's tranquil, with little violent crime or apparent ugliness and with few indigents," Charles explains. He returned to his original plan and began investigating island life. He subscribed to *Island Properties Report* and began reading up on the advantages and disadvantages of different islands: political climate, utilities and functional services, amenities and entertainment opportunities. Through his reading and research, he eliminated some islands (including the Bahamas) as too expensive or not viable, and eventually decided on St. Croix, in the U.S. Virgin Islands.

Charles decided not to offer his townhouse for sale until he had experienced simulated living abroad, so he found a house sitter for his Philadelphia home base while he tried living on St.

Croix. With only a few necessities such as clothing and his camera equipment, he set out for the island with a plan to live there for a few months. If he liked it, he would return home, sell his house, buy a small condominium for return trips and make the island his primary home.

After a few days in a hotel, he found an apartment. His life centered around the beaches and cafes, but after a few months he found the tranquil life a bit too mild, and even his photographic opportunities seemed to dry up.

As he continues his retirement exploration, Charles Yarby may have some difficulty finding the items on his wish list. He wants both tranquility and stimulation, simplicity along with sophistication, all in an affordable location abroad. But he continues his quest—and his latest destination is Portugal, where he may just find what he's been looking for: a country rich in culture and architectural heritage, easy access to stimulating European cities and an opportunity to cultivate international friendships and enjoy a varied social life.

Exploring Solo

For many people, planning a retirement is a pleasant excuse for a couple vacation—but when one partner isn't able to take the time because of work or family commitments, the other spouse may be glad to assume the role of explorer. Cost savings (the price of one expedition instead of two) is one advantage. Or one partner may be more enthusiastic about living abroad than the other, who relies on the spouse to make the first cut among options for living abroad, and trusts that if the scout finds the right locale, the other partner is likely to enjoy it, too. An example is Brian Jones.

Since retiring from a position in aerospace a year ago, Brian has been the primary scout in his family, exploring various countries in search of a home base abroad. With a son still living at home, and with Brian's wife still employed as an elementary school principal, the Joneses rely on Brian to preview retirement locales.

His wife joined him on a trip to Spain, where they were bitten by the bug for living abroad. One of the criteria they agreed on at the time (but have since eliminated as unimportant) was their preference for a high altitude. Brian set out on a second trip to Andorra, which provided a high altitude and the advantage of a

227

tax haven, but he found that Andorra had a higher cost of living and more air pollution than anticipated, and he found it lacking in cultural interest.

His next trip was to Costa Rica, which is now his first choice for retiring abroad. When Brian suggested Costa Rica, Ellen had some reservations: "Somewhere she got the idea that Central America is always humid, which it isn't. And I think she wasn't too interested in a Latin country, perhaps because she was concerned about the attitude toward women," explains Brian. He liked Costa Rica, didn't experience a humidity problem, saw many women in professional positions and concluded, "I think she would like it here." One of the persuasive points about Costa Rica is its beautiful beaches, which he and Ellen would enjoy as a couple. Not least important, he found prices in line with his budget plan.

As a move abroad becomes more likely, Brian will need to modify his hobby, which he describes as "a study of the complexities of history, politics and religion, and their influence on a culture." He will store his current library and papers, and start a new collection of material related to the culture of his second home.

Seeking Compatible Neighbors

Nathan Barsely of Connecticut is also interested in history, culture and travel, but after six decades in the Northeast his first requirement is a pleasant winter climate. Nathan plans to have a "traveler's retirement": his goal is to maintain a condominium or small home in the U.S., since as he explains, "I don't want to be a permanent expatriate." He does not plan to buy property abroad and one reason is mobility, since he hopes to experience more than one country, or as he explains, "We may stay six months or more perhaps in Portugal, Spain or Greece."

On his preferred lifestyle, Nathan says: "I like good food, good books, pleasant company—and I don't want total resort living." He assumes that the "club complex" life would limit his opportunity to meet a variety of people. But most resort developments abroad attract residents of many different nationalities, although it does require outreach to make friends in the native community. Nathan accepts the likelihood that most of his acquaintances will be American expatriates, so he is concerned about the type of Americans who are in residence and says, "I will try to determine the percentage of soldiers of fortune and ex-military compared with those who formerly were teachers or professors or who had other kinds of careers before moving abroad."

For his leisure time, Nathan looks forward to learning new languages, studying history and possibly writing with an eye toward eventual publication. In recent years, his experience as a former judge has proven useful off the bench. He is often the mediator of disputes in the neighborhood, finds this kind of busman's holiday satisfying—and is sure there will be ample opportunity to similarly assist his American neighbors abroad. Nathan sums up his plan as an adventure with a home base, and says, "I think we all want to try something new. What the hell— we can always go back. Let's try it."

Deciding to Stay Home

Retirement exploration can lead to the conclusion that you prefer to stay home—or that you prefer to live in some other region of the U.S. After considering alternatives, you may decide that an occasional trip abroad is sufficient to satisfy your need for adventure. But you will have the satisfaction of a decision based on exploratory experience, rather than always wondering: What is it like to be an insider rather than a tourist?

Paul and Cindy Blair, in their 50s, practice real estate in Southern California. Cindy says of their exploration of Spain, Mexico and Costa Rica: "Every place we have seen is right for somebody." Cindy may be that "somebody"—as she is more enthusiastic about living abroad than her husband Paul. One area that appealed to her was Spain's Costa del Sol, but Paul was reluctant to move across the Atlantic and says: "I didn't think we'd move *that* far, another continent away."

As their exploration progressed, they came close to deciding on Mexico. "One of the appealing things about it is transportation. It's inexpensive to get to Guadalajara, and it's an inexpensive cab ride to Lake Chapala from the airport," offers Cindy, who says she would look forward to visits from family and friends. Another plus, she notes, is good transportation to Mexico City for special shopping and entertainment, since it is only four hours away from Guadalajara on a comfortable and well-appointed train.

The Blairs were surprised to discover furnished property from $55,000, and were tempted by a nice home with a pool on Lake Chapala, priced at $100,000 (in 1989). The low cost of living was appealing, since their operating expenses are $3,000 per month in Orange County, California, and someday they will need to live on a fixed income. The Blairs' initial strategy was to buy abroad in a locale with a modest cost of living, so that they could enjoy retirement without reducing their style of living.

As they looked at property around Lake Chapala, one special home won Cindy's heart: a large, furnished, lake-view property with an asking price of $350,000. "I would describe it as comfortably elegant. The home was out of this world—and I've seen a lot of residential property in my career," says Cindy, adding, "it would have cost two million dollars in Palm Springs."

But the Blairs were beset by doubts as they continued their retirement exploration. Cindy was dismayed by the fact that across the street from her elegant dream home was "a little typical Mexican house." Paul liked the golfing facilities, but Cindy was concerned about another aspect of their leisure time, as she explains: "The Americans here obviously do most of their entertaining at home. In California we are out almost every night at different restaurants." Gourmet dining is important to the Blairs, but they cast a critical eye on restaurant fare in Mexico (and decided that San Miguel de Allende's food was preferable to cuisine sampled in Guadalajara). Cindy knew that home help was abundant and affordable, but since her life in the U.S. does not include home entertaining, she felt that this would be a big adjustment.

San Miguel de Allende was their next stop, where they liked the city's architecture, culture and altitude. When they arrived, the resort hotel in an outlying area turned out to be pleasant and spacious, but transportation to San Miguel by minibus was too inconvenient for serious exploration. Next, they moved to a hotel on the city square, arranged for a home tour and found ample opportunity to meet resident Americans and find out more about life in San Miguel.

An affable, outgoing couple, the Blairs found it easy to make friends in both Guadalajara and San Miguel. Cindy liked the artistic spirit of San Miguel's American community and observes: "They all know one another—art seems to be the source of their social activity." She found it easy to meet Americans just about everywhere, from a piano bar to the English-language library to an evening art exhibition. "I think it's easy to meet people—I could get very involved in San Miguel," says Cindy.

After exploring Spain, Costa Rica and Mexico (and enjoying the adventure, since as a business couple their research gives an extra edge to travel), the Blairs have come to a conclusion: "We're hitting all points of the compass, but at this point I don't feel we'll live outside the U.S.," says Paul.

Cindy, on the other hand, shows some disappointment with Paul's conclusion and is concerned about his eventual retirement and how he will spend his leisure time. Although she is involved with the arts community in Southern California, so far Paul has not developed outside interests, and Cindy remarks, "We live, eat and breathe real estate." For now, they plan to stay home and remain active in their business beyond the traditional retirement age. At some point, however, they will have to face the issue Cindy raises about living abroad when she says: "It would give us something interesting to do."

Moving On

If your first retirement site disappoints you, move on. Wanda Grieg is one of the solo explorers who seeks an international alternative while her spouse prefers to await a report back home. During the early years of their marriage, Wanda and Jim lived in Germany. Now that he is retired, they live in Hemet, California, a desert community with a large retirement population. "I already know what our priorities are," says Wanda.

Hemet was a village when she and Jim moved to the area over a decade ago, but it has become very crowded. "In the winter there are 10,000 snowbirds. It's one of the most inexpensive places you can live in Southern California, so everyone is going there." After an exploratory trip to Costa Rica, Wanda concluded that it met several of her criteria including ease of access and another benefit that the retirement community of Hemet does not provide, or as she explains: "I need independent public transportation."

Costa Rica has efficient and frequent bus service in San José and to outlying towns and rural and beach areas. Although today Wanda (who is in her late 50s) drives a sporty classic Porsche, she has an eye on her future. Hemet has no public transportation and she has seen problems that result when a large group of older drivers are concentrated in one area—a problem that will increase in coming years with the graying of the Baby Boomer population. Wanda has seen numerous accidents with older drivers, whose eyesight or judgment is not as keen as when their latest licenses were issued, or who drive with expired licenses because they have no alternative transportation. But she points out that independence is essential for an older person's self-esteem. "It comes back to transportation. It has become dangerous to drive in Hemet. I want to grow old gracefully—independent and healthy."

Another of her criteria for a retirement locale is stimulation, for herself, her husband and visitors. "If my grandchildren visit, there would be so many things to show them," she says of Costa Rica, where Wanda considers the University in San José a great resource. "I consider the potential of a country for my grandchildren to visit—my five-year-old grandson is already learning Spanish, and I'll learn it there."

Other items on her agenda for retirement are: a place where she can take walks ("You have to get exercise to be healthy. I take a long walk every morning.") and the availability of fresh fruits and vegetables, preferably in neighborhood markets. She points out that the convenience stores, which are increasingly becoming the neighborhood markets in the U.S., stock only processed foods; many elderly people in the U.S. rely on convenience stores, especially if transportation isn't available.

Wanda describes herself as "a doer not a joiner" and intends to be active in retirement. She is in good health and rarely has occasion to visit her physician, but is not daunted by the prospect of medical care abroad: "In Hemet, most of the doctors are of different nationalities, so it certainly doesn't bother me to think of going to a clinic or doctor's office in another country."

Previously, Wanda worked as a dietitian and with institutional food management—one reason she is concerned about fresh food, opportunities for healthful walks and water quality. "I am pretty particular about manageable soft water. I've lived where you have to use softeners, and it can be a pain. Hard water leaves stains on things. I can tell if it's hard or soft the minute I take a shower, and Costa Rica has soft water."

Although Wanda and Jim have traveled widely together, often she takes trips by herself or with a friend. A few years ago, she made an exploratory trip to Greece with her college-age daughter, Barbara. Wanda decided that Greece would be too far from home for a retirement locale, but the trip resulted in a pleasant surprise: during a bus trip their seatmates were a French couple with a daughter Barbara's age. For two years, Barbara had expressed interest in arranging an exchange with a European family, but this was only a vague wish until the trip to Greece. The subject came up naturally during a conversation on the bus. Wanda and Barbara exchanged addresses with the French couple, arrangements were made through letters and the following year Barbara's hoped-for exchange became a reality. The Griegs' enjoyment of international experiences is shared by their children—who encourage their parents to retire abroad. "Ever since we lived in Germany 30 years ago, we have thought about living abroad," says Wanda. "It puts a new lease on life. When you get older, I think you can get too complacent—you have to keep moving to stay agile."

A Hacienda in Mexico

The expatriate boating community is the center of Matt and Joan Feldman's social life in La Paz (Baja Sur), Mexico, a quiet enclave near the more reknowned tourist spot, Cabo San Lucas. "We prefer not to see it become a Cabo, but more ecologically oriented," explains Joan. "Our access to desert islands and the location on the bay is really unique."

The Feldmans knew where they wanted to live, so the only question was whether to choose La Paz or a more isolated locale. "Even though we might live on a prettier beach out of town, in La Paz we have markets and services. It's challenge enough moving to a foreign country without making it hard on yourself by living 60 miles from a supermarket," says Joan, who shops at American-style markets that carry a variety of local and imported goods and where prices are similar to those in the U.S. For bargains in a more charming but less convenient setting, she notes: "There are also farmers markets, and they're fabulous." If the supermarkets aren't a great bargain, the restaurants are: "You can go out to a good restaurant and have a complete meal for two with drinks for under $20," Joan says, although she admits that she and Matt miss California wine (and bring some back every trip home). They also miss oriental food; there is one Chinese restaurant in La Paz, but no Japanese or Thai. "Once in a while I miss Italian food, so I cook it at home," says Joan.

Many of the American expatriates are related to the boating community. "The marina is the communications center for everyone. Many of our friends cruised down years ago and bought a home," explains Joan. Although some expats live on their boats, the Feldmans—who own a boat in partnership with another couple—bought a two-bedroom home in a new multi-unit development for $100,000 at the end of 1989. "It would cost $400,000 in Marin County [California], " says Joan. "It's beautifully designed in the Mexican style with arches and tile everywhere—floors, roof, counters and bath." The designer, Max Shroyer, is well known in Baja, and in addition to residential architecture is also the designer of the fiberglass Panga boat.

Although the Feldmans are full-time residents, they maintain tourist status with a return to the U.S. every six months. "We've done our research to become retired residents," explains Joan, who is 43. (Her husband is 63.) "We might pursue it, mainly to avoid the six-month exit requirement. It also regularizes your status because you feel more a part of the country. The government encourages people to apply for resident status rather than to go back and forth." The Feldmans are still weighing the pros and cons of changing from tourist to resident. "We know people who have been here many years on a tourist visa and others who are residents. We've heard arguments on both sides."

Matt's interest in this part of Mexico dates back three decades, when he first began fishing in Baja. Early in their marriage the Feldmans vacationed in the area once or twice a year, then in 1988 they decided to rent an apartment for a few weeks. "That was when we started to feel connected with the community and saw there was a viable lifestyle for us," says Joan.

They bought their home through a development. Since it was under construction, they knew from the specifications exactly what they would need to furnish their home. Unlike some Americans who prefer to move with few belongings, the Feldmans decided to take "a household full of goods." Transportation of personal property was much easier than they expected, as Joan explains: "We exported through Columbia Export (Chula Vista, California). There were 200 tagged items and a computer printout of declared value. We paid duty at Tijuana and La Paz. Everything arrived safely with no damage or loss. We feel that is the correct legal way to do it—and we did not have to pay *mordida* (a bribe), either." She found that as long as duty is paid, you can bring virtually anything you want. "Within two weeks of consignment, everything was in our house. It cost $3,500, including delivery to our door. It surprised me, since when we moved 10 miles in California, it cost $1,000 for a one-day trip for the same size load. The Feldmans also brought along their Chevrolet pickup truck and a Jeep Cherokee, with no red tape involved. "If we have resident status, I don't think there will be any effect on keeping our cars," she notes.

The Feldmans' activities in La Paz include charity work through Club Cruceros, a gringo organization that began its auction as a chance to swap old boating equipment with proceeds donated to the area's needy children. The charity auction has expanded to include goods from residents and businesses in the area; last year it raised money to buy presents for 2,500 children.

Another way to become more involved with the community, Joan feels, is to learn Spanish. After her first six-week course, she found it beneficial to study with a private teacher. "The one-on-one is intense and extremely rewarding," says Joan. "I now read the daily newspaper in Spanish, although I don't understand every word. I can converse with a patient person and get my daily business done—I feel good about that. I'd like to become fluent. It frustrates me to talk like a three-year-old. But many Americans live here for years and never learn more than *gracias* and *una cerveza mas*—and they manage to function very well." Matt, she observes, has a grasp of "menu Spanish" but hopes to make more progress. A good way to practice is to cultivate acquaintances in the Spanish-speaking community. The Feldmans were pleased when a Mexican neighbor made a friendly overture. "He's an architect," explains Joan. "We take walks in the evening and we have been to each other's homes. That is an honor for us." Most of their friends, she notes, are Americans and Europeans.

For entertainment, the Feldmans have satellite TV with over 100 channels, and the English-speaking community also has video exchanges. The only movie theater in town often plays American films and the municipal theater occasionally offers symphony or ballet. La Paz, however, is not a cultural center. Most expatriates get together to share satellite broadcasts of major sports events or entertain friends at home or on their boats.

"We love to have people come down to visit, but we don't have room for houseguests so we put them up in an apartment or hotel," says Joan. "It works out nicely," she adds, "and makes it a more comfortable visit both for them and for us."

The Feldmans carry Blue Cross health insurance in the U.S. and are interested in researching other international insurance options. For now, Joan reports, "We've been very happy with medical care here. The military hospital—the best hospital in La Paz—takes care of tourists. You only pay for medicine and a doctor's visit costs under $20. We have an English-speaking doctor who has taken care of all our woes. Prescription drugs are much cheaper than in the U.S. and on my husband's blood pressure medicine alone we save hundreds of dollars a year." Joan believes a person doesn't really need insurance, but she would feel more comfortable having a major medical policy that would cover them outside the U.S.

In the past year there have been surprisingly few drawbacks, notes Joan. "The summer is hot but not humid, so we didn't find it that uncomfortable. The house is well designed and cooled with cross ventilation. In the summer you get up earlier and at midday you take it easy." One of the few frustrations has been the lack of a telephone. "We're anxious to get our telephone and don't know when that will be—we've been told a few months. We haven't missed it too much. We just fax at the Marina," explains Joan, who adds: "Other than that, I can't really think of any frustrations. We really love it and feel more comfortable here than anywhere. It's a different pace."

Matt adds: "We live in beautiful, clean air on the edge of a gorgeous sea that presents us with all kinds of marine life to observe. The city is exciting—you have a chance to see people go about their lives. They take the time to enjoy themselves, the time to talk and laugh and celebrate. People ask us 'What do you do all day?' We have our social work and other activities. Some days we get up in the morning with nothing to do and somehow we only get it half done."

Chapter 20

Future Developments and Forecasts

Global developments—some predictable, others unexpected—will affect your choice of a country in which to sojourn for a few months or live for several years. Some of the changes now on the horizon are sure to make international living smoother and reduce red tape in the future. These include expanded international and electronic banking and improved telecommunications (including fax, so that you can tend to business, if necessary, from thousands of miles away).

Some observers of the international scene believe there will be more accessible worldwide medical insurance—possibly even a type of Medicare for retired U.S. citizens abroad. With inexpensive health care available in many countries, a credit/reimbursement system might turn out to be a cost saver for both government and private insurers when the huge post-World War II generation reaches retirement age.

A Vacation Home in Cuba?

The opening of Eastern Europe increases the options for low-cost international living. A sentimental journey—possibly extended to a stay of months or years—in the country of your grandparents or great-grandparents may be both viable and desirable. Yugoslavia, for example, is a potential holiday and retirement haven, especially its sunny coastal region. The rich cultural tradition of Hungary may attract Hungarian descendants whose families emigrated to the U.S. in the 1950s. The next generation might look to Cuba or Nicaragua for holiday homes or retirement living—unthinkable until the Berlin Wall turned into souvenirs, but in the future, who knows?

The Arrival of the EC

The impact of the European Community, which will be fully in effect in 1992, could have several consequences for Americans who desire to live or retire abroad.

The less-developed member countries will receive subsidization by the EC to improve infrastructure: many primary roads that are now narrow and unnerving if not perilous could be reconstructed as smooth and safer highways; utilities, including unreliable electrical service and telephone systems, will be upgraded to enable international business to flow across borders. Today in many countries you must wait months or even years for telephone installation; this is almost certain to improve in the future.

Imported food from all EC countries will be available throughout Europe—you will find an array of Northern European cheeses in Southern Europe if you wish, or a packed-with-fiber Scandinavian cereal if you are tired of fresh bread from the local baker. Along with the flow of imports, some flavor of local tradition could be lost. To recapture it, you may need to travel away from the larger commercial and tourist areas, to where small towns are not likely to have Euro-supermarkets. The global market will first reach areas with the largest, most potentially profitable, population. So you might want to start working on your language skills—if you want to live or spend time where old traditions prevail.

Countries of the EC—the United Kingdom, Ireland, Germany, France, Luxembourg, Italy, Spain, Portugal, Greece, Denmark, Belgium and The Netherlands—are all expected to enjoy stronger economies as a result of the unified Euromarket. Northern Europeans are already buying holiday and retirement homes in the sunny South—and this trend will increase as the traditional inter-country barriers and bureaucratic red tape dissolve. Prices in countries that have been a bargain, such as Portugal, Spain and Greece, will continue to rise. Labor, in popular tourist areas, may become more expensive; with increasing employment opportunities for residents, household help (now extremely inexpensive in many countries) could cost more.

For investment purposes—a vacation home or future retirement home in any of the EC countries—coastal land is the most likely to increase in value. For a person interested in speculative investment, the place to buy may be European coastal areas that are not primary tourist destinations but have no apparent drawback other than a location rather far from the current center of development. As coastal land becomes less affordable, residents of major European cities will look for inland country property a reasonable distance from major cities. This trend is already under way; in France, for example, Parisians look for country homes within a few hours' drive of Paris as a *maison secondaire*.

International Retirement Communities

International investors are almost certain to pursue the demographic curve by building retirement villages in affordable, warm-weather countries—well-organized, full-service communities with recreational and health-care facilities. The demographics are clear: There will be a retirement boom in the U.S. starting around the year 2000 when the older Baby Boomers reach early retirement age and begin shopping for a high-quality and stimulating retirement-living concept.

Undeveloped or underdeveloped coastal areas in the Western Hemisphere are likely to become prime locations for holiday homes of the future. Even inland areas with a mild climate (which now may be very inexpensive) will become desirable for holiday and international retirement living. In Europe, the rampant development in areas such as Spain's Costa del Sol has provided a lesson in planned growth, as is now enforced by Portugal, Greece and other countries that impose density, height and architectural restrictions to preserve a region's desirability. So far, there is little evidence of long-term planning south of the U.S. border—the best investments will be in areas where some foresight is evident in the development plan.

From Cabaña to Coup

There is an element of unpredictability with any developing (a euphemism for "third world") country. Political change can transform a country with good potential for international living into a flyover: the Philippines, for example, was developing an attractive incentive program for American retirees in 1988. The appeal included several of the qualities that expatriate retirees prefer: a warm climate, low-cost housing and cost of living, inexpensive domestic help. But volatile political conditions—still as of spring 1991—make this an ill-advised retirement or holiday home destination.

The opening of Eastern Europe does not assure a similar change in troubled countries of Latin America. With vast economic problems and widespread poverty, there is always the possibility that a military strongman could step in and announce that Americans are unwelcome. A breakdown of basic services due to inefficiency or corruption could decimate the quality of life, no matter how inexpensive the cost of living for an American with hard currency, no matter how desirable the climate. In such countries, the best strategy is always to rent, not buy, and to avoid burning all your bridges to friends and family in the U.S.

Toward a Global Village

Despite these words of caution, the prospects are very good for an increasing number of desirable places to retire or vacation, to live part-time or permanently abroad. Investment potential in many countries is excellent. Bargains still exist, and are likely to expand with the entry of Hungary, Poland and other countries into the world marketplace. Hard currency is always welcome, and so are Americans, who—for all our faults—are appreciated for the best qualities of our expatriates: an openness and generosity of spirit. For a nation founded on countless nationalities, it is not surprising that the grandchildren and great-grandchildren of immigrants love to travel. In a land founded by adventurers, it is not surprising that many of us—especially those who want a different kind of retirement—are looking forward to adventures abroad.

Appendix

Lifestyle Values Inventory

After reading the preceding chapters, we hope you have gained a better idea of how you want to shape the coming years, whether your ideal location is a tropical setting, a rural cottage, a European city rich with tradition, or even a condominium in Florida.

Your retirement may be years away, or rapidly approaching. Whatever your timetable, retirement is inevitable for everyone except those who are self-employed and choose to work until failing health forces a retreat. The idea of retiring from a routine working life brings with it certain anxieties, but retirement can be a challenge instead of a crisis if it is anticipated with creative planning. Contrary to popular opinion, there can be a great deal of control over the aging process. Recent studies have shown that mental alertness may depend more on the efficiency of the heart and lung system than on chronological age. Exercise is one component; you also need to stay in good mental condition.

Your appetite for living and level of contentment are greatly dependent upon having a positive self image. When role identities change, a loss of direction and self-worth can result. People often complain of feeling adrift, a feeling labeled "retirement syndrome" which can be remedied once it is recognized.

Traditionally, men have experienced this loss of role identity to a greater extent than women, but clearly this is changing as more women pursue careers. Some goal or activity is needed to replace the lost endeavor or job in order to give meaning, focus and worth to retirement life. Moving to a different locale often opens new horizons: new friends, new surroundings, and a new culture all energize an individual and eliminate boredom and dullness as a cause of debility.

In the following Lifestye Values Inventory, by ranking your response to the 45 questions on the following pages you will be able to identify the personal values that are important when you decide to move abroad. The Lifestyle Values Inventory was developed from a study conducted by Dr. John C. Flanagan of American Institutes for Research, Palo Alto, California. The title of the study is "Identifiying Opportunities for Improving Quality of Life of Older Age Groups." It was prepared for the Administration on Aging (Department of Health & Human Services), to assist in policy making for the increasingly aging American population. A representative national sample was obtained from in-depth interviews with 2000 men and women between the ages of 50-70. The interviewees were from all walks of life and from diverse geographical locations throughout the United States.

After completing the questionnaire, in which you rank each factor in importance by assigning a value from 1 to 5 (highest), you will be able to derive a final score that offers important insights about what is important to you. The chapters of this book discuss these values as they arise when you live or retire abroad.

As noted previously, a relocation in retirement can be harmful when it threatens self esteem. What is the key to your self esteem? Is it linked to a certain type of social interaction, intellectual growth, creativity, helping others, or some other factor—perhaps one you have never seriously considered?

When you chose to read *Adventures Abroad*, you began to explore an option. The Lifestyle Values Inventory is an instrument that will sensitize you about what you value in your life and, eventually, in your retirement. The outcome may be a surprise to you, for often we are not really conscious of the strong motivating influences in our lives.

Note: For the most accurate results from the Lifestyle Values Inventory questionnaire, it is important to follow directions in the sequence given.

PART A: LIFESTYLE VALUES INVENTORY QUESTIONNAIRE

The statements below represent values which people consider important in retirement and often seek in later years.
Read each statement carefully and indicate how important it is for you.

Check the Number to Show How You Rate the Statement

5 means "very important"

4 means "important"

3 means "moderately important"

2 means "of little importance"

1 means "unimportant"

At this time in my life I value a retirement in which I......	5	4	3	2	1
1...can enjoy my spouse's companionship.					
2...can socialize with a variety of friends.					
3...can play golf/sports; take short sightseeing trips.					
4...have time for introspective thinking.					
5...can do things with close friends.					
6...can travel extensively.					

7...can attend concerts, plays, entertainment and sporting events.				
8...can have time to pursue my hobby.				
9...belong to a social/civic club.				
10...can live in an attractive house/apartment.				
11...can develop my contemplative skills.				
12...can meet new people.				
13...can have discussion sessions with friends.				
14...am living nearby my relatives.				
15...live in a neighborhood safe from robbery/assault.				
16...can use my abilities in a satisfying way.				
17...can participate in college lecture series/study groups.				
18...can be of help to my brothers/sisters or relatives.				
19...will be able to play with grandchildren frequently.				
20...am challenged in some type of productive activity.				
21...have time to express myself in an avocation.				
22...learn better communication skills/perceptions.				
23...receive care from competent physicians/dentists.				
24...can be appreciated by someone of the opposite sex.				
25...can help my children in their households.				

	5	4	3	2	1
26...can help in the organizations of my church.					
27...learn about a new topic through reading or adult education.					
28...have a meaningful part-time job.					
29...can express myself through some personal enterprise (painting, cooking, photography, writing).					
30...can be free to spend time in recreational reading.					
31...can play games, i.e. dominos, bowing, bridge, etc.					
32...can be a member of a social club or organization.					
33...am free of chronic/major illness.					
34...can improve my skill in some activity I've not had time for.					
35...can watch TV or listen to music.					
36...become politically active in my community or neighborhood group.					
37...will have someone to love and share with.					

38...can have a comfortable income.				
39...be free to attend social gatherings.				
40...will be active in a singing or dance group.				
41...will be able to see and visit my children frequently.				
42...can be a volunteer for a group that needs help.				
43...can read periodicals to keep informed about social and political problems.				
44...can celebrate the holidays with relatives.				
45...will be an active member of state or national political groups.				

Turn to Part B

Part B:

Self Scoring Procedure For Lifestyle Values Inventory

1.15 value codes (MF, HS, etc.) are listed below, each with three assigned statement numbers.

2. Record your score from **PART A: *Lifestyle Values Inventory Questionnaire*** for each statement opposite its number. Example: if you checked 5 (very important) for Statement 6 (can travel extensively) put a 5 next to statement number 6 below.

3. Be sure you assign a score to each statement number.

Statements	Statements	Statements	Statements
6-	15-	1-	19-
10-	23-	24-	25-
38-	33-	37-	41-
MF total-	HS total-	SP total-	CH total-

Statements	Statements	Statements	Statements
14-	2-	9-	36-
18-	5-	26-	43-
44-	13-	42-	45-
REL total-	FR total-	HLP total-	GVT total-

Statements	Statements	Statements	Statements
17-	4-	16-	8-
27-	11-	20-	21-
34-	22-	28-	29-
LN total-	UND total-	JOB total-	CR total-

Statements	Statements	Statements
12-	7-	3-
32-	30-	31-
39-	35-	40-
SO total-	PR total-	AR total-

4. Total the three numerical amounts you have listed for each VALUE. This is your **totaled score**. The highest possible total is 15. If you have a totaled score for any value greater than 15 or less than three, check your scoring.

5. Turn to the chart titled **Part C: *Lifestyle Factors*** and do steps **6** and **7**.

Procedure for Scoring Parts C & D

6. On Part C: titled *Lifestyle Factors* under the Points 5-1, circle the number or set of numbers which match your totaled score for each factor on Part B.

Example: If your totaled score for MF is 11 you would circle 12-10 under Point 3.

7. On Part D: *Ranking of Importance to You* put a ✓ in one of the three columns (High, Medium or Low) opposite each of the 15 factors (MF, HS, etc.) according to the point under which you circled your raw score on Part C: *Lifestyle Factors.* For example: if your raw score for MF was 3 on part C, you would check Medium: 3

You have now ranked which of the 15 factors are of high, medium or low importance to you in your retirement.

Turn to Part E for an interpretation of this ranking.

PART C: LIFESTYLE FACTORS

POINTS	5	4	3	2	1
FACTORS	(Circle your raw score)				
MF	15	14-13	12-10	9-6	5-1
HS	15	14	13	12-10	9-1
SP	15	14-13	12-7	6-4	3-1
CH	15	14	13-8	7-4	3-1
REL	15	14-12	11-8	7-4	3-1
FR	15	14-13	12-8	7-5	4-1
HLP	15	14-13	12-9	8-4	3-1
GVT	15	14-13	12-6	5-4	3-1
LN	15	14-13	12-5	4-3	2-1
UND	15	14	13-11	10-6	5-1
JOB	15	14	13-10	9-5	4-1
CR	15-14	13-9	8-5	4-3	2-1
SO	15-14	13-11	10-8	7-4	3-1
PR	15-14	13-11	10-8	7-5	4-1
AR	15-14	13	12-7	6-4	3-1

Part D: Ranking of Importance to You

Points	High: 5-4	Medium: 3	Low: 2-1
MF			
HS			
SP			
CH			
REL			
FR			
HLP			
GVT			
LN			
UND			
JOB			
CR			
SO			
PR			
AR			

Turn to Part E for an interpretation of your ranking.

Part E: Quality of Life Values

The following key is designed to help you interpret the results of the Lifestyle Values Inventory. Chapters in which these values are discussed are noted in parentheses.

PHYSICAL AND MATERIAL WELL BEING

MF - Material well-being and financial security

Continued expectation of having good food, comforts, possessions and a home. Money and financial security are important factors. (Chapters 3, 4, 13, 14, 20)

HS - Health and personal safety

Enjoying freedom from illness, posessing physical and mental fitness, avoiding accidents and other health hazards; effective treatment of health problems, aging and death is also included in this category. (Chapters 15, 16, 17)

INTERPERSONAL RELATIONS

SP - Relations with spouse or other close personal relationship.

Marriage or having a long-term personal relationship involving love, companionship, sexual satisfaction, understanding and communication. (Chapters 5, 19)

CH - Relationships with your children.

Raising children, observing their development, spending time together as a family. Molding character, offering guidance and help, appreciation of children and of learning both from and with them. (Chapters 10, 11)

REL - Relations with parents, siblings or other relatives.

Relationships in which one experiences communication, sharing experiences, visiting, helping each other. The feeling of belonging and having someone with whom to discuss matters is a major component in this category. (Chapters 10, 11, 19)

FR - Relations with friends.

Having close friends, sharing activities, interests and views. Important aspects include acceptance, visiting each other, exchanging help and advice, love, trust and support. (Chapters 5, 10, 11)

HLP - Activities related to helping others.

Helping or encouraging adults or children (other than relatives or close friends). This can be expressed through individual efforts or as a member of an organizaion such as a church, school or volunteer group. (Chapters 6, 12, 14)

GVT - Activities related to local and national government.

Keeping informed through the media; participating by voting and communicating one's political (as well as social and religious) viewpoint. A component of this is living conditions as they are affected by regulations, laws and policies of governing agencies. (Chapters 5, 12, 17)

PERSONAL DEVELOPMENT AND FULFILLMENT

LN - Intellectual development.

Learning, attending classes, acquiring knowledge, exercising mental abilities, problem solving, certification or attaining degrees. Other aspects include improving comprehension or appreciation in or out of a school environment. (Chapters 6, 9)

UND - Personal understanding and maturity.

Developing orientation, purpose, and a personal philosophy. This may involve gaining insight into, and acceptance, of your assets and limitations; awareness of persnal growth and development, realizing the ability to influence the course of your life. It includes decision-making and planning of activities. For come people, a component is religious or spiritual experiences. (Chapters 5, 6, 12)

JOB - Work-related interests.

Having interesting, challenging, rewarding work in a job or within the home. This includes achievement, using your abilities, learning and productivity, obtaining recognition and job accomplishment. (Chapters 5, 6, 13, 14)

CR - Creativity and personal expression.

Showing ingenuity, originality, imagination in music, art, writing, crafts, drama, photography or practical scientific or technical endeavors. This also includes expression through a personal project, collection or other achievement. (Chapters 6, 7, 8, 19)

RECREATION

SO - Social Activities

Entertaining at home or elsewhere, attending parties or other social gatherings, meeting new people, interacting with others. This may include participation in social organizations and clubs. (Chapters 5, 10, 12)

PR - Passive and observational recreational activities.

Participating in passive recreation such as television, listening to music, reading, watching films or going to entertainment or sports events; this category includes appreciation of art and beauty in various aspects of life. (Chapters 2, 4, 7, 19)

AR - Active and participatory recreational activities.

Participation in active recreation, such as sports, running, hunting, fishing, boating, camping, vacation travel and sightseeing. This may include sedentary or active games, singing, playing a musical instrument, dancing and acting. (Chapters 2, 5, 6, 7, 10, 19)

Banking & Tax Worksheet

Banking From Home

1. Does your U.S. bank offer the type of services you need for part-time or full time residency abroad, such as fast (electronic) and reasonably priced transfer of funds? Y____N____

2. What are the fees involved in international fund transfer, and are there different kinds/different costs?_____
_____

3. What type of bank statement would your U.S. bank provide to you (mailed to your foreign address)?
_____

4. If you arrange for a regular amount to be deposited in your overseas account, should you designate someone with power of attorney (or a trusted co-signer on the account) in case you need an emergency fund transfer? Y____N____

5. Does your U.S. bank have a convenient branch, or a working relationship with another convenient bank, in the country where you plan to live or sojourn? Y_____N____
(Name of bank, locations)_____
_____

Banking Abroad

Expatriate bank accounts are grouped in several different categories, not all of which may be available to you. A tourist may not be permitted to have a bank account, or only to have a dollar account—a resident may not be permitted to maintain a local account in dollars. Banking laws vary by country, and individual banks may offer different services.

1. What types of bank accounts (checking, savings, long-term interest bearing account such as Certificate of Deposit) are generally available abroad for any of the following categories, if relevant:

Visitor/tourist _____

An expatriate with work permit_____

A pensioner/resident_____

A part time resident (usually six months)_____

A full time resident (there may be different categories of full time resident status, so check for any that may apply to you now or in the future
_____

2. Given the banking laws of this country, as they pertain to expatriates, which (foreign) bank offers the services you need?

_____

_____

3. Are there restrictions on withdrawals for any of the above accounts (some of which may require several days notice)?

_____

4. What are the legal requirements for importing U.S. dollars, either for living (operating) funds, or for a major purchase such as a home or car? _____

_____

INVESTMENTS

1. What kind of sheltered investment opportunities are available, such as tax-free (or reduced) incentives to invest in tourist-promoting ventures, or in certain industries this government is promoting with tax incentives?

_____

_____

_____

2. Is it advisable to form a corporation for tax reasons in this country? Y____N____

If yes, what are the advantages? (these may include writing off some living expenses such as a car, or to lessen red tape or tax liability for your heirs) _____

_____

_____

3. What are the drawbacks of unusual investment opportunities in this country (such as cases of fraudulent offerings and other risks; long time period before showing a profit as with some types of exotic agricultural investment; or need for unusual expertise to monitor progress of investment)?

_____

_____

_____

INCOME TAXES

Are you liable for income tax as a part-time (six month) or full-time resident of this country?

I. Income tax on earnings (work or business) in that country (note percentage, exemptions, etc.)

_____

_____

2. Income tax on worldwide income (including Social Security or other pension or annuity income from the U.S.)

_____

_____

3. Tax on unearned income (interest in foreign account) _____

_____

_____

4. Do you receive credit for U.S. taxes paid (i.e., is there a tax treaty to avoid double taxation, between this country and the U.S.? Y____N____

5. Names of recommended lawyers or agents who will help with preparation of your foreign taxes:_____

_____

_____

6. If you are considering purchase of property, what is your capital gains liability? (In some countries, the buyer may be required to pay tax on the increase in value between the last assessment (sale) and your current purchase price.) _____

_____

_____

7. What are the laws pertaining to inheritance taxes? Is your will valid/must it be redrawn and translated? Y____N____

8. What is the inheritance tax liability for your spouse? _____ and for your children in the U.S., should both parents expire, (for instance, in an accident)?_____

_____

_____

9. Does your designated executor in the U.S. have the effective power to implement your will, or must you make other arrangements abroad?

_____

Home Planning Worksheet

Your Needs

At this time (exploratory visit, simulated living, part-or full-time residency) you prefer _____bedrooms, _____baths, and (yes/no) dining room_____,terrace or balcony _____, elevator access if multi-story _____,parking _____, security _____.

Rental

1. For what length of time will you need rental accommodations?
_____

2. What type of accommodations are available (apartment, house, townhouse) which are scarce?_____

3. Are there times of the year when this area is crowded with vacationers, resulting in a seasonal rate change? If so, which months comprise the high season? From _____ to _____

Rental prices during high season range from $_____to $_____

Rental prices during low season range from $_____ to $_____

4. What type of rental housing is available and at what cost? Hotels or "aparthotels" range from $_____ to _____;

Apartments in smaller buildings $_____ to _____;

High rise apartments $_____ to _____

Villas or townhouses $_____ to _____

Single family homes $_____ to _____

5. Does the residence (and price) include appliances_____, installed telephone_____, utilities _____, maid service or gardener _____

What is meant by "furnished" _____
_____

If telephone not included, how long does it take for installation?
_____

Ownership
(Also review the above questions, when relevant)

1. Are there restrictions on ownership either by resident status or by location (e.g. coastal or border land)?_____

2. Can you own free title or only through bank trust (if so, what does this entail regarding eventual disposition; if land lease, what is the period of renewability, etc.)_____

_____

How do you determine clear title?_____

_____

4. Is financing available?_____If so, at what rate?_____

What percentage down is required? _____

5. (Cash) What deposit is required (percentage of price) _____

When is balance due? _____

6. If you cannot be in the country to finalize the transaction, who will act with limited power of attorney and for what fee?_____

_____

7. What is the property tax rate? (% of assessed or market value, or in some cases based on rental value) _____

8. Is there a sales tax (transfer tax, stamp tax) or other taxes for which buyer is liable at time of purchase or within a few months thereafter?

_____

9. What are the other fees involved (such as notary, deed registry,etc.)

_____

10. What is the legal procedure for home purchase (use separate sheet to detail the sequence of events, estimated time involved, and necessary documents). _____

_____

11. How do you arrange for transfer of U.S. funds for property purchase and also document importing of purchase price for future repatriation? _____

_____

12. How long will it take to import purchase price?_____

_____

I3. Can your U.S. bank arrange for the transfer or must you make other arrangements, and at what cost?_____

_____

14. What kind of homeowners insurance is available (if recommended)?_____

_____

15. How do you repatriate U.S. dollars upon the sale of the property? _____

16. Is there a capital gains tax? _____

17. What are the implications of inheritance tax for your heirs? How should you take title (if with spouse, for example) to simplify inheritanceprocedures_____
_____

Building And Remodelling

1. What zoning restrictions and building regulations might affect your plans to build or remodel?_____
_____
_____

2. What type of materials and construction are commonly used for building? _____

3. Which other materials might you wish to use, and are they available at a reasonable cost? _____
_____
_____

4. What kind of heating/cooling system is needed? (for example, you may need more heat than local residents are accustomed to)_____
_____

5. What services does the contractor or developer provide?_____
_____
_____

6. What is the practical and legal relationship between the builder-owner, the architect, contractor and other suppliers (and what are the terms for these professionals)? _____
_____
_____

Career Worksheet

Defining Your Needs
Are you interested in working full-time___ earning extra income____ or pursuing a hobby or avocation with sufficient income to offset its cost____?

Business Ownership
1. Do you need a local partner to own a business? Y__ N__

2. What kind of resident legal status or special visa do you need to own or be a partner in a business? _____

3. If a partnership is necessary, will you be allowed to work in the business (or only plan and supervise)? Y___ N___

4. If required to be a hands-off owner, will you be able to find and/or train local help to work key positions in the business? Y___ N___

5. What jobs would need to be filled by local employees—what skills would be needed (or taught) and could language pose a problem?
_____
_____

6. What kind of competition already exists in this market or field?
_____
_____

7. If there is no competition, is there a potential demand for this kind of business, or is there a reason no one has done it?_____
_____
_____

Professional Practice
1. Would you like to work in your field of experience or expertise, if offered the opportunity? Y____ N____

2. Is an expatriate allowed to practice your profession in this country? Y___ N___

3. If not, might you be able to practice as a consultant or liaison with the English-speaking community, perhaps in association with a local firm? Y___N___

4. Which institutions or governmental agencies should you contact to inform them of your availability for consulting?
_____
_____

5. What form of compensation is possible without affecting your tax status or requiring complicated paperwork (e.g., honorarium)

_____

_____

6. What are the possibilities for teaching (primary and secondary grades in English language schools) in your field of experience or expertise? Is there demand for teachers in a subject in which you are qualified to teach? _____

_____

Hobby and Avocation Income

1. If you wish to pursue your hobby or avocation abroad (for extra income or to cover costs), are there any legal restraints for you (as a pensioner or with resident status) for your area of interest? (e.g. woodcraft, interior decorating, promotional photography, freelance journalism, publicity, graphic design, event catering, etc.) Y___ N___

2. If there are restraints on any of the above, is a barter arrangement possible, and what (if any) are the laws regarding barter exchange of goods and services? How strictly are these laws enforced?_____

_____

_____

3. Will you be able to purchase sufficient supplies on a regular basis to fulfill orders or otherwise perform the service you intend to offer? Y___N___

Legal Worksheet

1. What are the various categories of visitor, and resident status (including pensioner status, if offered)? _____

_____

2. What privileges are extended with these categories of visitor/resident, if any?

_____

_____

3. For a sojourn or a period of simulated living (between 30 days and six months), what permit, visa or documentation is required?

_____ _____

_____

4. May permits and extensions (i.e., for the period of time that you intend to stay) be issued in the country, or must they be arranged in the U.S. prior to departure? If the latter, how long would it take to process such permits? _____

_____

5. If you need permit renewals, by what date must you do so? _____ (mark your calendar, checking against unexpected holidays when offices may be closed).

6. Where do you go for the necessary renewal?_____

_____

7. Is it necessary to exit the country at any time during the period you plan to remain abroad (such as an extended visitors permit) Y____N____. If so, how long must you remain away?_____

8. What is the fee for each entry/exit, if any? _____

9. How long may you remain outside the country before you lose your status (such as if you return to the U.S. for an extended stay)?

_____

10.What are the fees/processing costs for permits?_____

_____

Resident Status
11. What financial requirements (if any) must you meet to qualify for resident status?_____

_____

12. What privileges are extended for resident or pensioner/resident?

_____

Can you import personal goods, appliances, or a car duty free or at a reduced rate?_____

Purchase a new car in the country with no tax or a reduced tax?_____Other privileges of residency:_____
_____

13. For residence papers (including pensioner status in those countries which offer this), what costs will be incurred for legal assistance, document processing, etc.? _____

14. How long does it take for resident papers to be processed?
_____

15. What documentation is needed, such as (always) passport ____, clearance of police record_____ and (often) proof of income or financial responsibility ____, marriage certificate or divorce decree _____, medical exam_____(rarely) proof of relative in country or invitation by resident_____, proof that you have assurance of housing in the country (where there are housing shortages)_____

16. For the above (especially financial assets or guaranteed income), exactly what form of documentation will qualify?
_____

17. Names of lawyers recommended to help with residency processing:
_____
_____
_____
_____

18. Must any of the above documentation be provided in translation; if so, which documents?_____
_____

19. If pensioner status is offered, at what age do you qualify?
_____   _____

20. If a property owner, do you need a will in the native language?
Y____N____

Health Care Worksheet

Access And Quality

1. Areas/cities in this country with good medical care include :
_____

2. The best hospital and clinic facilities are:_____
_____
_____

3. Are English-speaking doctors available? Y____N____

4. If you require specialized medical care, are there good physicians, preferably English-speaking, at a reasonable distance from where you plan to live? Y____N____

5. What is the distance and available transportation between the area where you plan to live and an emergency medical facility?_____, and are English-speaking physicians available? Y____N____

Costs

1. Cost of average routine office visit $_____

2. Cost of office visit to specialist $_____

3. Cost of prescription (ideally, compare one you are familiar with or require on a regular basis) $_____

4. One day of hospitalization in semi-private room $_____

Private room $_____

5. Average cost of X-ray $_____

6. Average cost of visit to dentist $_____

Insurance

1. Does your current insurance (e.g. Blue Cross) offer coverage (usually a supplement) if you are outside the U.S.? Y____N____

2. If not, is there alternate medical coverage, either by a U.S. insurer or insurance program offered abroad for expatriate residents?
_____

3. Does the policy cover the cost of evacuation to the U.S. or to a medical facility in another country (e.g. England) if necessary? Y____N____

4. Is payment made directly to the hospital and doctor or must you pay costs and seek reimbursement? _____

5. What are the exclusions and limitations (preexisting conditions, surgical procedures or illnesses that may be excluded from coverage, age limit)_____

6. What is the deductible? _____

7. What is the maximum time period available for coverage (some U.S. policies are short term for holiday travelers—you will need long-term coverage for simulated living or part-time/full-time residency abroad)?

_____

Embassies

Embassy of Britain
3100 Massachusetts Ave. NW
Washington, D.C. 20008
(202) 462-1340

Embassy of Costa Rica
2112 S. Street NW
Washington, D.C. 20008
(202) 234-2945

Embassy of France
4101 Reservoir Road NW
Washington, D.C. 20007
(202) 944-6000

Embassy of Greece
2211 Massachusetts Ave. NW
Washington, D.C. 20008
(202) 667-3168

Embassy of Ireland
2234 Massachusetts Ave. NW
Washington, D.C. 20008
(202) 462-3939

Embassy of Italy
1601 Fuller St. NW
Washington, D.C. 20009
(202) 328-5500

Embassy of Mexico
2224 Wyoming Ave. NW
Washingon, D.C. 20008
(202) 234-2501

Embassy of Poland
2640 16th St. NW
Washington, D.C. 20009
(202) 234-3800

Embassy of Portugal
2125 Kalorama Rd. NW
Washington, D.C. 20008
(202) 328-8610

Embassy of Spain
2700 15th St. NW
Washington, D.C. 20009
(202) 265-0190

Embassy of Thailand
2300 Kalorama Rd. NW
Washington, D.C. 20008
(202) 483-7200

Embassy of Uruguay
1918 F Street NW
Washington, D.C. 20006
(202) 331-1313

International Housing Costs

The following is a sampling of housing costs cited in this book, with original purchase price and, where available, estimated 1991 market value.

Costa Rica:

Carl and Nancy Thalmeyer's three-bedroom, custom-bult home near San Jose cost $100,000 in 1987; estimated 1991 value: $120,000.

France:

Arlene and Paul Dexter's two-bedroom home in the Dordogne region cost $50,000 in 1987; estimated 1991 value: $100,000.

Greece:

Lily Cairns' two-bedroom townhouse on the island of Mykonos cost $30,000 in 1983; estimated 1991 value: $60,000.

Ireland:

Pamela and Tom Winger's two-bedroom farmhouse near Kerry-on-Shannon cost $34,000 in 1990.

Italy:

Linda and Bob Martinelli's two-bedroom duplex in Albisano cost $150,000 in 1989.

Mexico:

Matt and Joan Feldman's two-bedroom home (with a shared pool) in La Paz, Mexico, cost $100,000 in 1990.

Portugal:

Bert Rampling's four-bedroom home (on a large view lot) in the Algarve cost $180,000 in 1989.

Spain:

Veronica and George Alta's two-bedroom condominium in Malaga cost $40,000 in 1984; estimated 1991 value: $80,000.

Thailand:

David Mead's three-bedroom, custom built home on a large lot in Chiang Mai cost $40,000 in 1987; estimated 1991 value: $100,000.

Uruguay:

George and Marie Frank's two-bedroom view condominium in Montevideo cost $65,000 in 1983; estimated 1991 value: $125,000.

Residency Information

The following is an abbreviated sampling of residency requirements in several different countries. Tourist status usually allows a 30-day visit which may be extended up to 90 days, or longer in some cases. Be sure to update all information using the worksheet.

For resident or pensioner status, most countries require a birth certificate, marriage (or divorce) certificate, proof of clean police record, financial profile, and some countries also require a medical report or health insurance.

Prior to a long-stay visit of more than a few weeks, contact the country's consular office or embassy in the U.S. for the latest requirements.

Britain

Tourist may stay up to 180 days. Applicant for residency must apply in the U.S., but this is not encouraged except for U.S. citizens who demonstrate close family or business ties with the U.K.

Must show independent means of financial support.

Costa Rica:

Tourist may stay 90 days then exit required; pensionado (pensioner) resident must reside at least four months each year. Rentista status available for non-pensioners with guaranteed income; investor/resident status for minimum of $50,000 investment in CR. Resident financial requirement: $600 per month for pensionado, $1,000 per month for rentista.

France:

Tourist may stay 90 days then exit required. May apply for renewable one-year resident card (long-stay permit takes 3-4 months to process). Resident applicant must show proof of health insurance coverage in France as well as proof of financial support.

Greece:

Tourist may stay 60 days, extensions available. Applicant for residency must show means of financial support.

Ireland:

Tourist may stay 90 days (round trip airline ticket required). Extensions available. If parents or grandparents wre born in Ireland, residency is easy to establish (also eligible for EEC passport). Proof of financial support required.

Italy:

Tourist may stay 90 days, maximum six months (must apply in U.S.). Applicant for residency must show proof of adequate means of support.

Mexico:

Tourist may stay up to 180 days, renewable for total of 18 months. There are over a dozen categories of visitor and resident status, any of which may change so it is important to update information. A few examples: Visitante rentista (pensioner over age 50) required to exit after two years. Immigrante rentista (semi-permanent resident) good for up to 5 years with renewals. Inmigrado (permanent resident) staus may be applied for after 5 years, allows right to work. Residency financial requirement: proof of minimum of $1,000 per month income for head of house, $80 additional for each dependent.

Poland:

With visa may stay 90 days. Candidate for residency must show reason (family, business). Can apply for residency either in U.S. or Poland. No minimum income requirement; Social Security benefits document is sufficient financial proof for retiree.

Portugal:

Tourist may stay 60 days, renewable but must exit for 24 hours after total of 90 days. Applicant for residency must show proof of financial support (no minimum).

Spain:

Six-month stay allowed (permit available for 3-month extensions up to a total of 180 days); After two extensions, you may apply for resident permit. Proof of medical insurance required; Financial requirement of minimum of $7500 per year plus $1,500 for spouse.

Thailand:

Visa allows stay of 60 days, or with reason up to 90 days. May be extended with letter of purpose; no minimum financial requirement for resident applicant, but must show proof of financial support.

Uruguay:

May stay up to 90 days; extensions available. New regulations are pending for resident applicant so check before planning long-stay visit.

Taxation Source List

All countries tax income earned in that country. Usually if you are a resident for 180 days or more each year, you are liable for income tax based on imported income (e.g., Social Security, pension, interest income) but credit is given for tax paid in the U.S. Some countries do not credit U.S. taxes paid, as noted below.

The following is a sampling of the variations on personal and property tax found in different countries. Contact consulate or embassy for the latest information to update your worksheet.

	Income Tax	Inheritance Tax	Capital Gains	Property Tax
Britain	Credit for tax paid in U.S.	Yes	Residence Exempt	Yes
Costa Rica	Only on income earned in C.R.	No	No	No
France	Credit for tax paid in U.S.	Yes	Yes	Yes
Greece	Credit for tax paid in U.S.	No	Yes	Yes

	Income Tax	Inheritance Tax	Capital Gains	Property Tax
Ireland	Social Security taxed 15%. Individual works of art—if deemed of value to Ireland—are not liable to income tax.	Yes	Yes	No
Italy	Credit for tax paid in U.S.	Yes	Yes	Yes
Mexico	Credit for tax paid in U.S.	No	Yes	Yes
Poland	No tax on Social Security income	Yes	Yes	Yes
Portugal	Social Security taxed (some exemptions) if reside over 180 days	Yes	No	Yes

	Income Tax	Inheritance Tax	Capital Gains	Property Tax
Spain	Credit for tax paid in U.S.	Yes	Yes	Yes
Thailand	Social security taxed	Yes	Yes	Yes
Uruguay	Credit for tax paid in U.S.	Yes	Yes	Yes

Bilingual Medical List

Prepared by the Foundation for Nursing Studies (FEE)

For translation into the language of the country in which
you will be living (if not Spanish).

In the hospital or doctor's office you will be asked the following:

First name (Nombre)   Surname (Apellido)
Address (Direccion)   Telephone (Telefono)
Date of Birth (Fecha de Nacimiento)   Age (Edad)
Nationality (Nacionalidad)   Country/Passport Number
                                         (Pais/numero de pasaporte)

Mother's name (Nombre y apellido de la Madre)
Fathers name (Nobre y apellido del Padre)
Marital status: Single (soltero/a); Married (Casado/a)
Widow/Widower (Vuido/a)

Health insurance (Seguro de Salud)   Policy number (Numero de
                                         Poliza de Seguro)

English - Symptoms   Spanish - Los Sintomas

**Below, indicate which one by
pointing to left, right, both, all:**

1. My ankle hurts	1. Me duele el tobillo
2. My arm hurts	2. Me duele el brazo
3. My back hurts	3. Me duele la espalda
4. My buttocks hurts	4. Me duele el trasero
5. My chest hurts	5. Me duele el pecho
6. My ear hurts	6. Me duele la oreja
7. My elbow hurts	7. Me duele el codo
8. My eye hurts	8. Me duele el ojo
9. I have something in my eye	9. Tengo algo estrano en el ojo
10. My finger hurts	10. Me duele el dedo
11. My foot hurts	11. Me duele el pie
12. My hand hurts	12. Me duele la mano
13. My head hurts/headache	13. Me duele la cabeza
a. right side b. left side	a. lado derecho b. lado izquierdo
c. forehead d. on top	c. frente d. por encima
e. migraine	e. migrana, jaqueca
14. My hip hurts	14. Me duele la cadera
15. My knee hurts	15. Me duele la rodilla
16. My leg hurts	16. Me duele la pierna
17. My neck hurts	17. Me duele el cuello
18. My rib hurts	18. Me duele la costilla
19. My shoulder hurts	19. Me duele el hombro
20. My stomach hurts	20. Me duele el estomago

21. My throat hurts	21. Me duele la garganta
22. My toe hurts	22. Me duele el dedo del pie
23. My tooth hurts	23. Me duele el diente, la muela
24 .I can't breathe, I am choking	24. No puedo respirar, me atraganto
25. I am dizzy I am fainting	25. Estoy mareado/a Me desmayo
26. I am nauseated	26. Tengo nausea
27. My heart is pounding	27. Tengo palpitaciones
28. I've cut myself	28. Me he cortado/a
29. I've burned myself	29. Me he quemado/a
30. I have a bad cough	30. Tengo una tos fuerte
31. I have diarrhea	31. Tengo diarrea
32. I am constipated	32. Estoy estrenido/a
33. I can't urinate	33. No pued orinar
34. I have gas	34. Tengo flatulencia
35. I have heartburn	35. Tengoo acidez estomacal
36. I have a cold, I have a stuffy nose	36. Tengo un catarro Estoy constipado/a
37. I can't move	37. No puedo moverme
38. I can't walk	38. No puedo andar
39. I am bleeding I have a nosebleed	39. Estoy sangrando tengo hemorragia nasal
40. My skin itches	40. La piel me pica

Previous Medical History

1. I am diabetic	1. Soy diabetico/a
2. I am epileptic	2. Soy epileptico/a
3. I am asthmatic	3. Soy asmatico/a
4. I am deaf	4. Soy sordo/a
5. I can't see without my glasses	5. No puedo ver sin mis gafas
6. I wear contact lenses	6. Yo llevo lentillas
7. I have an ulcer	7. Tengo una ulcera
8. I have Parkinson's disease	8. Sufro la enfermedad de Parkinson
9. I suffer migraine headaches	9. Sufro migranas, jaquecas
10. I have had hepatitis	10. He sufrido hepatitis
11. I have had heart surgery	11. He sido operado de corazon
12. I have had a heart attack	12. He sufrido un infarto
13. I have had a stroke	13. He tenido una hemorragia cerebra
14. I have high blood pressure	14. Tengo hipertension
15. I have had a hysterectomy	15. He sido intervenido de histerecto
16. I have had prostate surgery	16. He sido operado de la prostata
17. I have had cancer of the a. breast b.lung c.uterus d.liver e. kidney f.bladder g.colon h. stomach i.mouth	17. He sufrido carcinoma del/de la a.pecho b.pulmon c.utero d.higado e.rinon f.vejiga g.colon h.estomago i.boca

j.prostate k.testicle l.brain | j .prostata k.testiculo l.cere

18. I have had leukemia
(of the blood)
19. I am allergic to:
a. penicillin
b. sulfa c. aspirin

18. He sufrido leucemia
(de la sangre)
19. Tengo alergia a:
a. penicilina
b. sulfa c. aspirina

Medicines I take regularly

20. Thyroid
21. Insulin
22. Tranquilizers
23. Medicine for my heart
24. Medicine for high blood
pressure
25. Medicine for depression

20. Tiroides
21. Insulina
22. Tranquilizantes
23. Medicina para el corazon
24. Medicina para hipertension

25. Medicina para la depresion

In the Hospital

1. When will the doctor come?
2. Answer: a. soon b.afternoon
c. tonight d.tomorrow morning

3. Please phone the doctor

4. The catheter hurts
5. I can't sleep
6. I can't eat
7. I am cold. I am hot.
8. I am thirst. I am hungry.
9. I would like water, milk,
coffee, tea, juice, please
10. I need a blanket,
a pillow
11. The bed is wet, dirty
12. I need the bedpan, the urinal
13. Please raise the bed

14. Please lower the bed

15. The bandage is too tight

16. The bandage is too loose

1. Cuando viene el medico?
2. Repuesta: a. pronto
b. por la tarde c. esta noche
d. manana por manana
3. Llame al medico por telefono
por favor
4. Me duele la sonda
5. No puedo dormir
6. No puedo comer
7. Tengo frio. Tengo calor.
8. Tengo sed. Tengo hambre.
9. Quisiera tomar agua, leche,
cafe, te, zumo, por favor.
10. Necesito una manta,
una almohada
11. La cama esta mojada, sucia
12. Necesito la cuna, el orinal
13. Que suba un poco la cama
por favor
14. Que baje un poco la cama
por favor
15. La venda esta demasiado
apretada
16. La venda esta demasiado
loja

What Are You Doing?

17. Taking a blood sample

18. Giving an injection:

antibiotic, sleep, nausea

17. Haciendo un examen de la
sangre
18. Poniendo una inyeccion
(pinchar)
antibiotico, sueno, nausea

19. Electrocariagram
20. Putting on a cast
21. Introducing a catheter
22. Giving a suppository

19. Una electrocardiograma
20. Poniendo un yeso
21. Introduciendo una sonda
22. Dandole un sopositoria

Where Am I Going?

23. To X-Ray
24. To the operating room
25. To Intensive Care
26. To another room
27. To the delivery room

23. A Rayos X, Radiografia
24. A la sala de operaciones
25. A la unidad de vigilancia intensivo
26. A otra habitacion
27. Al Paritorio

Having a Baby

1. Midwife
2. The contractions are every
   5 minutes, one after the other
3. The waters have broken
4. The baby is coming
5. My breasts hurt
6. The baby is crying a lot

1. Comadrona, Madrona
2. Las contracciones me dan cada
   cinco minutos, me dan segudas
3. Ha roto la bolsa de agua
4. Esta naciendo el nino
5. Me duelen los pechos
6. El bebe llora mucho

Sources

1. Further Reading:

Cooper, Marian, ed. *The World's Top Retirement Havens.* Baltimore, MD: Agora Books, 1989.

Dickinson, Peter A. *Travel and Retirement Edens Abroad.* Glenview IL: Scott, Foresman and Co., 1989.

Howells, John. *Choose Latin America.* San Francisco: Gateway Books, 1986.

Howells, John and Don Merwin. *Choose Mexico.* San Francisco: Gateway Books, 1988.

Howells, John and Bettie Magee. *Choose Spain.* San Francisco: Gateway Books, 1990.

Also:

Handbook of Consular Services. U.S. Department of State, 220 C Street NW, Washington D.C. 20250.

Background Notes on the Countries of the World. Superintendant of Documents, U.S. Government Printing Office, Washington D.C. 20402.

2. Periodicals:

The Retirement Newsletter, editor: Peter A. Dickinson; Phillips Publishing, Inc., 7811 Montrose Rd., Potomac, MD 20854; (301) 424-3700.

International Living 824 E. Baltimore St., Baltimore MD, 21202; (800) 433-1528.

Island Properties Report P.O. Box 58, Woodstock, VT 05091; (802) 457-3734.

3. English Language Periodicals Abroad:

Costa Rica:
Tico Times
Apartado 4632
San Jose, Costa Rica

Costa Rica Report
Apartado 6283
1000 San Jose, Costa Rica

France:
Free Voice
American Church
65 Quay d'Orsay
75005 Paris, France

Passion (sold at newsstands in some U.S. cities)
18 rue du Pont-Neuf
75001 Paris, France

Ireland:
Property Ireland
Rockwood, Stocking Lane
Ballyboden, Dublin 16, Ireland

Mexico:
The News
Balderas 87 - 3rd Floor
Mexico 1 DF, Mexico

The Colony Reporter
Lopez Cotillo 2057
Guadalajara 44140, Jalisco, Mexico

Adventures in Mexico
Apartado Postal 32-96
Guadalajara, Jalisco, Mexico

Atencion San Miguel
Apdo 119
San Miguel de Allende, Guanajuato, Mexico

Portugal:
Anglo-Portuguese News
Ave de Sao Pedro 14-D
2765 Monte Estoril, Portugal

Algarve Magazine
Rua 25 Abril
8400 Lagos, Algarve, Portugal

Spain:
Lookout
Puebla Lucia
29640 Fuengirola (Malaga), Spain

4. Living and Retiring Abroad Services:

American-Canadian Club
Hotel Plaza del Sol
Lopez Mateos y Mariano Otero
45050 Guadalajara, Jalisco, Mexico
tel. 47-87-90 extension 1413

Lifestyle Explorations, Inc.
World Trade Center, Suite 400
Boston, MA 02210

For tour information:
(508) 371-4814 (24 hours)
(508) 369-9192 (FAX)

For other information write:
Jane Parker
3722 Blue Lake Drive, Spring, TX 77388

About the Authors

Jane Parker is director of Lifestyle Explorations, an international travel/seminar service. Founded in 1979 as Retirement Explorations, the program has introduced more than 500 people to living options in countries around the world. Jane Parker, a graduate of California State University at Northridge, created Lifestyle Explorations as she approached retirement from a teaching career. She lived in Africa for two years, and now resides near Houston, Texas.

Allene Symons is a contributing editor for *Publishers Weekly* magazine in New York, where she was formerly a senior editor. She is the author of a novel, *Vagabond Prophet,* published by Avon Books in 1982. She has also written for *Details, Physicians Travel & Leisure, Small Press* and *New West* (now called *California* magazine). Allene Symons graduated from San Francisco State University and received her M.A. from Claremont Graduate School. She lives in the Los Angeles area.

Index

Our books are available in most bookstores. However, if you have any difficulty finding them, we will be happy to ship them to you directly. Mail us this coupon with your check or money order and they'll be on their way to you within days.

ADVENTURES ABROAD Exploring the Travel/Retirement Option	$12.95	_____
WHERE TO RETIRE Your Travel Guide to America's Best Places	12.95	_____
CHOOSE MEXICO: Retire on $400 a Month	9.95	_____
RV TRAVEL IN MEXICO The Complete How-to-do-it Book	9.95	_____
CHOOSE SPAIN Leisurely Vacations or Affordable Retirement	11.95	_____
CHOOSE LATIN AMERICA Seasonal or Retirement Living	9.95	_____
GET UP AND GO: A Guide for the Mature Traveler	10.95	_____
THE GRANDPARENT BOOK A Commonsense Guide	11.95	_____
TO LOVE AGAIN: Intimate Relationships After 60	7.95	_____

Subtotal: _____

Add $1.75 for postage and handling for the first book,
.50 for each additional one.
(Canadian orders: $ .75 additional postage)   _____

California residents add sales tax   _____

Total Enclosed: _____

Name_____

Address_____

City_____State_____Zip_____

Books should reach you in two or three weeks.
If you are dissatisfied for any reason, the price of the book(s) will be refunded in full.

Mail to : Gateway Books • 13 Bedford Cove • San Rafael, CA 94901